THE EASTERN COUGAR

Historic Accounts, Scientific Investigations, and New Evidence

edited by
Chris Bolgiano and
Jerry Roberts

STACKPOLE
BOOKS

0 11557 03218 5

Library of Congress Cataloging-in-Publication Data

on file with the Library of Congress

Contents

Acknowledgments

I AM GRATEFUL TO JERRY ROBERTS FOR PROPOSING AN ANTHOLOGY, WHICH seemed to me to solve the problem of authenticating the eastern cougar story. Much of the historical research for the first chapter was originally done during a summer grant from the Virginia Foundation for the Humanities and Public Policy. My colleagues at Carrier Library, James Madison University provided essential interlibrary loan support. Many thanks go to Todd Lester, who established the nonprofit Eastern Cougar Foundation and asked me to work with him as vice president, and who has inspired me ever since with his vision of wild cougars in the East. The indefatigable Helen McGinnis sent me numerous cougar stories. Thanks are also due to Ken Miller, Mark Dowling, Bob Wilson and others in the Eastern Cougar Network for their devotion to tracking down and recording the accumulating evidence of cougars in the East. Several members of the Eastern Cougar Foundation's Board of Directors—David Maehr, Melanie Culver, and Mark Jenkins—wrote original essays for a small token of an honorarium. I appreciated the efforts of various copyright managers at newspapers and journals to expedite the necessary permissions and keep fees as low as possible.

—CHRIS BOLGIANO

THE NOTION TO WRITE ABOUT SUPPOSEDLY VANISHED PENNSYLVANIA wildlife germinated after I took a day trip into the Clarion River region on New Year's Eve, 2001, with old schoolboy friends. The project was pared to one animal after I read the chapter "The Spiritual Challenge of the Eastern Panther" in Chris Bolgiano's book *Mountain Lion: An Unnatural History of Pumas and People.* After forging a long-distance alliance, I met Chris and her husband, Ralph, at their idyllic home in the mountains of Virginia. This book exists because of Chris's professionalism, grace, integrity, forbearance, eloquence, exactitude, guidance, trust, hospitality, humor, vision, and toughness.

Thanks also go to Joanne Mallillin of Carson, California; Joe Kosack and Jerry Feaser of the Pennsylvania Game Commission in Harrisburg; old friend John Beale and Corey Waugaman of the *Pittsburgh Post-Gazette;* research librarian Carl Spadoni at McMaster University in Hamilton, Ontario; Gerry Parker of Sackville, New Brunswick, for generously supplying photographs; David Seitz of the Rights & Permissions Department of the *New York Times;* Doug List for his help with file transfers; Marjeanne Blinn and Andrea Dickerson of the Palos Verdes Library District; George Schaller of the Wildlife Conservation Society for his encouragement; David Dougherty of the University of New Brunswick; Rob Andregg of the Vermont Institution of Natural Sciences in Woodstock; Alex and Ann Roberts and Mark and Patty Roberts for their support; Don Lechman, Boots LeBaron, and Dick Loftus for keeping tabs on the project; Kyle and Tyler Kolfschoten for their company while I wrote; and public libraries in the California cities of Torrance, Redondo Beach, and Long Beach as well as libraries at the University of California at Los Angeles and California State University, Long Beach. I would also like to thank Kevin Sanders and Jim Martillotti in Kittanning, Pennsylvania, and John Perry in Kennedyville, Maryland.

—JERRY ROBERTS

Preface

WE HOPE THAT THIS ASSEMBLAGE OF DOCUMENTS—AND THE OPPORTUNITY it affords to read, analyze, and decide for oneself—will propel the public discussion about cougars past its current stalled state. Arguments over where a cougar comes from and what human-defined subspecies it may or may not be, while reflecting legitimate concerns for preserving unique genomes, have become arcane and academic. The important questions about eastern cougars are not scientific, they are cultural—and some would even call them spiritual. How will we as a society respond to the possibility of cougars in the East?

The literature of cougars in eastern North America is enormous. We have tried to select the most influential or representative documents in the realms of both science and culture but have inevitably left out many important works. Except for occasional minor changes in format such as paragraph indentations, the selections are presented exactly as they appeared in the sources, including misspellings, odd capitalization, and use of obsolete terms. Our sources are somewhat biased to the mid-Atlantic states, because we are both originally from that region, but we feel that the selections accurately mirror the widespread attitudes and practices of their times.

Historic Range of Cougars in Eastern North America

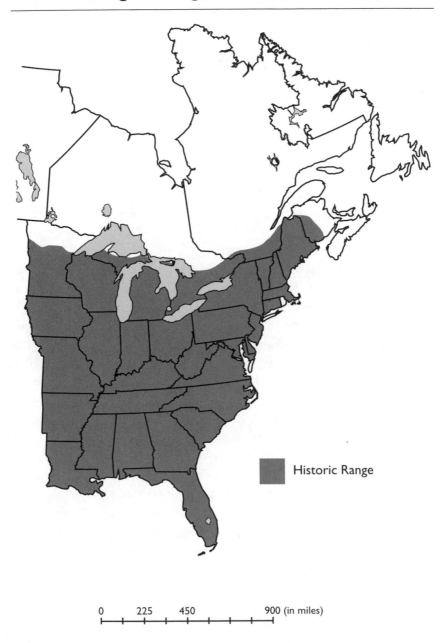

Historic Range

0   225   450   900 (in miles)

SOURCE: Young, Stanley P. and Edward A. Goldman, The Puma: Mysterious American Cat. Washington, D. C.: American Wildlife Institute, 1946
© 2004 Chris McGough, Meghan Gemma, Melanie Benda, James Madison University Geospatial Data Lab, Harrisonburg, VA

1

Identity:
What Is an Eastern Cougar?

WHEN CHRISTOPHER COLUMBUS SIGHTED THE NEW WORLD IN 1492, Europeans had accumulated thousands of years of experience with wolves and bears. Small cats were familiar in the form of the European wildcat and the somewhat larger lynx. But the big, tawny cat that silently stalked the woods of the New World was unlike any animal known in the Old.

Cougars *(Puma concolor)* are native only to North, Central, and South America. They ranged at the time of Columbus from the shores of the Caribbean islands where he landed to the coast of British Columbia, and southward all the way to the windswept plains of Patagonia. Avoiding only tundra, which offers no cover to an ambush predator, cougars claimed habitats as varied as mountainsides, swamps, and deserts.

FIRST ENCOUNTERS
It was only natural that the earliest explorers described what they saw in terms of what they had known in Europe. Amerigo Vespucci scooped Columbus by being the first to give a name to the New World animal we know today as cougar—actually two names, beginning the long, confusing history of multiple names for this cat. On his first voyage in 1497, skirting the Caribbean coast of Central America, Vespucci saw a land "full of animals, few [of which] resemble ours excepting lions, panthers and even these have some dissimilarities of form."

Those dissimilarities of form would be ignored for many years. Columbus, too, in a 1503 letter to King Ferdinand and Queen Isabella of Spain about his fourth and final voyage to the New World, named lions as one of the animals he saw along the coast of Central America: "I saw some very large fowls (the feathers of which resemble wool), lions, stags, fallow-deer and birds."

What Columbus and Vespucci meant by lions and panthers were the medieval images of African lions and Asian leopards. These animals were last encountered in the flesh by Europeans during the Crusades several centuries before Columbus sailed. In medieval iconography the lion was seen as both noble and brutal; the panther was beautiful and treacherous. Over the course of the next three centuries, cougar folklore absorbed all of these ambivalent images and developed unique twists of its own.

Cougars are almost magically elusive, able to appear and disappear with hardly a trace. This characteristic made early settlers uncertain about the kind or number of cats that lurked on the frontier. It also made understanding the cat's behavior extremely difficult, and what is not understood is often loathed. The cougar's secretive nature even made many Native Americans uneasy; the cat seems to have been generally respected but not necessarily beloved.

In the centuries of initial exploration and settlement, the cougar received a plurality of names like no other mammal: mountain lion, panther, painter, Indian devil, red lion, deer tiger, catamount, wildcat, puma, and cougar (the last two are derived from Native American names, of which there must have been hundreds, perhaps thousands, to correspond with the diversity of native cultures). More than half a century after Columbus and Vespucci offered the first names for the new American cat, M. John Hawkins, Esq., added several more while exploring Florida in 1565: "Of beasts in this countrey besides deere, foxes, hares, polcats, conies, ownces, and leopards, I am not able certeinly to say: but it is thought that there are lions and tygres as well as unicornes; lions especially" (Sparke, in Burrage). *Ownce* (ounce) is an Old World term that referred originally to lynx but had broadened to include leopards. French explorer Rene Goulaine de Laudonniere added yet another name in his 1587 account of four voyages to Florida: "Beasts well known here are ownces, luserns and a certain kind of beast that differeth little from the lion of Africa." *Lusern* (lucern) was also an Old World term for lynx, and perhaps referred to the American bobcat. The bobcat has a short tail and is less than half the size and weight of a cougar but to this day remains the source of much confusion about the larger cat.

Cougars are distinguished from African lions in several ways: They are physically unable to roar due to a different throat structure, are significantly smaller, and lack the tuft at the end of the tail and the prominent mane of the males. Nonetheless, early explorers continued to ascribe African lion qualities to American cougars. The first doubts about lions may have been raised by William Strachey in 1612, although his manuscript, *Historie of Travell into Virginia Britannia,* was not published until 1849:

> *Lyons I will not positively affirme that the Country hath, synce our people never yet sawe any, howbeit in their discoveryes to the Mangoagues they did light once upon twoo skynns, which by all the Judgements in the Fort were supposed to be Lyons skyns, and this last yeare myself being at the Falls with Sir Thos. Dale I found in an Indian howse certain Clawes tyed up in a string which I brought awaie, and into England, and they are assured unto me to be Lyons Clawes.*

Doubt of the existence of lions was also recorded in New England by author Thomas Morton in his 1632 *New English Caanan,* in which he wrote that such a snowy climate could not support lions. Two years later, however, William Wood published in *New England's Prospect* a poem describing the region's animals that began with the phrase "The kingly Lyon." After eight more lines of rhythmic mammalian inventory, Wood broke into prose to describe the roaring that he attributed to the lion:

> *Concerning Lyons, I will not say that I ever saw any my selfe, but some affirme that they have seene a Lyon at Cape Anne which is not above six leagues from Boston; some likewise being lost in woods, have heard such terrible roarings, as have made them much agast; which must eyther be Devills or Lyons; there being no other creatures which use to roaring saving Beares, which have not such a terrible kind of roaring: besides, Plimouth men have traded for Lyons skinnes in former times.*

Referring to the Old World belief that jackals hunted prey for the benefit of lions, Morton continued: "But sure it is that there be Lyons on that Continent, for the Virginians saw an old Lyon in their plantations, who having lost his Jackall, which was wont to hunt his prey, was brought so poore that he could goe no further." John Josselyn also cited the jackal theory in his 1672 publication, *New England's Rarities Discovered,* in which he reasoned that a jackal-like animal in the woods was "a shrew'd sign that there are lions upon the Continent." In 1669, Nathaniel Shrigley listed lions, panthers, and leopards as native animals in *A true relation of Virginia and Maryland; with the commodities therein,* and in 1682 Thomas Ash added to that list when he stated, in *Carolina, or a description of the present state of that country,* that planters must often share their hogs with tigers.

The lack of a mane was explained in 1649 by Adriaen van der Donck in New Netherlands, the future New York, who stated that lions were "only known by the skins of the females, sometimes brought in by Indians for sale; who on inquiry say, that lions are found far to the southwest, distant fifteen or twenty days, in very high mountains, and that the males are too active and fierce to be taken." Gentlemen in the colonies sometimes sent skins back to friends and family in England that they labeled as lions.

As decades passed and no maned lion was ever caught, the name panther became more common throughout the eastern U.S., sometimes corrupted to "painter" by backwoods folk. John Banister, the first English university-trained naturalist to visit America, mentioned panthers in his 1679 letter home and used that term exclusively (Ewan 1970). Yet John Clayton, the great Virginia botanist, in a 1694 account published in *Philosophical Transactions,* added yet another name when he wrote, "I never heard of any lion, they told me of a creature killed . . . which I conceived to be a sort of pard or tiger." *Pard* was a term of Greek and Persian derivation referring to the leopard.

Despite the confusion generated by all these Old World names, the remarkable English naturalist John Ray, considered the greatest taxonomist prior to Carl Linnaeus, was able in 1693 to designate the roe-colored cat as a unique American species that he named the *cuguacuarana,* a native Brazilian name. The word "cougar" is derived from it and by the 1760s was in use in the form of "couguar" in Europe. "Cougar" was in common use in the eastern U.S. at least by 1812, when Virginian William Nelson wrote to his friend St. George Tucker about some cougar bones that had been found in Williamsburg.

SCIENTIFIC ESTABLISHMENT

From the earliest days of European exploration in eastern North America, accounts of cougars contained biological truths embedded in untruths. One of the most persistent themes concerns the behavior of cougars toward humans. In both cougar folklore and natural history, there are two distinct motifs: cougars as mild, even cowardly, and cougars as blood-thirsty predators that readily attack humans. In *The History and Present State of Virginia,* the first American colonial history to be published by a native son (albeit in London, in 1705), author Robert Beverley wrote that hunting bears, panthers, and wild cats yielded "pleasure as well as profit to the sportsman" but reassured readers that these animals were not dangerous to people: "All these creatures ever fly from the face of man, doing no damage but to the cattle and hogs."

John Bartram, the brilliant field botanist from Philadelphia, reinforced Beverley's assessment in a 1738 letter to his influential English natural history patron Peter Collinson, and also sounded a refrain that would echo throughout cougar lore—that of cougars following people:

> Panthers have not seized any of our people, that I have heard; but many have been sadly frightened with them. They have pursued several men, both on horseback and foot. Many have shot them down, and others have escaped by running away. But I believe, as a panther doth not much fear a single man, so he hath no great desire to seize him; for if he had, running from him would be a poor means to escape such a nimble, strong creature, which will leap about twenty feet at one leap.

The debate over whether cougars are inherently dangerous to humans continues to this day, and is further documented in Chapter 3.

John Lawson, a surveyor in North Carolina, did not address the threat of cougars to humans in his 1709 *History of North Carolina,* but he was clear about the threat to livestock: "This Beast is the greatest Enemy to the Planter of any Vermine in Carolina." His accusation gains credence from his accurate observations about cougar behavior, comprising perhaps the best field description to date:

> He climbs Trees with the greatest Agility imaginable, is very strong limbed, catching a piece of Meat from any Creature he strikes at. His

Tail is exceeding long; his Eyes look very fierce and lively, are large and of a grayish Colour; his Prey is Swine's-Flesh, Deer, or anything he can take; no Creature is so nice and clean as this in his Food. When he has got his Prey he fills his Belly with the Slaughter and carefully lays up the Remainder, covering it very neatly with Leaves, which if anything touches, he never eats any more of it. He purrs as Cats do; if taken when Young is never to be reclaimed from his wild Nature. He hollows like a Man in the Woods when killed, which is by making him take a Tree, as the least Cur will presently do.

Lawson's brief description appeared in recognizable form in natural history books by other writers for more than a century. "As for lions," Lawson continued, "I never saw any in America, neither can I imagine how they should come here."

The realization that cougars were not lions was by now widespread. William Byrd II, scion of a wealthy Virginia plantation family, expressed some lingering tension between myth and reality when he wrote *History of the Dividing Line* in 1728 (not published until 1841):

The Indian killd a very fat Doe, and came across a Bear, which had been put to Death and was half devour'd by a Panther. The last of these Brutes reigns absolute Monarch of the Woods, and in the keenness of his hunger will venture to attack a Bear; tho' then 'tis ever by surprise, as all Beasts of the cat kind use to come upon their Prey—As formidable as this Beast is to his Fellow Brutes, he never has the confidence to venture upon a Man, but retires from him with great respect, if there be a way open for his Escape. However, it must be confesst, his Voice is a little contemptible for a Monarch of the Forrest, being not a great deal lowder nor more awful than the Mewing of a Household Cat.

So much for the mighty roar of the lion. In a footnote to this passage, Byrd thought to clarify the confused identity of the American cougar but merely perpetuated the confusion of Old World identities: "Some authors who have given an Account of the Southern Continent of America wou'd make the World believe there are lyons when in all likelihood they were mistaken, imagining these Panthers to be Lyons."

In the same era, many of the increasing number of books published by New World travelers told tales about animals that thoroughly confused Old and New World ideas. In *Journal of a Voyage to North America,* for example, published in 1761, author P. de Charlevoix described a cat called the carcajou with a tail so long it twisted three times around his body and who lacked a sense of smell so that he depended on three foxes to hunt for him. This description of what was probably meant to be a cougar was repeated by several other authors, including Jonathon Carver in his very popular *Travels through the interior parts of North America in the years 1766, 1767, and 1768,* which by 1781 had already sold out three editions. Carver described both "the cat of the mountain" and the carcajou in ways that commingled traits of cougars and bobcats. Other authors continued to meld more accurate descriptions with age-old themes of blood lust attributed to the panthers of the Old World.

The thread of scientifically minded observation was picked up by Mark Catebsy in his 1731 *Natural History of Carolina, Florida, and the Bahama Islands.* Although Catesby did not include a drawing of a panther in his book, he listed it among other beasts of the same genus but of a different species than animals of Europe. By the time Catesby was writing his tome, panthers and other large animals were already being pushed to the far edges of settlements, as described by Virginia botanist John Clayton in a letter to his estate manger in England in 1739: "Panthers, Buffaloes and Elks and wild cats are only to be found among the mountains and desert parts of the countrey where there are as yet but few inhabitants."

By the mid-1700s, works of classification and taxonomy became a torrent. One of the first major compendiums of natural history, *Histoire naturelle, generale et particuliere,* published in 1761 by French naturalist Georges Louis Comte de Buffon, included a chapter on "The Couguar." Buffon published a supplement in 1766 that contained a chapter on "The Couguar of Pennsylvania." In 1771, as Buffon's work was being translated into English, Linnaeus published his famous taxonomy in which the cougar was given the species name *Felis concolor,* the cat of one color. Citations to Linnaeus and other authors are given for the cougar in William Smellie's 1812 English translation of Buffon, *Natural History, General and Particular.* Differences among cougars from different locations were being recognized, a hint of the subspecies taxonomy to follow. Buffon's chapter on "The Couguar of Pennsylvania" is given here:

The jaguar, as well as the couguar, inhabits the warmest regions of South America. But there is another species of couguar (of which we have given a figure) found in the temperate climates of North America, as on the mountains of Carolina, Georgia, Pennsylvania, and the adjacent provinces. The drawing of this couguar was sent me from England by the late Mr. Colinson, with the following description: if it is exact, this couguar must differ greatly from the common kind.

Plate 176

"The couguar of Pennsylvania," says Mr. Colinson, "differs much from the couguar of Cayenne. . . . His limbs are shorter, his body much longer, and his tail is also three or four inches longer. But, in the colour of the hair, and the form of the head and ears, they have a perfect resemblance to each other. The couguar of Pennsylvania," adds Mr. Colinson, "is an animal remarkable for thinness and length of body, shortness of legs, and length of tail. The length of the body, from the muzzle to the anus, is five feet four inches; and that of the tail is two feet six inches. The forelegs are one foot long, and the hind-legs one foot three inches. The height of the body before is one foot nine inches, and one foot ten inches behind. The circumference of the thickest part of the body is two feet three inches."[1]

Mr. Edwards, who, for skill in the art of drawing, and knowledge of natural history, merits the applauses of all lovers of science, sent me some engravings, which corresponded with the drawing communicated by Mr. Colinson.

Buffon's 1766 supplement also included a chapter on one of the most mysterious aspects of cougar folklore, "The Black Couguar." Sightings of black cougars are frequently reported today in eastern North America, but despite all the cougars ever killed—including more than sixty-five

---

[1]Mr. Colinson's letter to M. de Buffon, April 30, 1763.

thousand taken during government predator control programs in the West beginning in the late nineteenth century—no black specimen has ever been scientifically confirmed. The one credible North American reference to a black cougar is by reputable author Claude Barnes, who in his 1960 book, *The Cougar, or Mountain Lion,* wrote that the only black cougar he had ever personally seen was the skin of a cat killed by a hunter in Colorado. That skin has disappeared into history. Another reputable author, Jim Bob Tinsley, included a photo of a black cougar killed in Costa Rica in 1959 in *The Puma, Legendary Lion of the Americas* (1987).

Buffon's chapter described the black cougar as quite small and known only in particular areas of South America and offered an explanation: "This black couguar may be the same animal which Piso and Marcrave call the jaguarette." This reference could possibly be to the jaguarundi, a small American wildcat that exists in both a red and black phase. Biologists today believe that fishers and other animals are confused for a rare cougar form apparently limited to Central and South America. White cougars have also been reported, but far less often than black cats, and again, never verified. In an 1891 report to the U.S. National Museum (part of the Smithsonian Institution), Frederick True wrote: "The occurrence of albino Pumas in the Alleghany Mountains and in New Mexico has been reported, but not authoritatively."

Shortly after Buffon and Linnaeus published their works, a 1792 book published in Great Britain entitled *The animal kingdom, or zoological system, of the celebrated Sir Charles Linnaeus,* by Robert Kerr, assigned the name *Felis concolor couguar* to the cougar known in eastern North America. Except for the change in genus from *Felis* to *Puma* by the American Society of Mammalogists in 1993, *Puma concolor couguar* remains the scientific designation for the variant, or subspecies, of cougars that originally lived in eastern North America north of Florida. Accounts of cougars based on experience in eastern North America appeared in many natural history books, such as George Ord's "North American Zoology" (published in *Guthrie's Geography* in 1815), Thomas Bewick's *A General History of Quadrupeds* (1824), Richard Harlan's *Fauna Americana* (1825), and John Godman's *American Natural History* (1826). Constantine Rafinesque's 1832 article in the *Atlantic Journal* and *Friend of Knowledge* was one of the more accurate of a burgeoning number of popular as well as scientific magazine pieces on zoology in general or cougars in particular. Some authors listed several species of cats, reflecting the continuing confusion over the many names of the cougar, but perhaps also reflecting regional differences by the adaptable cat.

By the mid-1800s, many Americans were moving westward, and cougar stories from western territories began to swamp the knowledge of eastern cougars, which by now were becoming quite scarce. One of the last major descriptions of cougars in the East based on personal experience was written by the famous naturalist and artist, John James Audubon (with coauthor John Bachman) in *Viviparous Quadrupeds of North America* (1846). (Audubon also painted the eastern cougar.) Their account is a combination of the hunting stories that were extremely popular at the time with serious natural history.

The excerpt below shows that Audubon and Bachman dealt correctly with some of the most persistent motifs that by then had become fixed in cougar folklore—attacking sleeping humans (in some stories, a sleeping human is not attacked but covered with leaves), following and attacking horses while humans are riding them (many stories have the human dropping food or clothes one by one to distract the threatening cougar), acting in a cowardly yet bloodthirsty manner, and crying like a child (or a woman being murdered). The theme of cougar numbers declining in the East is also persistent. Only the mention of adult cougars hunting in pairs is completely erroneous; cougars are usually solitary except for mothers with young and siblings who have just left their mother. It would take the development of radio telemetry in the 1970s, when wild western cougars were treed, tranquilized, and fitted with radio tracking collars, before the habits of cougars were more thoroughly understood.

Description
Body, long and slender; head, small; neck, long; ears, rounded; legs, short and stout; tail, long, slender and cylindrical, sometimes trailing; fur, soft and short.

Colour
Body and legs, of a uniform fulvous or tawny colour; under surface, reddish-white; around the eyes, grayish-yellow; hairs within the ears, yellowish-white; exterior of the ears, blackish; lips, at the moustache, black; throat, whitish; tail of the male, longer than that of the female,

Paintings of a male and female cougar by John James Audubon, from his *Viviparous Quadrupeds of North America.*

brown at tip, not tufted. We have seen several specimens differing from the above in various shades of colour. These accidental variations, however, are not sufficient to warrant us in regarding these individuals as distinct species. The young are beautifully spotted and barred with blackish-brown, and their hair is soft and downy.

Habits

The Cougar is known all over the United States by the name of the panther or painter, and is another example of that ignorance or want of imagination, which was manifested by the "Colonists," who named nearly every quadruped, bird, and fish, which they found on our continent, after species belonging to the Old World, without regard to more than a most slight resemblance, and generally with a total disregard of propriety. . . . [T]he Cougar . . . is but little more like the true panther than an opossum is like the kangaroo! Before, however, entirely quitting this subject, we may mention that for a long time the Cougar was thought to be the lion; the supposition was that all the skins of the animal that were brought into the settlements by the Indians were skins of females; and the lioness, having something the same colour and but little mane, it occurred to the colonists that the skins they saw could belong to no other animal!

The Cougar is found sparsely distributed over the whole of North America up to about latitude 45°. In former times this animal was more abundant than at present, and one was even seen a few miles from the city of New York within the recollection of Dr. Dekay, who speaks of the consternation occasioned by its appearance in Westchester County, when he was a boy.

The Cougar is generally found in the very wildest parts of the country, in deep wooded swamps, or among the mountain cliffs and chasms of the Alleghany range. In Florida he inhabits the miry swamps and the watery everglades. . . . This species at times attacks young cattle, and the male from which our drawing was made, was shot in the act of feeding upon a black heifer which he had seized, killed, and dragged into the edge of a thicket close adjoining the spot. The Cougar, is however, generally compelled to subsist on small animals, young deer, skunks, raccoons, &c., or birds, and will even eat carrion when hard pressed by hunger. His courage is not great, and unless very hungry, or when wounded and at bay, he seldom attacks man. . . .

Dr. Dekay mentions, that he was told of a Cougar in Warren County, in the State of New York, that resorted to a barn, from whence he was repeatedly dislodged, and finally killed. "He shewed no fight whatever. His mouth was found to be filled with the spines of the Canada porcupine, which was probably the cause of his diminished wariness and ferocity, and would in all probability have finally caused his death."

The panther, or "painter," as the Cougar is called, is a nocturnal animal more by choice than necessity, as it can see well during the day time. It steals upon its intended prey in the darkness of night, with a silent, cautious step, and with great patience makes its noiseless way through the tangled thickets of the deepest forest. When the benighted traveller, or the wearied hunter may be slumbering in his rudely and hastily constructed bivouac at the foot of a huge tree, amid the lonely forest, his fire nearly out, and all around most dismal, dreary, and obscure, he may perchance be roused to a state of terror by the stealthy tread of the prowling Cougar; or his frightened horse, by its snortings and struggles to get loose, will awaken him in time to see the glistening eyes of the dangerous beast glaring upon him like two burning coals. Lucky is he then, if his coolness does not desert him, if his trusty rifle does not miss, through his agitation, or snap for want of better flint; or well off is he, if he can frighten away the savage beast by hurling at him a blazing brand from his nearly extinguished campfire. For, be sure the animal has not approached him without the gnawing hunger—the desire for blood; engendered by long fasting and gaunt famine.

Some very rare but not well authenticated instances have been recorded in our public prints, where the Cougar at such times has sprang upon the sleeper. At other times the horses are thrown into such a fright, that they break all fastenings and fly in every direction. The late Mr. Robert Best of Cincinnati, wrote to Dr. Godman, that one of these animals had surprised a party of travellers, sprung upon the horses, and so lacerated with its claws and teeth their flanks and buttocks, that they with the greatest difficulty succeeded in driving the poor creatures before them next morning, to a public house some miles off. This party, however, had no fire, and were unarmed.

A planter on the Yazoo river [Mississippi], some years ago, related the following anecdote of the Cougar to us. As he was riding home alone one night, through the woods, along what is called a "bridle-path" (i. e. a horse-track), one of these animals sprang at him from a fallen log, but owing to his horse making a sudden plunge forward, only struck the rump of the gallant steed with one paw, and could not maintain his hold. The gentleman was for a moment unable to account for the furious start his horse had made, but presently turning his head saw the Cougar behind, and putting spurs to his horse, galloped away. On examining the horse, wounds were observed on his rump corresponding with the claws of the Cougar's paw, and from their distance apart, the foot must have been spread widely when he struck the animal.

Another respectable gentleman of the State of Mississippi gave us the following account. A friend of his, a cotton planter, one evening, while at tea, was startled by a tremendous outcry among his dogs, and ran out to quiet them, thinking some person, perhaps a neighbour, had called to see him. The dogs could not be driven back, but rushed into the house; he seized his horsewhip, which hung inside the hall door, and whipped them all out, as he thought, except one, which ran under the table. He then took a candle and looking down, to his surprise and alarm discovered the supposed refractory dog to be a Cougar. He retreated instanter, the females and children of his family fled frightened half out of their senses. The Cougar sprang at him, he parried the blow with the candlestick, but the animal flew at him again, leaping forward perpendicularly, striking at his face with the fore-feet, and at his body with the hind-feet. These attacks he repelled by dealing the Cougar straight-forward blows on its belly with his fist, lightly turning aside and evading its claws, as he best could. The Cougar had nearly overpowered him, when luckily he backed toward the fire-place, and as the animal sprang again at him, dodged him, and the panther almost fell into the fire; at which he was so terrified that he endeavoured to escape, and darting out of the door was immediately attacked again by the dogs, and with their help and a club was killed.

Two raftsmen on the Yazoo river, one night encamped on the bank, under a small tent they carried with them, just large enough to cover two. They had a merry supper, and having made a large fire, retired, "turned in" and were soon fast asleep. The night waned, and by degrees a drizzling rain succeeded by a heavy shower pattering on the leaves and on their canvas roof, which sheltered them from its fury, half awakened one of them, when on a sudden the savage growl of a Cougar was heard, and in an instant the animal pounced upon the tent and overthrew it.

Our raftsmen did not feel the full force of the blow, as the slight poles of the tent gave way, and the impetus of the spring carried the Panther over them; they started up and scuffled out of the tent without further notice "to quit," and by the dim light of their fire, which the rain had nearly extinguished, saw the animal facing them and ready for another leap; they hastily seized two of the burning sticks, and whirling them around their heads with loud whoops, scared away the midnight prowler. After this adventure they did not, however, try to sleep under their tent any more that night!

We have, given these relations of others to show that at long intervals, and under peculiar circumstances, when perhaps pinched with hunger, or in defence of its young, the Cougar sometimes attacks men. These instances, however, are very rare, and the relations of an affrightened traveller must be received with some caution, making a due allowance for a natural disposition in man to indulge in the marvellous.

Our own experience in regard to the habits of this species is somewhat limited, but we are obliged to state that in the only three instances in which we observed it in its native forests, an impression was left on our minds that it was the most cowardly of any species of its size belonging to this genus. In our boyhood, whilst residing in the northern part of New York, forty-eight years ago, on our way to school through a wood, a Cougar crossed the path not ten yards in front of us. We had never before seen this species, and it was, even at that early period, exceedingly rare in that vicinity. When the Cougar observed us he commenced a hurried retreat; a small terrier that accompanied us gave chase to the animal, which, after running about a hundred yards, mounted an oak and rested on one of its limbs about twenty feet from the ground. We approached and raised a loud whoop, when he sprang to the earth and soon made his escape. He was, a few days afterwards, hunted by the neighbours and shot. Another was treed at night, by a party on a raccoon hunt; supposing it to be a raccoon, one of the men climbed the tree, when the Cougar leaped to the ground, overturning one of the young hunters that happened to be in his way, and made his escape. A third was chased by cur-dogs in a valley in the vicinity of the Catskill mountains, and after half an hour's chase ascended a beech-tree. He placed himself in a crotch, and was fired at with duck-shot about a dozen times, when he was finally killed, and fell heavily to the ground. A Mr. Randolph, of Virginia, related to us an amusing anecdote of a rencontre which he and a Kentuckian had in a valley of one of the Virginia mountains with a Cougar. This occurrence took place about thirty years ago. They had no guns, but meeting him near the road, they gave chase with their horses, and after a run of a few hundred yards he ascended a tree. Randolph climbed the tree, and the Cougar sprang down, avoiding the Kentuckian, who stood ready to attack him with his club. The latter again followed, on his horse, when he treed him a second time. Randolph again climbed after him, but found the animal was coming down, and disposed to fight his way to the ground. He stunned him with a blow, when the Cougar let go his hold, fell to the earth, and was killed by his comrade, who was waiting with his club below.

From all the conversations we have had with hunters who were in the habit of killing the Cougar, we have been brought to the conviction that a man of moderate courage, with a good rifle and a steady arm, accompanied by three or four active dogs, a mixture of either the fox-hound or grey-hound, might hunt the Cougar with great safety to him-self, and with a tolerable prospect of success.

This animal, which has excited so much terror in the minds of the ignorant and timid, has been nearly exterminated in all our Atlantic States, and we do not recollect a single well authenticated instance where any hunter's life fell a sacrifice in a Cougar hunt.

Among the mountains of the head-waters of the Juniatta river [Pennsylvania], as we were informed, the Cougar is so abundant, that one man has killed for some years, from two to five, and one very hard winter, he killed seven. In this part of the country the Cougar is hunted with half-bred hounds, the full-blooded dogs lacking courage to attack so large and fierce-looking an animal when they overtake it. The hunt is conducted much in the manner of a chase after the common wild-cat. The Cougar is "treed" after running about fifteen or twenty minutes, and generally shot, but sometimes it shews fight before it takes to a tree, and the hunters consider it great sport: we heard of an instance of one of these fights, in which the Cougar got hold of a dog, and was killing it, when the hunter in his anxiety to save his dog, rushed upon the Cougar, seized him by the tail and broke his back with a single blow of an axe.

According to the relations of old hunters, the Cougar has three or four young at a litter. We have heard of an instance of one being found, a very old female, in whose den there were five young, about as large as cats, we believe, however, that the usual number of young, is two.

The dens of this species are generally near the mouth of some cave in the rocks, where the animal's lair is just far enough inside to be out of the rain; and not in this respect like the dens of the bear, which are sometimes ten or twelve yards from the opening of a large crack or fissure in the rocks. In the Southern States, where there are no caves or rocks, the lair of the Cougar is generally in a very dense thicket, or in a cane-brake. It is a rude sort of bed of sticks, weeds, leaves, and grasses or mosses, and where the canes arch over it; as they are evergreen, their long pointed leaves turn the rain at all seasons of the year. We have never observed any bones or fragments of animals they had fed upon, at the lairs of the Cougar, and suppose they always feed on what they catch near the spot where they capture the prey.

The tales related of the cry of the Cougar in the forest in imitation of the call of a lost traveller, or the cry of a child, must be received with much caution, and may in many of their exaggerations be set down as vulgar errors. In a state of captivity, we have never heard the male uttering any other note than a low growl; the female, however, we have frequently heard uttering a kind of mewing like that of a cat, but a more prolonged and louder note, that could be heard at the distance of about two hundred yards. All the males, however, of the cat kind, at the season when the sexes seek each other, emit remarkable and startling cries, as is evidenced by the common cat, in what is denominated caterwauling. We have observed the same habit in the leopard, the ocelot, and in our two species of lynx. It is not impossible, therefore, that the male Cougar, may at the rutting season have some peculiar and startling notes. The cries, however, to which persons have from time to time directed our attention, as belonging to the Cougar, we were well convinced were uttered by other animals. In one instance, we ascertained them to proceed from a red fox which was killed in the hunt, got up for the purpose of killing the Cougar. In other cases the screams of the great horned, the barred, or the screech owl are mistaken for the cries of this animal.

The female Cougar is a most affectionate mother, and will not leave her young cubs, unless occasionally to procure food to support her own strength; she therefore often becomes very lean and poor. The female we have figured, was in this condition; we procured one of her cubs and fig-

ured it, presenting its beautiful spots, seldom before noticed. The other made its escape.

The whelps are suckled by the dam until about half grown, and then hunt with the old ones (which generally go in pairs) until the mother is with young again, or the young ones find mates for themselves, and begin to breed.

The period of gestation of the Cougar is ninety-seven days, as has been ascertained at the Zoological Society of London. (Proceedings, 1832, p. 62.) In the Northern and Middle States, the young are produced in the spring. In the Southern States, however, where the animal is supplied with an abundance of food, and not much incommoded by the cold, the young have in some instances been discovered in autumn. . . .

Geographical Distribution
This species has a wide geographical range. It was formerly found in all the Northern and Eastern States, and we have seen a specimen procured in Upper Canada. The climates of Lower Canada, New Foundland, and Labrador, appear to be too cold for its permanent residence. In all the Atlantic States it was formerly found, and a few still exist in the less cultivated portions. It is occasionally shot in the extensive swamps, along the river courses of Carolina, Georgia, Mississippi, and Louisiana; it is found sparingly on the whole range of the Alleghanies, running through a considerable portion of the United States. . . .

General Remarks
The variations of size, to which this species is subject, have created much confusion among our books of Natural History, and added a considerable number of supposed new species. After having examined very carefully very many specimens, both in a prepared state, and alive in menageries, procured in most parts of North and South America, we have arrived at the conclusion that the Cougar of North America and the Puma of our Southern Continent are one and the same species, and cannot even be regarded as varieties.

After Audubon wrote his description, tales of cougars in the East began to fade, although many were captured in local and county histories published toward the end of the nineteenth century, and by writers hired in the 1930s by the federal Works Progress Administration to preserve rural heritage. Books of natural history written for many eastern states in the late 1800s tended to describe cougars as a native animal already or soon to be exterminated by the press of human population. Frederick True's aforementioned 1891 statement about albino cougars was embedded in an eighteen-page chapter on "The Puma, or America Lion," in which he gave a state-by-state list of cougar occurrence: "On the Atlantic coast of North America the species has apparently not been found in the States of New Hampshire, Rhode Island, New Jersey, or Delaware. On our northern boundary I find no mention of its having been found in Michigan or Indiana. In Ohio it was extirpated prior to 1838, and probably more recently in Illinois and Indiana. The Puma has retired before the advance of civilization, and in many of the more thickly populated States it is improbable that even stragglers could be found at the present day."

Ernest Thompson Seton, an extremely popular wildlife writer in his day, agreed in his 1929 book, *Lives of Game Animals:* "In the Eastern States, [the cougar] is virtually extinct. If there is a pair of Cougars in the Green Mountains, Vt., now, it is the highest possible number. If there are six pairs in the mountains between the Catskills and Georgia, I should be agreeably surprised."

True's geographical assessment and Seton's numbers were cautiously challenged in 1976 by U.S. Fish and Wildlife Service biologist Ronald M. Nowak in his report "The Cougar in the United States and Canada": "By about 1900 a significant population still was present in southern Florida, but it apparently declined steadily until the present. There is evidence that certain other populations also survived or became re-established in the central and eastern parts of the continent, and that there may have been moderate increases since the 1940s." Nowak's statement reflects the increasing number of reports of cougars in the East. This phenomenon began to catch the attention of popular writers, as described in the next section.

By the early twentieth century, the practice of natural history was fracturing into specialized areas of biological science. Cougars, like most animals, as well as plants, were increasingly identified by particular morphological characteristics, meticulously measured and compared, believed to have evolved in particular localities. The taxonomy of cougar subspecies (a number ranging from twenty-seven to thirty-two) in North, Central, and South America that grew out of this approach would be challenged in the twenty-first century. In Chapter 3, geneticist Melanie Culver explains her DNA analysis that suggests decreasing the number of subspecies to six.

The seminal description of the eastern cougar subspecies can be found in the 1946 book *The Puma, Mysterious American Cat,* by Stanley P. Young and Edward A. Goldman:

Type locality.—*Pennsylvania.*

Distribution.—*Extinct. Formerly eastern United States as far north as Maine and to southern Ontario and Quebec. Doubtless intergrading to the southward with* coryi. *[i.e.,* Felis concolor coryi, *the Florida panther].*

General characters.—*A medium sized or rather large, dark subspecies. Similar to* coryi, *of Florida, but cranial characters, especially the anteriorly more convergent zygomata and narrower, flatter nasals, distinctive. Similar in general to* hippolestes, *of Wyoming, but smaller, and skull differing in detail.*

Color.— *"Body and legs of a uniform fulvous or tawny hue . . . Ears light-colored within, blackish behind. Belly pale reddish or reddish white. Face sometimes with a uniform lighter tint than the general hue of the body." De Kay (1842: 47).*

Skull.—*Similar to that of* coryi, *but less elongated; nasals narrower and flatter; zygomata more widely spreading posteriorly, turning more abruptly inward and converging anteriorly; postorbital processes shorter; jugal less extended posteriorly; auditory bullae usually smaller, bulging less prominently below exoccipitals; dentition about as in* coryi. *Compared with that of* hippolestes, *the skull is somewhat smaller, less elongated; zygomata more strongly bowed outward posteriorly, more abruptly turned inward and converging anteriorly; nasals broader posteriorly, and narrower, less widely spreading anteriorly over nares; auditory bullae smaller, bulging less prominently below exoccipitals; dentition about the same.*

Measurements.—*Emmons (1840: 35) gives the "whole length" of one of the largest individuals, presumably male, from New York as 9 feet (= 2,743 mm.); tail of a male, 2 feet, 3 inches (= 686 mm.); tail of a female, 1 foot, 9 inches (= 534 mm.). Skull. (Two adults, sex unmarked but obviously females, from the Adirondack Mountain region, New York, respectively): Greatest length, 184,—; condy-*

lobasal length, 168.7, 165; zygomatic breadth, 134.5, 127.8; height of cranium, 66.4, 62.5; interorbital breadth, 35.8, 35.9; postorbital processes, 73.2, 71; width of nasals (at anterior tips of frontals), 16.4, 14.5; width of palate (across interpterygoid fossa), 27.8, 295.8; maxillary tooth row, alveolar length (front of canine to back of carnassial), 55.8, 54.3; upper carnassial, crown length, 22.2, 20.3, width, 10.9, 10.7; lower carnassial, crown length, 16.7, 15.2; upper canine, alveolar diameter (antero-postero), 11.8, 10.9.

Remarks.—The puma formerly ranged throughout the Eastern States, but apparently became extinct many years ago. Surprisingly few specimens found their way into museum collections. Skulls from the State of New York are assumed to represent typical couguar which was described from Pennsylvania. The skulls indicate that it was a well-marked form, differing from coryi and hippolestes in cranial features such as commonly distinguish other subspecies. Unfortunately no skins that have not been exposed to light for a long period are known to be available for comparison, and the color is therefore imperfectly known.

A fragmentary skull from Capon Springs, W. Va., has wide spreading zygomata and in other characters appears to be near typical couguar. Among early specimen records, according to R. M. Anderson, a skin in the National Museum of Canada was taken at Three Rivers, Quebec, in 1828. A mounted specimen in the Museum of the Boston Society of Natural History was captured at Wardsboro, Vt., November 20, 1875.

Felis dorsalis Rafinesque (1832: 19) from Alleghany Mountains of Pennsylvania was described as spotted on sides with a black band all along the middle of the back, the total length 10 feet, and "very different from Felis pardalis, by size four times larger."

Specimens examined.—Total number, 8, as follows:

New York: Adirondack Mountains, 1 (skull only); Catskill Mountains, 1 (skull only);[1]

Essex County, 2 (1 skin only; 1 skull only); "St. Lawrence County," 2 (skulls only).[1]

Pennsylvania: Elk County, 1 (skull only). West Virginia: Capon Springs, 1 (skull only).

---

[1]New York State Mus.

Note that in Young and Goldman's summary, the eastern cougar subspecies was determined on the basis of a total of eight incomplete museum specimens, a surprising paucity remarked upon even by the authors. This inadequate sample undermines the legitimacy of both the traditional and the proposed new taxonomy. Not only are there too few specimens from which to extrapolate the morphology of an entire population, but there is also too little DNA to create a valid genetic profile (see further discussion of genetics in Chapter 3). It seems that the cougar subspecies *Puma concolor couguar* can be defined only as simply cougar.

POPULAR PERCEPTION

The dearth of eastern cougar specimens is explained in part by authors Jackie R. Esposito and Steven L. Herb in *The Nittany Lion* (Pennsylvania State University Press, 1997), the story of one of the most famous cougar mascots in the East. The authors write that in 1942, as Edward A. Goldman began researching the cougar book cited above, he arranged to

CHRIS BOLGIANO

The original Nittany Lion, shot in 1856 by Samuel Brush in Susquehanna County, Pennsylvania. Now displayed behind glass in Pattee Library at Pennsylvania State University, the Brush Lion may be the most complete remaining specimen of the original eastern cougar. The vicious snarl frozen by the taxidermist reflects the human view of cougars at the time.

borrow all cougar specimens owned by the Carnegie Museum. These were placed on a train, but "a freak accident . . . seemed to affect only the car containing the lions, which burst into flames, destroying all the specimens. From that day forward, museums would never again ship or share entire collections of any species."

The Penn State Nittany Lion mascot and its colorful history over the last century and a half began with a real cougar, shot in 1856 by Samuel Brush of Brushville, Susquehanna County, Pennsylvania. At that time, most people considered cougars to be completely undesirable, and getting rid of them was the proper thing to do. The depth of popular loathing of the cougar is clear in the poetry of Daniel Bryan, brother of Daniel Boone's wife, Rebecca Bryan, of Virginia's Shenandoah Valley. Bryan's epic celebration of the frontier heroism of Daniel Boone, *The Mountain Muse,* published in 1813 in Harrisonburg, Virginia, included this passage:

A thousand, thundering feet, with heavy sound,
Like a tornado hurried swiftly on,
And shook the shuddering ground, when lo! appear'd,
O'erspreading many a rood of the drear waste,
A mighty multitude of Buffaloes huge,
Resistless, raging, mad! In their dark van,
One, more enrag'd and furious than the rest,
Vociferous bursts of awful agony pour'd;
His pain-set eyes like burning Globules glar'd;
Upon his knees he oft impetuous pitch'd,
Goring the ground, while, to and fro, in vain
His rough hair'd head he dash'd; for on his back
With rending talons in the flesh infix'd,
A murderous PANTHER plied the work of Death!
Adown the sufferer's brindled sides ran blood,
Profusely streaming. Cruelly, with teeth
Of spear-accuminated sharpness, gnaw'd
The merc'less monster through the strength-strung loins,
And buried deeply in the smoking chasm,
His gory, life-destroying snout; until
Full half his blood-smear'd body disappear'd,

Deep sunk mid sunder'd muscles, mangled flesh,
And bubbling blood!—The roaring sufferer reel'd
And sank and rose, and staggering fell again,
His pain-protruded eyes, with glaring green,
Were deeply died, and Death's destructive shaft
Drew from his heaving heart the strug'ling life!
Around their fallen fellow gather'd thick
The furious herds, and yells and groans, and clash
Of crowded horns, in horrid tumult broke
From the close-clustering circle's brindled bounds.
They snuff'd the sanguine steam the purple spouts
Sent through the air, and catching thence the rage
Of fiercest bestial madness, sidelong tore,
With buried horns, the valley's blood-stain'd breast,
And fiercely furrow'd up, with pawing feet,
Its flower-bespangled soil, wild-bellowing, crush'd
The yielding shrubs, and gored the rough-bark'd trees.
The ferine Murderer startled at the din,
And disinterring his blood-buried half,
Look'd wild and grimly on the pressing foe;
And finding dangers thick beset him round,
With agile Spring, Leap'd on a Buffalo's back,
And thence a neighboring poplar reached, up which
He swiftly fled. Where, on a lofty bough,
Viewing the scene below, 'out-stretch'd he lay,
With head declining o'er his gory paws.
Boone the gorg'd prowler marked, aim'd at his eye
The unerring rifle, and brought headlong down
His brain-bespatter'd carcase. Terror-shock'd
At the unwonted peal, the wide-mouth'd herds
Hoarse-yelling, burst resistless through the Brakes.

The blood lust ascribed to Old World panthers is apparent here. As decades passed and most easterners lost contact with the kind of wilderness that supported cougars, this negative imagery began to be balanced by an ambivalent admiration for some cougar qualities. W. Gilmore Simms' serialized novel, *The Cub of the Panther,* published in twelve installments throughout 1869 in the New York magazine *The Old Guard,* was allegedly based on a real story that took place in the mountains of South Carolina in the 1840s. A boy was born with a birthmark shaped like a panther cub as his mother was being stalked by a panther in a snowstorm. He was rescued in the nick of time, and grew up to be lithe, graceful, strong, fearless, solitary, and above all widely respected as a superb hunter, but quick to quarrel—and thereon turned the plot.

Magazines and dime novels that became popular in the late nineteenth century told tales of cougars as worthy—if often sneaky—adversaries for intrepid heroes, but these were mostly about western cougars. Although the cougar had largely disappeared from nearly all of eastern North America by the early twentieth century, its notoriety as the lord of the forests was kept alive by several regional writers. These chroniclers extolled the old days of frontier cougar hunting as a nostalgic highlight of a vanished way of life and a blood sport that provided unparalleled excitement. Among the most notable was Henry W. Shoemaker, a wealthy and prominent conservationist and political Progressive who published several Pennsylvania newspapers, including the *Altoona Tribune.*

Shoemaker used his wealth and position to celebrate the natural and cultural aspects of Pennsylvania history. His hundred-plus publications include *The Pennsylvania Lion or Panther: A Narrative of Our Grandest Animal* (1914) and the eulogy *Extinct Pennsylvania Animals, Part 1: The Panther and the Wolf* (1917). In the latter, he notes that the text has been prepared "from the point of view of the old hunters, whom the writer has interviewed. While there are some statements which are liable to be declared scientifically incorrect, they are printed for what they are worth, as the authorities were as reliable as unscientific observers can be. The statement is herein made that Pennsylvania panthers were the largest known in the East, and this the writer believes to be correct. This animal, above all others, added most to the legendary lore of the state." Shoemaker made an unusual case on behalf of the cougar for the sake of the old hunters: "This is done in case a time should come when 'red-blooded' sportsmen will decide to reintroduce the panther as our leading game animal. Then there would be at least one published work which would show the misjudged 'cougar' in a favorable light."

Shoemaker also stated that the last confirmed cougar kill in Pennsylvania was in 1905 in Clearfield County, but he mentioned two uncon-

John Gallant shot this cougar while squirrel hunting in Crawford County, PA, in 1967.

firmed kills as late as 1916 in Mifflin County. Unfortunately, Shoemaker wasn't able to remark on the 1967 incident in Crawford County in which a young female cougar was killed by squirrel hunter John Gallant and confirmed by a curator at the Carnegie Museum of Natural History in Pittsburgh (as reported by investigative naturalist Helen McGinnis in *Pennsylvania Game News,* February 1982). Questions about the origins of this cougar and another seen with her immediately arose, as would be the case in every subsequent confirmation across the East (see Chapter 2). Nonetheless, this 1967 confirmation, in conjunction with the accumulating sighting reports, helped put the eastern cougar subspecies on the federal Endangered Species List in 1973.

More reliable than Shoemaker's mix of legend and fact was John Spargo's 1950 chronicle, *The Catamount in Vermont.* Spargo used the colloquial adaptation of the Spanish *gatmonte,* meaning "mountain cat." Director of the Bennington Historical Museum and Art Gallery, Spargo described the traditional attitude toward cougars: "Frightful and terrifying in mien, its every appearance anywhere in the vicinity of human habitation has caused it to be hunted by resolute men armed with shotguns and muskets and rifles bent upon its extermination. Not even the savage wolf, formerly numerous in many parts of the State aroused the farmers and woodsmen to equal efforts at extermination."

Spargo inventoried the most reliable Vermont cougar stories, particularly those that yielded physical and photographic evidence, like the Wardsboro Panther of 1875 and the Barnard Panther of 1881, said to be the last verified cougar in the state. Some Vermonters refused to believe that. Spargo also reported on a tongue-in-cheek "secret society," the Irrepressible and Uncompromising Order of Panthers, formed in 1934 by a group of people who were convinced they had seen cougars. Unfortunately, Spargo, like Shoemaker, was unable to remark upon the 1994 case that once again confirmed cougar presence in his state (see Chapter 2).

The mid-century writing that probably had the greatest impact on the common perception of cougar status was Herbert Ravenel Sass's 1954 piece in the venerable *Saturday Evening Post,* "The Panther Prowls the East Again!" Sass concentrated on sightings in South Carolina by reputedly reliable sources but also included most of Appalachia and eastern

VERMONT HISTORICAL SOCIETY

Hunter Alexander Crowell poses with the Barnard Panther, shot in 1881 and believed to be the last eastern cougar killed in Vermont.

Canada. "In New York State each hunting season brings a new batch of panther stories. In Pennsylvania, West Virginia and North Carolina, stories of panthers seen in the woods are a regular accompaniment of each hunting season." Sass admitted to having no physical evidence for the existence of the animal but proclaimed that the large number of sightings couldn't be ignored. "It is the scientist's business, we are often told, to be skeptical," he wrote. "But skepticism didn't split the atom."

Among the sightings cited by Sass are those resulting from fieldwork by one of the foremost advocates for cougars in the East, wildlife biologist Bruce S. Wright of the Northeastern Wildlife Station in Fredericton, New Brunswick, Canada. Wright spent decades investigating cougar sightings, looking for field evidence, and interviewing cougar experts, including America's most famous and beloved conservationist, Aldo Leopold, who, said Wright, "believed before anybody else and who gave me the necessary encouragement."

Wright published his findings in two books, *The Ghost of North America: The Story of the Eastern Panther* (1959) and *The Eastern Panther: A*

The skin of a cougar killed in New Brunswick, Canada, in 1932.

Question of Survival (1972). In them he published the first twentieth-century photo of a cougar in the East (and the only New Brunswick specimen ever photographed), shot in 1932.

Wright grounded his work on scientific methods, but despite the difficulty of documenting the cat's existence, he believed that the many sightings by credible people indicated at least a few cougars living in the East. He seems to have been the first biologist to castigate his professional colleagues for their refusal to even consider the possibility of cougars. He recommended the establishment of cougar refuges and worried about the impact of ever-increasing roads on cougar habitat.

Wright's tradition of objective scrutiny was carried on by New Brunswick wildlife biologist Gerry Parker, who in 1998 published his own investigation into past and present cougar reports in *The Eastern Panther, Mystery Cat of the Appalachians:* "This book will not answer whether the panther still remains with us. After years of involvement with this enigma, especially in Atlantic Canada, I remain optimistic. The panther now represents for me all the lost wilderness of the vast, virgin American continent and the mystery and challenge of its Adirondack forests."

Far to the south, in the state of Tennessee, the listing of the eastern cougar as a federally endangered species in 1973 prompted the Great Smoky Mountains Natural History Association to fund a report on "Status and History of the Mountain Lion in the Great Smoky Mountains National Park." Written by Nicole Culbertson of the park's Uplands Field Research Laboratory, the report recorded the last cougar killed in the park, in 1920, and documented cougars in Tennessee in 1971 and North Carolina in 1976. After analyzing prey abundance, human disturbance, and carrying capacity of the park, the report concluded that "the number of mountain lion sightings through the years suggest that the mountain lion may never have actually been extinct in the Great Smoky Mountains area. The lion may have been able to maintain itself in small numbers in the more inaccessible mountainous regions in or around the park . . . while a conservation [*sic*] population estimate for 1975 would be three animals, the estimate could be as high as five or six."

The possibility that cougars, now an endangered species, might exist on national forest lands adjoining the Great Smoky Mountains National Park had implications for logging policies on public lands. In 1978 the

Biologist and author Bruce S. Wright with a mounted cougar trapped in
Somerset County, Maine, in 1938.

U.S. Forest Service and the U.S. Fish and Wildlife Service collaborated to
fund a field study by U.S. F&WS biologist Robert L. Downing. For six
winters he looked for cougar tracks in the Southern Appalachians whenever it snowed, and tracked them through history when it didn't. He
reported his results in a 1984 issue of the journal *Cryptozoology*, including
the most detailed list of cougar evidence to date.

Although Downing found only one track and one scat suspected to
have been made by cougars, he figured that even after allowing for false
reports, "as many as 20 cougars may have been killed in or near the
mountains in Georgia, Alabama, Tennessee, North Carolina, and South
Carolina during the last 50 to 80 years." Nonetheless, he was pessimistic
about being able to prove that breeding populations of cougars exist:

> *Public agencies have adopted the defensive attitude that they will not*
> *consider such radical measures [as closing hunting season where cougars*
> *are seen] until breeding populations of cougars have been proven to*

exist. All that I have been able to prove in six years of effort is that proof
of their existence is difficult to obtain . . . "non-occurrence" is virtually
impossible to prove conclusively. I must conclude, unless we accept the
unlikely possibility that everyone who reported seeing a cougar in the
East was mistaken, that the animal has existed in small numbers in sev-
eral areas at least within the last ten years. I do not know if it still exists
at the present time.

Instead of acknowledging the possibility that a few remnant clusters
of cougars might remain, state and federal wildlife management personnel hardened their already stiff resistance and generally refused to consider sightings without physical proof. People trying to report sightings
often experienced (and still do) ridicule and rudeness. In response to
agency hostility, grassroots groups dedicated to documenting cougar
reports began to proliferate.

Undoubtedly the most controversial of these groups was founded by
John Lutz, a radio reporter in Baltimore, Maryland, who started investigating cougars in the 1960s after he covered a story about a mysterious
predator along the Gunpowder River. By the 1980s, Lutz had become
seriously alienated from wildlife officials and formed a multi-state collab-
oration of like-minded individuals called the Eastern Puma Research
Network. His newsletters contained reports sent in by his contacts. The
January 2003 newsletter gave a summary of statistics for 2002 (the latest
year available): 475 total sightings from 25 states (New York contributed
the most with 69) and three Canadian provinces. Of the total, 100 were
black cougars, and 69 were cubs.

Many people felt that Lutz's criteria for evaluating reports were
weak, and in the 1990s he lost credibility when he claimed to have physical proof but refused to make it accessible. Conspiracy theories held by
some members of Lutz's group were described by writer Jay Kirk in an
article for *Harper's Magazine* (April 2004).

In New Hampshire, businessman Ted Reed, who believed he had
seen a cougar in Nova Scotia, founded a more conservative group,
Friends of the Eastern Panther. His newsletter, "Panther Prints," published from 1990 to 1994, contained well-documented reports.

During that same time period, Ohio native Jay Tischendorf, who
studied western cougars as a wildlife biology student and eventually

became a veterinarian in Montana, also published a newsletter, "Eastern Panther Update." Tischendorf's articles went beyond sighting reports to discuss broader issues of cougar habitat, behavior, and management. In 1994 he collaborated with Ted Reed and Gannon University in Erie, Pennsylvania, to organize the first Eastern Cougar Conference. The proceedings, published in 1996, followed the standard scientific conference format and included presentations by nationally respected carnivore expert Susan Morse of Vermont and Dr. Ranier Brocke of the State University of New York at Syracuse.

Ten years later, Tischendorf helped organize the second Eastern Cougar Conference, in Morgantown, West Virginia (proceedings were in publication as this book went to press). This time, Tischendorf collaborated with a new group, the Eastern Cougar Foundation. Established in 1998 by West Virginia coal miner Todd Lester, who used email and the Internet (www.easterncougar.org) to develop a network of contacts, the Eastern Cougar Foundation seems to be the first such group to acquire IRS nonprofit status (see Todd Lester's essay in Chapter 3). Science-based, with several prominent biologists on its board of directors, the foundation's goals as stated on its website are: "1. Conduct investigations to document cougar presence in eastern North America. 2. Promote full legal protection of all cougars living wild in the East, regardless of origins. 3. Build tolerance through education." In 2003, the Eastern Cougar Foundation won several grants and began a remote camera field survey for cougars in West Virginia in full cooperation with state and federal agencies.

The task of documenting cougar confirmations elsewhere in the East was taken over by a group of volunteers who formed the Eastern Cougar Network (later renamed the Cougar Network). This group does not advocate any position and aims only to report the increasing number of verified cases of cougars on a website (www.easterncougarnet.org) maintained by Ken Miller, a retired computer expert living in New England. Confirmations are defined on this website as:

> 1. The body of a dead cougar, or a live captured animal. 2. Photographs (including video) that clearly identify one or more cougars, and which can be certified as to date, time and place by the original photographer. 3. Evidence which has been analyzed and identified as DNA material

from Puma concolor *(cougar). DNA can be extracted from scat (the most common source of DNA evidence) or from hair. Note: ECN is interested in documenting evidence of wild, free-roaming cougars. As a result, animals of known captive origin are not included as confirmations or probables.*

The search for cougars in the East is now focused on field evidence, but unconfirmed sightings continue to pour in. Chris Bolgiano's 1995 book, *Mountain Lion: An Unnatural History of Pumas and People,* explored the phenomenon of eastern cougar sightings:

> *The people who think they've seen a cougar resist the obvious and logical explanations. They want to believe they've seen the rarest and arguably the most dangerous animal possible where they live. Surely these cougars are cultural projections, drawn perhaps from guilt for our collective ravaging of the continent, and from yearning for the exoneration that the survival of cougars would confer. Psychologists say that knowledge of humankind's assault on the natural world is a painful source of modern Angst. Surely, too, there is an element of thrill-seeking in the sightings, in a culture addicted to the fastest, biggest, highest, and fiercest, whether in machines, mountains, or animals. Maybe the image of cat goes deeper than culture. Maybe it has been permanently etched on human consciousness by eons of fear and admiration. Cat sightings may be a primal expression of the human understanding of nature.*

Confirmed Cougar Evidence in Eastern North America

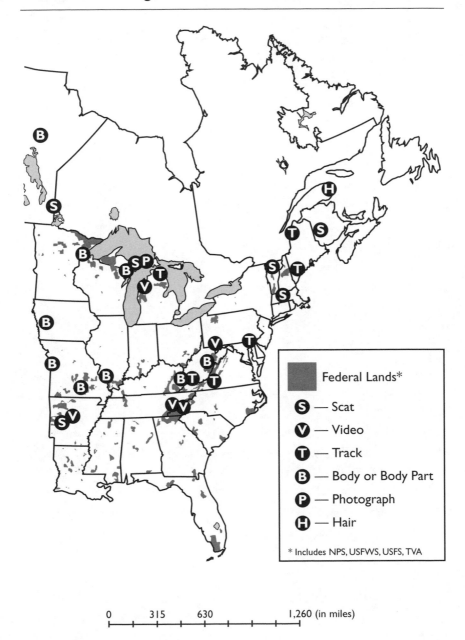

Federal Lands*

S — Scat
V — Video
T — Track
B — Body or Body Part
P — Photograph
H — Hair

* Includes NPS, USFWS, USFS, TVA

0   315   630   1,260 (in miles)

2

Reappearance:
Where's the Evidence?

The previous chapter described the accelerating pace of cougar encounters reported by both rural and urban residents throughout the twentieth century. The response of the wildlife establishment—state and federal wildlife agency scientists and administrators, plus academic research biologists—was simple: deny, deny, deny. Sightings were attributed to delusion, deception, or drunkenness. "There's never any field evidence," was the common refrain of the officials to whom sightings were reported—until the 1990s, when the situation changed dramatically.

Confirmed field evidence began to accumulate, and at an astonishing rate. This continuing phenomenon may be due to increasing numbers of cougars throughout the East, increasing numbers of people living in rural areas, increasingly sophisticated DNA technology, or increasing interest by the press in reporting alleged encounters—or all of the above. Now, instead of dismissing the possibility of wild cougars, biologists acknowledge that there might be a few, but maintain that these cats couldn't possibly be remnant natives and must all be FERCs (feral escaped or released captives) from subspecies other than that designated as the endangered eastern cougar.

By calling into question the genetic heritage of cougars living wild in the East, wildlife officials can sidestep the Endangered Species Act, which lists only the Florida panther (Puma concolor coryii) and the eastern cougar (Puma concolor couguar). Never mind the intent of the act to preserve rare life forms, or the scientific impossibility of defining unique eastern cougar genes, or the common practice of substituting subspecies from elsewhere in many official wildlife projects (including the Florida Panther Program) when the original genome is extinct or debilitated from inbreeding.

The following section contains the most credible confirmations of field evidence of cougars living wild in the East for which reprint permissions could be obtained: papers in peer-reviewed scientific journals, reputable newspaper articles, governmental agency file memos and reports, and on-the-record interviews with authorities. But the documents gathered here represent merely the tip of a cougar's tail, so to speak—an enormous body of additional literature exists in varying shades of credibility.

The paper that begins this section is the first compilation of documented field evidence of cougars in the East to be presented at a scientific forum. The Mountain Lion Workshops, held in western North America every three to six years since the 1970s, are the major gatherings of researchers and managers. One of the first actions of the newly formed Eastern Cougar Foundation was to collaborate on the following paper.

Field Evidence of Cougars in Eastern North America

by Chris Bolgiano, Todd Lester, Donald W. Linzey, and David S. Maehr
In L. A. Harveson, P. M. Harveson, and R. W. Adams, editors. *Proceedings of the Sixth Mountain Lion Workshop.* Austin, Texas, 2000.

Abstract

Confirmed physical field evidence of cougars living wild in several regions of eastern North America is beginning to accumulate. Related issues of legal status, habitat management, and social acceptance are also emerging. We document twelve instances in which various items of field evidence have been confirmed by biologists: three cases involving live animals, a dead body or body part; four cases of scats; three cases of tracks; and two videos. The geographic range of these incidents is New Brunswick, Canada, to Missouri, and the date range is 1976 to 2000. Each case entails consideration of significant details, including the history of cougars in the local area, the circumstances of local habitat and prey, evidence of reproduction, credentials of confirming biologists and the possibility of fraud. Possible sources of these animals include remnant natives, escaped or released captives, and colonizers from known cougar populations in Florida, Texas and elsewhere. Since spring of 1998 at least 3 radio-collared Florida panthers have crossed north of the Caloosahatchee River for the first time since fieldwork began 20 years ago. The potential for reestablishment of a viable breeding population is more likely to be limited by human intolerance than biological constraints, especially in rural communities near public lands. An ecological benefit of a cougar population in the east might be to return an evolutionary selection force and population check on over-abundant deer. Outdoor recreationists and hunters are also likely to express interest in cougars.

Introduction

Native eastern cougars were believed extirpated throughout the east by the 1940s, but a growing number of sightings prompted the listing of *Felis concolor couguar* on the 1973 Endangered Species List (Bolgiano 1995). A field survey in the southern Appalachians by the U.S. Fish and Wildlife Service (USF&WS), however, failed to find conclusive evidence of cougars by the early 1980s, although a small number of possible deer kills, scrapes, and scats were identified (Downing 1981).

Confirmed field evidence began to accumulate in the 1990s. The presence of at least a few individuals living wild in the east is now acknowledged by the USF&WS (Clark 2000). Issues of legal status, population viability, habitat management, and human acceptance are emerging. The Eastern Cougar Foundation (ECF), a 501(c)(3) organization, was founded by independent researcher Todd Lester in West Virginia in 1998 to compile the accumulating evidence, and to grapple with these issues.

As Vice President of the ECF, I'm here to present the evidence, and to grapple. Our Board of Directors includes David Maehr, former leader of Florida panther field research; Donald Linzey, in charge of mammal research for the All-Taxa Biodiversity Inventory in Great Smoky Mountains National Park; Melanie Culver, cougar geneticist who is also presenting a paper at this workshop; and Sue Morse, carnivore expert who gave the keynote address at the Third Mountain Lion Workshop in Prescott, AZ in 1988.

Methods

Todd Lester of WV and Donald Linzey of VA have for many years passed out flyers asking people to call them if a cougar was seen, so communication networks were already established. Todd Lester expanded them through an eastern cougar web site and a listserv, which at times has included well over 100 people from South America to Alaska. Lester and Linzey standardized the procedures they use to narrow the large volume of sightings to the small percentage of credible prospects (Miller 1998). For those within a day's drive, they conduct field searches for hard evidence and scrutinize evidence collected by others. For more distant cases, one or more of us investigates through phone and email interviews. Written confirmation from recognized authorities is the only validation we accept. Melanie Culver at VA Tech tests samples and validates tests conducted by others.

Results

Over the past two years we have compiled one dozen confirmed incidents from Ontario to North Carolina, some of them representing clusters of cougar activity (copies of any or all documentations are available from the ECF for the cost of photocopying and postage). Cases are categorized by type of evidence.

Three cases involve live animals, a dead body or a body part:

In 1976, a male cougar was killed while killing sheep, and a pregnant female was captured two days later in Pocahontas County, WV. The dead cougar was pictured in the local paper with WV Dept. of Natural Resources (WVDNR) officer Larry Guthrie. Correspondence between the USF&WS and the WVDNR focuses on discussion about whether the captured cougar is tame and would therefore constitute a threat to humans if released in the wild, but no documentation seems to exist on the actual fate of the cougar or any progeny.

In 1998, a cougar pelt was found along a road in Texas County, MO, near the Mark Twain National Forest and approximately 125 air miles west of the IL site below. It is believed to be from a cougar that was treed and killed by raccoon hunters in 1994, the first cougar killed in MO since 1927. The MO Department of Conservation (MDC) uncovered a photo of the dead cat and successfully prosecuted two hunters, who admitted dumping the pelt. Gary Cravens of the MDC determined from witnesses that the hunted cougar had no tattoos and long, sharp claws, found also on the pelt. Genetic analysis of the pelt indicated a North American genotype. In addition, in the same general area, a video of a cougar was made by MDC agent Jerry Elliott in 1996, and two deer kills were confirmed as cougar kills by the MDC in 1998.

In July of 2000, a cougar was killed by a train in western Randolph County, IL near the Mississippi River and the Shawnee National Forest. A necropsy by Alan Woolf of the Cooperative Wildlife Research Laboratory at Southern Illinois University found a normal, healthy male aged 4 to 6 years belonging to the North American genotype, with normal claws, stomach contents of 100% fawn, and no tattoos. Many, if not most captive cougars are declawed and/or have tattoos.

There are four cases of scats:

In 1992 in central New Brunswick, Canada, Provincial wildlife biologist Rod Cumberland documented tracks and collected a scat that was analyzed by the Canadian Museum of Nature in Ottawa and found to contain showshoe hair bones and foot and leg hairs of cougar.

In 1994, a scat recovered by agents of the VT Fish & Wildlife Dept. near Craftsbury in north central VT was sent to the USF&WS Forensics Lab in Ashland, OR, where cougar foot hairs were found in it. These are presumed ingested during self-grooming. The sighting that prompted the search involved three cougars, and three sets of tracks were found, possibly indicating a family group.

In 1997, a scat collected in central MA by John McCarter, a staff member of the Paul Rezendes Tracking School, was sent to George Amato of the Wildlife Conservation Society in New York. DNA tests indicated cougar, a finding confirmed by Melanie Culver, who also found that the animal was of the North American genotype. The large, wild Quabbin Reservoir area of central MA has for many years been a locus of cougar sightings.

In 1999 in Ontario, Canada, Provincial wildlife biologist Lil Anderson collected a scat that was sent to the Alberta Natural Resources Service forensics lab in Edmonton for thin layer chromatography and found to be cougar.

There are three cases of tracks:

In 1990 in southwestern VA, Donald Linzey collected photos and cement casts of tracks that he confirmed as cougar. This is approximately

140 air miles from an incident in Russell County, VA in 1997, in which 25 goats were killed by an alleged cougar (not confirmed), and where personnel of the VA Dept. of Game and Inland Fisheries reported two separate cougar sightings, one of which included a kitten.

In 1994 in northwestern ME, approximately 150 air miles east of the confirmed New Brunswick site, two game wardens investigated a sighting of three cats near the St. Johns River and found tracks which they officially reported as cougar to Richard Hoppe, wildlife biologist for the ME Dept. of Inland Fisheries and Wildlife.

In 1996 in southern WV, approximately 100 air miles from the confirmed tracks in VA, Todd Lester made plaster casts of tracks that were confirmed by Lee Fitzhugh of the Extension Wildlife Service at University of CA, Davis, and by David Maehr. This is an area with a long history of cougar sightings and deer kills thought to be cougar.

There are two videos:

In the early 1990s in the western mountains of MD, a home video was obtained and verified by Leslie Johnston, District Wildlife Manager of the MD Dept. of Natural Resources, who made it available to MD public TV, where it was shown many times, and to various biologists' meetings.

A still picture made from a home video taken near Friendsville, MD, around 1993.

PAUL R. SCHROYER FAMILY AND MARK JENKINS

In 1991 in NC just east of the Great Smoky Mountains National Park, a home video was obtained and verified by Donald Linzey. The Great Smoky Mountains was one of the areas that Bob Downing, who did the USF&WS field survey mentioned earlier, felt could have supported native cougars through the twentieth century, because roughly 20% of the park's 500,000 acres was never logged and remained an undisturbed refuge.

Discussion

Fail-safe chain of custody documentation for all evidence is unattainable, and it's possible that one or a few incidents may be forgeries. But it is unlikely that all of them are. Questions are shifting to: 1) whether these are escaped or released animals other than the native eastern cougar or Florida panther subspecies *(Puma concolor couguar* and *Puma concolor coryi,* the only ones listed in the Endangered Species Act); and 2) whether these are individual, transient animals or a breeding population(s). The answer to the first question may never be resolved, because of the low genetic variability of North American cougars and perhaps more importantly because of the small sample size of known eastern cougars (Culver 1999).

In addition to remnant natives and escaped/released captives, a third possible source is colonizers from known cougar populations in Florida, Texas, and Montana, and suspected populations in Saskatchewan and Manitoba (Anderson 1983; Wrigley 1982). Since spring of 1998, at least three radio-collared Florida panthers have crossed north of the Caloosahatchee River west of Lake Okeechobee for the first time since fieldwork began twenty years ago (Maehr 2000). There is also evidence of increasing cougar activity in Kansas, Nebraska, Oklahoma, and other areas of the West that could indicate that cougars are reclaiming former ranges or even expanding into new areas (Henderson 1992; Duggan 2000; Pike 1999).

It's also possible that cougars from two or all three sources are interbreeding in the east. Three clusters of confirmation raise intriguing questions about reproduction. First, the 1994 VT confirmation involved a possible family group, and New England, especially Maine, continues to report sightings of mothers with kittens, some with field evidence awaiting confirmation. Although there are concerns about development of the North Woods, at present there is a substantial amount of wild land there.

Second is a cluster in the Southern Appalachians. The ECF is biased toward receiving reports from this region because we are based there. However, there are some seven million acres of national forests and parks spread from Virginia to Georgia, the largest complex of public lands east of the Mississippi River. Included are 47 Congressionally designated wilderness areas, many of which are so remote and rugged that they still contain old growth that was never logged. It seems likely that if cougars are breeding, it would be in this region. A habitat analyses based on GIS layers of forest cover and human population, road, and deer densities showed that good cougar habitat in the central Appalachians does exist in and around these public lands (Taverna 1999).

Third is the cluster of activity in MO and the confirmation just across the Mississippi River in IL. It seems unlikely that cougars could cross the river, but it was also deemed highly unlikely that Florida panthers could successfully navigate through intense human development and cross the Caloosahatchee River. Given the remarkable capabilities of this animal, no possibility should be absolutely ruled out.

Conclusion

Given the well-known regrowth of forest cover and resurgence of deer herds across the east, it's likely that human rather than biological constraints will limit the establishment of viable cougar populations. There is a potentially positive public reaction to the animals. Fifty-six conservation groups across the east endorsed the recent ECF request that the USF&WS expand the Similarity of Appearances rule of the ESA from Florida throughout the east (Lester 2000). That request was denied pending documentation of a breeding population. If viable cougar populations with their potential for depredations are to be tolerated, however, much educational outreach remains to be done in rural communities, especially around public lands. It may be possible to persuade hunters to accept perceived cougar competition for deer, and simultaneously to reduce the possibilities of cougar attacks on humans and livestock, by allowing non-consumptive chasing with dogs in restricted areas as a means of aversive conditioning (Hebert 1996). There may also be possibilities for future ecotourism. Most importantly, a viable cougar population would return a native predator and offer ecosystem benefits such as an evolutionary selection force and population check on currently over-abundant deer.

Acknowledgements

We wish to thank the Sierra Club and the Southern Appalachian Forest Coalition for making it possible to present this paper.

Bibliography

Anderson, Allen E. 1983. A critical review of literature on puma *(Felis concolor)*. Special report no. 54. Colorado Division of Wildlife. 91 pp.

Bolgiano, Chris. 1995. *Mountain lion: an unnatural history of pumas and people.* Mechanicsburg, PA: Stackpole Books. 209 pp.

Brocke, Rainer H., and Fred G. VanDyke. 1985. "Eastern cougars: the verifiability of the presence of isolated individuals versus populations (comment on Downing, *Cryptozoology,* 3:31–49, 1984)." *Cryptozoology* 4:102–105.

Clark, Jamie R. 2000. Letter of June 21 to Todd Lester, President, Eastern Cougar Foundation. 1 p.

Culbertson, Nicole. 1976. Status and history of the mountain lion in the Great Smoky Mountains National Park. Research/Resources Management Report no. 15. Gatlinburg, TN: National Park Service Southeast Region, Uplands Field Research Laboratory, Great Smoky Mountains National Park. 51 pp.

Culver, Melanie. 1999. Molecular genetic variation, population structure, and natural history of free-ranging pumas *(Puma concolor)*. Dissertation. College Park, MD: University of Maryland. 225 pp.

Downing, Robert L. 1981. "The current status of the cougar in the Southern Appalachian [sic]." In: *Proceedings of The Nongame and Endangered Wildlife Symposium,* Athens, GA, August 13–14.

Downing, Robert L. 1984. "The search for cougars in the eastern United States." *Cryptozoology* 3: 31–49.

Duggan, Joe. 2000. "Examinations reveals [sic] shot cat was healthy." *Lincoln Journal Star* [NE], November 2. 1 p.

Hebert, D., and L. Lay. 1997. "Cougar-human interactions in British Columbia." In: *Proceedings of the Fifth Mountain Lion Workshop,* 27 Feb.–1 March, 1996, p. 44–45. Southern California Chapter of The Wildlife Society.

Henderson, F. Robert. 1992. Update: Puma in Kansas? Kansas State University Cooperative Extension Service. 22 pp.

Lester, Todd. 2000. Letter of March 20 to Jamie Clark, Director, U.S. Fish & Wildlife Service. 2 pp.

Linzey, Donald W. 1999. "Cougars in the Southern Appalachians." In: *Proceedings of the New River Symposium,* April 15–16, Boone, NC, p. 10–15.

Maehr, David S. 2000. Personal communication.

McBride, Roy T., et al. 1993. "Do mountain lions exist in Arkansas?" In: *Proceedings of the Annual Conference of the Southeastern Fish and Wildlife Agencies* 47:394–402.

Miller, Janet. 1998. Evidence for an eastern cougar reassessment. M.S. Thesis. Oxford, OH: Miami University.

Nowak, Ronald M. 1976. The cougar in the United States and Canada. New York Zoological Society and U.S. Fish & Wildlife Service.

Pike, Jason R., et al. 1999. "A geographic analysis of the status of mountain lions in Oklahoma." *Wildlife Society Bulletin* 27(1): 4–10.

Roof, Jayde C., and David S. Maehr. 1988. "Sign surveys for Florida panthers on peripheral areas of their known range." *Florida Field Naturalist* 16(4): 81–104.

Taverna, Kristin, et al. 1999. Eastern Cougar *(Puma concolor couguar):* Habitat suitability analysis for the central Appalachians. Charlottesville, VA: Appalachian Restoration Campaign. 23 pp. www.heartwood.org/arc

Tischendorf, Jay W., and Steven J. Ropski, eds. 1994. *Proceedings of the Eastern Cougar Conference,* Gannon University, Erie, PA, June 3–5. Ft. Collins, CO: American Ecological Research Institute. 245 pp.

Wrigley, Robert E., and Robert W. Nero. 1982. Manitoba's big cat: the story of the cougar in Manitoba. Winnipeg: Manitoba Museum of Man and Nature.

Young, Stanley P., and Edward A. Goldman. 1946. *The puma, mysterious American cat.* Washington, D.C.: American Wildlife Institute. 358 pp.

As noted in the above paper, cougar movements eastward from established popula-tions in Rocky Mountain states to midwestern states have become a major focus of active documentation. Probably using riparian strips as corridors, cougars are appearing in Oklahoma, Kansas, and Nebraska, where they have not been seen for decades, even a century or more. South Dakota now has a breeding population in the Black Hills. States on both sides of the Mississippi River are reporting cougars. The documents in the rest of this section are organized by geographic area, starting with the most southerly states along the Mississippi River and moving northward around the Great Lakes states into the Canadian provinces of Ontario, Quebec, and New Brunswick, then south down the Appalachian Mountain chain. Coyotes are believed to have traveled this general route to inhabit every state in the East, and it's at least theoretically possible that cougars are following a similar course.

A Survey of Recent Accounts of the Mountain Lion (*Puma concolor*) in Arkansas

by David W. Clark, Steffany C. White, Annalea K. Bowers, Leah D. Lucio, and Gary A. Heidt[1]
Southeastern Naturalist 1(3): 269–278, 2002

Abstract

We collected physical evidence (scats and tracks) that suggested the presence of 1 or more mountain lions (*Puma concolor*) in Arkansas from 1998–1999, and conducted a survey of mountain lion occurrences in Arkansas from 1996–2000. Mountain lions were reported statewide, with most in the Ozark and Ouachita Mountains. In addition to the surveys, we collected 7 pieces of tangible evidence (e.g., scats, tracks, and video) from 1996–2000. A survey of the U.S. Department of Agriculture, state veterinarians, and an Arkansas Game and Fish Commission (AGFC) internal survey of their wildlife officers documented at least 101 captive *P. concolor* in the state. The origins of reported free-ranging animals could not be determined.

Introduction

The mountain lion's (*Puma concolor*) original range is the largest of any native terrestrial mammal in the Western Hemisphere, extending from the southern Yukon Territory of Canada to southern Chile (Dixon 1982;

---

[1]Department of Biology, University of Arkansas at Little Rock, 2801 South University Avenue, Little Rock, AR 72204.

Lindzey 1987), and covering most of North America (Currier 1983). With the exception of southern Texas and south Florida, it has been widely thought that mountain lions were largely extirpated from the central and eastern portions of the United States (Lindzey 1987).

In recent years there has been an accumulation of physical evidence and numerous sightings of mountain lions in areas where they were thought to be extirpated. For example, in 2001, a lactating female with 2 cubs was killed near Duluth, Minnesota, and a small population has since been acknowledged in the northern portion of the state (Zuidema 2002). Sightings by natural resource professionals and the public have also occurred in the Upper Peninsula and northern Lower Michigan; more recently a set of tracks and a photograph of an animal confirmed their existence (Zuidema 2002). Likewise, a few mountain lions may inhabit portions of northern Wisconsin (Zuidema 2002). In 2001, an apparently wild individual was killed by a car in Shelby County, Iowa, and tracks have been confirmed from other counties (Iowa Department of Natural Resources press release, 2001, Clear Lake, IA). In 2000, a wild mountain lion was killed after being struck by a train in Randolph County, Illinois (Illinois Department of Natural Resources press release, 2000, Springfield, IL). In 1999, an interagency Mountain Lion Response Team was formed in Missouri after 4 hunters killed and photographed a mountain lion, a second was videotaped, and rabbit hunter's dogs treed another (*Missouri Conservationist* 1999). Bischof and Morrison (2000) reported a mountain lion killed by a hunter and discussed 8 additional observations in Nebraska. Bolgiano et al. (2000) pointed out that physical evidence of mountain lions in eastern North America has been accumulating. This phenomenon may also be occurring in Arkansas.

The white-tailed deer *(Odocoileus virginiana)* in Arkansas had dwindled to about 300 animals by the early 1930s. At this time, it was widely believed that the mountain lion *(Puma concolor)* was extirpated from the state (Young and Goldman 1946). Deer numbers have increased in Arkansas since the late 1940s (Cartwright 1999). In 1949, a mountain lion was killed by a hunter in western Arkansas (Sealander 1951). In the 1950s and 1960s, sightings and discovery of sign increased and in 1969 a hunter killed a mountain lion in southeastern Arkansas (Lewis 1969, 1970; Noble 1971; Sealander 1956). Sealander and Gipson (1973) summarized 63 mountain lion records from 1945 to 1972 and suggested that a small and possibly increasing mountain lion population existed in the state.

In 1975, a hunter killed a mountain lion in western Arkansas and in 1978 a track, a sighting, and steroid analysis of a scat confirmed the presence of a second mountain lion in the area (Harvey and Barkley 1979). Reports of mountain lions by citizens, hunters, and biologists increased to over 30 reports per year in the mid-1980s (Arkansas Game and Fish Commission records). A field study from 1988–91 failed to discover mountain lions or their sign in Arkansas and concluded that there were "no wild reproducing populations of mountain lions in Arkansas" (McBride et al. 1993). As a result, the Arkansas Game and Fish Commission (AGFC) discontinued a database of reported free-ranging mountain lions.

More recently, tracks and scat from 5 localities in Pulaski, Perry, Garland, and Hot Spring counties were determined to be those of mountain lion (Witsell et al. 1999). This renewed an interest in the possible presence of free-ranging mountain lions in Arkansas. As a result, with cooperation from the AGFC, we (1) re-established a mountain lion clearinghouse; (2) determined the relation among reports, physiographic region, and deer harvest; and (3) examined the geographic relation between captive mountain lions and mountain lion sightings.

Methods
We used mail surveys, information from hunting groups, AGFC records, U.S. Department of Agriculture (USDA) records, and unsolicited reports from Arkansas citizens to evaluate the current status of mountain lions in Arkansas. Due to controversy regarding presence of reproducing mountain lions in Arkansas (McBride et al. 1993), we classified our reports in 1 of 4 reliability classes according to standards set by the Florida Panther Conference (Pritchard 1976) and used by the AGFC in the 1980s. Class I evidence includes a photograph of an animal, scat, track, or a cast of a track. Class II evidence are sightings made by an observer of known reliability (i.e., a biologist). Class III observations are made by an unqualified observer, but are accompanied by convincing descriptions or details and Class IV sightings are highly questionable. We restricted data to 1996–2000 to reflect recent patterns and minimize error in respondent recollection. We omitted reports referring to black animals. Reported sight-

ings were followed up by field searches when incidents had occurred within 3 days and since last rainfall.

Surveys

A survey of 850 natural resource professionals was conducted from fall 1999 to summer 2000 following the format of Berg et al. (1983) and Pike et al. (1999). Recipients included 124 AGFC biologists, 139 county agricultural and extension agents, 63 Arkansas State Park employees, 75 Arkansas Forestry Commission personnel, 419 members of the Arkansas Trappers Association, and 30 employees of the Arkansas Natural Heritage Commission, Nature Conservancy, Ozark Natural Science Center, as well as timber company biologists. All sampled individuals had relevant job descriptions and were distributed throughout the state. We requested information concerning mountain lions reportedly seen directly, those reported by other reliable individuals known to the respondent, sign observed by the respondent, and sign observed by other reliable individuals. The reliability of individual evaluations, even by biologists familiar with the characteristics of *Puma* sign, can often be problematic and these reports were interpreted with caution (Belden 1978; McBride et al. 1993). We also requested the date, location, and description of the event. A map of Arkansas was included for marking locations of sightings. A reminder mailing was sent in July 2000 to recipients who had not responded. Prior to the 1999 deer-hunting season, posters requesting information on mountain lion sightings and sign were mailed to 1200 hunting clubs that leased land from timber companies. It followed the format of Hardin (1996) and included information concerning identification of mountain lions, tracks, and scat. All unsolicited and poster-generated reports were followed with attempts to verify the information with a telephone interview. These reports were not used if the respondent was not the observer, the description of the event was too vague, or the respondent could not be contacted by telephone. A second survey was mailed to 251 Arkansas veterinarians to estimate numbers and locations of captive mountain lions in the state. A letter was also sent to the USDA State Veterinarian requesting locations of breeders, exhibitors, and brokers of captive mountain lions. Any individual may possess mountain lions if obtained from a person with a USDA Wild Animal Dealer permit and only breeders, exhibitors, and brokers are permitted and inspected.

Data Analyses

We used ARC/INFO (Environmental Systems Research Institute, Redlands, CA) to plot reported locations of sightings or sign relative to county boundaries, highways, lakes, and rivers. We included location data from Sealander and Gipson (1973) for comparison with this study. Sighting and sign location concentrations were calculated using the Spatial Analysis extension for ARC/INFO (ESRI, Version 2) as the number of locations per 60 km². We conducted statistical analyses using the Statistical Analysis System (SAS Institute, Inc. 1990). We used logistic regression to determine the association between the number of reported mountain lion sightings and statewide deer harvests (1996–1999). We used Chi-square analysis to test for changes in the number of sightings and sign across seasons.

Results

A total of 349 (41.1%) sighting/sign questionnaire surveys were returned. These included 98 sightings and 38 observations of sign throughout the state for 1996–2000. Forty-seven percent of the reports described observations by the respondent. Posters and unsolicited reports produced 13 usable records for the same time period.

Reliability ratings for all reports included: 7 (5%) in Class I, 23 (15%) in Class II, 107 (72%) in Class III, and 12 (8%) in Class IV. Class I evidence included a video (Montgomery County), 2 sets of tracks (Pulaski and White counties), and 4 scats (Hot Spring, Pulaski (2), and Garland counties). Five (3%) of the Class IV reports were of black animals.

Reports of sightings and sign were distributed throughout the state (Fig. 1). Most reports were from the Interior Highlands, including 23% from the Ozark Mountains and 40% from the Ouachita Mountains. The Gulf Coastal Plain accounted for 23% of sightings and sign, while the Mississippi Delta had the fewest reports (14%). Two concentrations were in the Ouachita Mountains of western Arkansas (primarily Yell, northern Pike, and southern Montgomery counties), and in the west central part of the state (including western Pulaski, northern Saline, and southern Perry counties). Other reports centered in northwestern Arkansas within the Ozark Mountains, including Crawford, Washington, and Benton counties.

More observations were reported during the fall (X^2 0.05.3 = 10.3465, P = 0.0175; winter 27; spring 22; summer 24; fall 44). Reports were associated with the 1996 to 2000 deer harvests ($R^2 = 0.9614$, $P = 0.0195$).

USDA reports indicated 12 breeders, exhibitors, or brokers in the state. However, the exact number of mountain lions could not be discerned due to frequent changes in the number of animals held by each entity. State veterinarians reported an additional 30 locations housing at least 1 mountain lion.

Discussion

The return rate of our survey (41.1 %) was similar to mountain lion surveys in Oklahoma (46%; Pike et al. 1999) and Wyoming (42.7%; Berg et al. 1983) and was comparable to that of a recent Arkansas mammal status survey (42.3%; Majors et al. 1996).

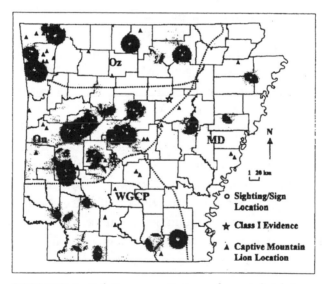

FIGURE 1. Relative concentrations of reported sightings and sign (1996–2000), locations of Class I evidence, and locations of known captive mountain lions in Arkansas. Darker shade indicates greater concentration (number of locations per 60 km²) of reported sightings and sign. Physiographic Regions: Oz = Ozark Mountains; Ou = Ouachita Mountains; WGCP = West Gulf Coastal Plain; MD = Mississippi Delta.

The Ouachita and Ozark Mountains consist of rugged and isolated habitat with sparse human populations and were expected to produce the most reports. These areas also have the highest black bear *(Ursus americanus)* densities in the state (Smith 1990). Along with the Gulf Coastal Plain, these 3 areas have experienced increases in white-tailed deer (Cartwright 1999). Furthermore, Jordan (1994) included these areas among the top 10 for reestablishment of the Florida panther *(P.c. coryi)*. The Mississippi Delta, with the exception of Crowley's Ridge and the White River National Wildlife Refuge, has little topographical relief, intensive agricultural development, and little forest cover, an apparent prerequisite for the species in the southeastern U.S. (Maehr et al. 2001).

Sealander and Gipson (1973) summarized what they considered to be all reliable mountain lion reports in Arkansas from 1945 through 1972. They concluded that the mountain lion was "holding its own" and possibly increasing in numbers due to an increasing deer population. They indicated that mountain lion populations were centered near the Saline and Ouachita River bottomlands in southeastern Arkansas, the White River National Wildlife Refuge near the confluence of the White and Arkansas rivers, the western Ozark Mountains north of the Arkansas River, and the Ouachita mountains in west central Arkansas south of the Arkansas River. Our data (Fig. 1) also implicate the Ozark and Ouachita mountains, but include more of the state as well. We recorded approximately the same levels as Sealander and Gipson (1973) in the southeastern bottomlands. We also show more reports in the southwestern part of the state where Sealander and Gipson (1973) had only scattered reports. There were no reports from the White River National Wildlife Refuge (a high use area for consumptive and nonconsumptive recreation). Although not specifically listed by Sealander and Gipson (1973), both studies show concentrations in the northeastern part of the Ozark Mountains.

Our classification approach (Pritchard 1976) included 30 reports from natural resource professionals. These Class I reports are the best evidence of mountain lions in the state. Of the Class I evidence, 3 scats and 1 set of tracks were previously verified (Witsell et al. 1999). While these data indicate the presence of individuals, they do not necessarily indicate an actual population of mountain lions.

Pike et al. (1999) and Berg et al. (1983) found a significant correlation between mountain lion sightings and deer harvests in Oklahoma and Wyoming; we found a similar correlation in Arkansas. Arkansas is experiencing a rapid increase in the white-tailed deer population, estimated at approximately 1 million, and harvest records show a corresponding increase (Cartwright 1999). White-tailed deer represent the major prey for mountain lions (Anderson 1983). Jordan (1993) found that the 3 previously mentioned potential reintroduction sites in Arkansas received an equal or greater prey density ranking compared to the northern Florida and southern Georgia feasibility reintroduction site as well as the panther-occupied site in southern Florida. Thus, Arkansas deer are likely capable of supporting a viable mountain lion population.

A tendency for hunters and wildlife professionals to be more active during fall may explain the increase in reported mountain lions at this time. There could be other explanations for a greater number of fall sightings such as reduced vegetation that would allow animals to be seen more easily.

A large captive mountain lion population apparently exists in Arkansas. Captive animals occasionally escape or are released. In 1987, the AGFC reported a dead, declawed mountain lion in Franklin County (Mosby 1988). However, the frequency and extent of other such events are unknown.

A survey of AGFC wildlife officers indicated a minimum of 101 captive animals in the state (Sasse 2001). The officers indicated the presence of captive mountain lions in Benton, Yell, Ashley, Union, and Calhoun counties, all of which are located in areas where mountain lion sightings are most frequent (Fig. 1). They also reported the release and unsuccessful recapture of a mountain lion in Yell County in 1997. Furthermore, one of us (GAH) knew of several mountain lions released in the area of Montgomery and Pike counties in 1988, another area of many reports. Although there is little evidence for this, others have suggested that released and even declawed mountain lions can persist in areas of suitable habitat and prey (Belden and Hagedorn 1993; R. T. McBride, pers. comm.).

Conclusion

With increasing numbers of mountain lion sightings and accumulation of hard evidence, it appears that free-ranging mountain lions have occasionally appeared in Arkansas. However, the number of animals, their origination, taxonomic status, and breeding status are unknown.

We have documented a minimum of 4 mountain lions in Arkansas over a span of 5 years based on Class I evidence. In all likelihood, they are the result of releases or escapes or animals dispersing from neighboring states. East Texas (Robertson and Altman 2000), Missouri (Hardin 1996; *Missouri Conservationist* 1999), and Oklahoma (Pike et al. 1999) have mountain lion populations, free-ranging animals, or persistent reports of sightings. However, given the large number of captive lions, the lack of regulation, and known releases and escapes, free-ranging animals in Arkansas may all be from captivity.

A renewed interest in Arkansas mountain lions has occurred with increased sighting reports and accumulation of hard evidence. The AGFC has classified them as a non-game mammal (B. D. Sasse, pers. comm.). Based in part, on the results of this study, regulations regarding captive animals and a protocol for recording and evaluating reported sightings throughout the state have been revised.

Acknowledgments

We wish to thank D. C. Goad and B. D. Sasse of the AGFC for their help and support. L. J. Dalby and K. Koone of the UALR GIS Spatial Laboratory provided guidance with the GIS data entry and analysis. S. A. Creek, D. S. Maehr, J. H. Peck, R. S. Sikes, and two anonymous reviewers provided helpful comments on an earlier draft. Additionally, we would like to thank T. Witsell and P. L. Dozhier for their contributions. The Arkansas Game and Fish Commission provided partial funding. The University of Arkansas at Little Rock Institutional Review Board reviewed all survey instruments prior to distribution.

Literature Cited

Anderson, A. E. 1983. A critical review of literature on puma *(Fells concolor)*. Colorado Division of Wildlife Special Report 54, Denver, CO. 91 pp.

Belden, R. C. 1978. How to recognize panther tracks. *Proceedings of the Annual Conference of the Southeastern Fish and Wildlife Agencies* 32:112–115.

Belden, R. C., and B. W. Hagedorn. 1993. Feasibility of translocating panthers into Northern Florida. *Journal of Wildlife Management* 57:388–397.

Berg, R. L., L. L. McDonald, and M. D. Strickland. 1983. Distribution of mountain lions in Wyoming as determined by mail questionnaire. *Wildlife Society Bulletin* 11:265–268.

Bischof, R., and B. Morrison. 2000. Status report on mountain lions in Nebraska. In L. A. Harveson. (Ed.). *Sixth Mountain Lion Workshop,* San Antonio, TX. In press.

Bolgiano, C., T. Lester, and D. Maehr. 2000. Field evidence of cougars in North America. In L. A. Harveson. (Ed.). *Sixth Mountain Lion Workshop,* San Antonio, TX. In press.

Cartwright, M. E. 1999. Strategic deer management plan. Arkansas Game and Fish Commission. 40 pp. M.I.P.1983. *Felis concolor. Mammalian Species* 200:1–7.

Dixon, K. R. 1982. Mountain lion. Pp. 711–727. In I. A. Chapman and G. A. Feldhamer. (Eds.). *Wild mammals of North America: biology, management, and economics.* Johns Hopkins University Press, Baltimore, MD. 1147 pp.

Hardin, S. E. 1996. The status of the puma *(Puma concolor)* in Missouri, based on sightings. Unpublished M.S. Thesis, Southwest Missouri State University, Springfield, MO.

Harvey, M. J., and S. W. Barkley. 1979. *Distribution and status of endangered mammals in Arkansas.* Arkansas Game and Fish Commission. 10 pp.

Jordan, D. B. 1993. *Preliminary analysis of potential Florida panther reintroduction sites.* United States Fish and Wildlife Service. 34 pp.

Jordan, D. B. 1994. Identification and evaluation of candidate Florida Panther population reestablishment sites. Pp. 106–120. In Jordan, D.B. (Ed.). *Proceedings of Florida panther conference.* U.S. Fish and Wildlife Service. 120 pp.

Lewis, J. C: 1969. Evidence of mountain lions in the Ozarks and adjacent areas, 1948–1968. *Journal of Mammalogy* 50:371–372.

Lewis, J. C. 1970. Evidence of mountain lions in the Ozark, Boston, and Ouachita Mountains. *Proceedings of the Oklahoma Academy of Science for 1968,* pp. 182–184.

Lindzey, F. G. 1987. Mountain Lion. Pp. 657–658. In M. Novak, J.A. Baker, M.E. Obbard, and B. Malloch. (Eds). *Wild furbearer management and conservation in North America.* Ontario Ministry of Natural Resources, Toronto. 1150 pp.

Maehr, D. S., T. S. Hoctor, and L. D. Harris. 2001. The Florida panther: A flagship for regional restoration. Pp. 293–312. In D. S. Maehr, R. F. Noss, and J. L. Larkin (Eds.). *Large Mammal Restoration: Ecological and Sociological Challenges in the 21st Century.* Island Press, Washington DC. 375 pp.

Majors, T. J., D. C. Brock, and G. A. Heidt. 1996. A mail survey to determine the status of the black-tailed jackrabbit, ringtail cat, long-tailed weasel, badger, and Eastern spotted skunk in Arkansas. *Proceedings of the Arkansas Academy of Science* 50:127–130.

McBride, R. T., R. M. McBride, J. L. Cashman, and D. S. Maehr. 1993. Do mountain lions exist in Arkansas? *Proceedings of the Annual Conference of the Southeastern Fish and Wildlife Agencies* 47:394–402.

Missouri Conservationist. 1999. Mountain lion history a mystery: Do you know where this cat came from? September: 30.

Mosby, J. Save Arkansas cougars—where? *Arkansas Gazette.* 31 December 1988; section 8D.

Noble, R. E. 1971. A recent record of the puma *(Felis concolor)* in Arkansas. *Southwestern Naturalist* 16:209.

Pike, J. R., J. H. Shaw, D. M. Leslie, and M.G. Shaw. 1999. A geographic analysis of the status of mountain lions in Oklahoma. *Wildlife Society Bulletin* 27:4–11.

Pritchard, P. E. H. (Ed.). 1976. *Proceedings of the Florida panther conference.* Florida Audubon Society, Gainesville, FL. 121 pp.

Robertson, P., and C. D. Altman Jr. 2000. Texas mountain lion status report. In L. A. Harveson. (Ed.). *Sixth Mountain Lion Workshop,* San Antonio, TX. In press.

Sasse, D. B. 2001. Status of pet mountain lions *(Puma concolor)* in Arkansas. *Journal of the Arkansas Academy of Science* 55:188.

SAS Institute, Inc. 1990. *SAS stet users guide. Version 6, fourth edition.* SAS Institute, Cary, NC.

Sealander, J. A. 1951. Mountain lion in Arkansas. *Journal of Mammalogy* 32:364.

Sealander, J. A. 1956. A provisional checklist and key to the mammals of Arkansas (with annotations). *American Midland Naturalist* 56:257–296.

Sealander, J. A., and P. S. Gipson. 1973. Status of the mountain lion in Arkansas. *Proceedings of the Arkansas Academy of Science* 27:38–41.

Smith, K. G., J. D. Clark, and P. S. Gipson. 1990. History of black bears in Arkansas: over-exploitation, near elimination, and successful reintroduction. *Proceedings of the Tenth Eastern Workshop on Black Bear Restoration and Management* 10:5–14.

Witsell, T., G. A. Heidt, P. L. Dozhier, T. Frothingham, and M. Lynn. 1999. Recent documentations of mountain lion *(Puma concolor)* in Arkansas. *Proceedings of the Arkansas Academy of Science* 53:157–158.

Young, S. P., and E. A. Goldman. 1946. *The puma, mysterious American cat.* American Wildlife Institute, Washington, DC. 358 pp.

Zuidema, M. 2002. Are there mountain lions in Michigan? *Fur-Fish-Game.* March.

The Arkansas Game and Fish Commission reacted to the possibility of cougars in a way that mirrors the argument formulated in the 1990s by Paul Nickerson and other officials in the U.S. Fish and Wildlife Service (the federal agency responsible for enforcing the Endangered Species Act): These cougars couldn't be remnant natives, so they aren't protected and are of no concern to us. Some of the incidents reported in this section clearly involve formerly captive cats, but other cases lack any evidence of prior captivity. Nonetheless, most wildlife agencies continue to assert that all confirmed cougars are released or escaped captives from elsewhere.

Memorandum

From: Ledbetter, Nancy S.
Sent: Friday, July 18, 2003 4:51 PM
To: AGFC
Subject: AGFC Mountain Lion Position Statement

Here is the AGFC mountain lion position statement that the commissioners approved this week. If you have any questions, please contact David Goad. Thanks.

Arkansas Game and Fish Commission
Mountain Lion Position Statement.

The purpose of this document is to articulate the official position of the Arkansas Game and Fish Commission relative to mountain lions in the state. Mountain lions, more recently known as the Florida panther *(Puma concolor coryi),* were historically present throughout Arkansas until their apparent eradication, which occurred by about 1920. Since that time efforts have been made to determine the existence or lack thereof of this animal. There is no verifiable evidence that there exists a wild, viable reproducing population of the original mountain lion that inhabited the state as settlers came from the east. There are known releases of captive mountain lions, most probably acquired from western states. Consequently, it is theoretically possible that a reproducing population exists from feral ancestry. Therefore, it is the position of the Arkansas Game and Fish Commission that this subspecies has been eradicated from the state and any mountain lion in the wild in Arkansas is not an endangered Florida panther unless proven otherwise.

Nancy S. Ledbetter
Director of Communications
Arkansas Game and Fish Commission
2 Natural Resources Drive
Little Rock, Arkansas 72205
Phone: 501-223-6318
Fax: 501-223-6448
Email: nledbetter@agfc.state.ar.us

Hunter's Remote Camera Captures Picture of Mountain Lion

by Austin Gelder
Arkansas Democrat-Gazette, Little Rock, Arkansas, Saturday, August 23, 2003

Don Scott of Little Rock often spots deer, coyotes, raccoons, foxes, bobcats and buzzards while in the woods of Arkansas but had never spied a big cat. At least not until two weeks ago, when a camera triggered by a heat sensor Scott had set up near the Winona Wildlife Management Area snapped a shot of a lithe, golden mountain lion creeping through the forest. "I've been hunting all my life and I'm 65," Scott said. "This is the first time I've ever come across a mountain lion."

And that's no surprise, considering the Arkansas Game and Fish Commission says the state's wild mountain lion population was wiped out by the 1920s after pioneers slaughtered them and decimated the white-tailed deer the cats relied on for food. In 2001, the Game and Fish Commission took mountain lions off the state's endangered species list and officially adopted the policy that there are no wild mountain lions in Arkansas. It's the only state to have done so. "We determined all of our native panthers were gone from the state," Game and Fish biologist Blake Sasse said. "We haven't come across any in Arkansas that we can't trace back to a pet animal that's escaped or intentionally been released."

More than 100 mountain lions—also called cougars, pumas or Florida panthers—live in captivity in Arkansas. While the state doesn't have a law regulating ownership of exotic animals, the U.S. Department of Agriculture requires owners to hold a livestock permit. "In the last five years we know of at least eight mountain lions that escaped or were released, but all of those were either killed or recaptured," Sasse said.

But is it possible that wild mountain lions are re-establishing themselves in Arkansas forests? "I wouldn't rule anything out," Sasse said. "There's a known mountain lion population in southern Texas, and they can travel long distances."

Plenty of people suspect the big cats may very well be moving back to the Natural State. People living near the Hot Springs Country Club reported seeing or hearing cougars this winter and spring, and some blamed the cats for attacks on pet dogs. And just this month, a Missouri motorist hit a 105-pound male mountain lion on a Jefferson City highway about 150 miles north of the Arkansas-Missouri border. The animals can weigh from 80 to 230 pounds and range from 5 to 8 feet in length.

Many biologists suspect wild mountain lions may be migrating eastward from South Dakota, Colorado and Texas. Male mountain lions have been known to travel hundreds of miles to stake out their own territory.

But even if wild mountain lions are here, Sasse said there probably aren't many of them. "If we had a large number we'd see them showing up hit by cars on the road or we'd have people shooting them."

Scott's camera caught the image of a mountain lion on private land near the Winona Wildlife Management Area west of Little Rock. He uses the camera to track deer in preparation for hunting season. The picture of the mountain lion was taken sometime between Aug. 6 and Aug. 13. The camera also captured the images of several deer during that time period.

Dr. Gary Heidt, a wildlife biologist and chairman of the biology department at the University of Arkansas at Little Rock, said he's not sure whether mountain lions spotted in the state are animals that escaped captivity or their offspring, or if they're immigrants from Western states.

"Until we finally get one and can run some DNA tests on it we won't know for sure," he said. Regardless of where they came from, it's important to study these animals, Heidt said. "If they're captive animals or if they're wild animals, if they're in the state they're part of our fauna."

Don Scott of Little Rock, Arkansas, took this photo with a remote camera while scouting for hunting places near the Winona Wildlife Management Area in 2003.

While some would welcome mountain lions back to their home habitat, others have no interest in re-establishing the big cats on Arkansas soil. Arkansas officials told the U.S. Fish and Wildlife Service last fall they want no part of a plan to expand the Florida panther population into wild areas of the Ozark and Ouachita mountains. Arkansas was the only southeastern state being considered for the relocation program that refused to join.

Public reaction is one reason. Wildlife experts said they would expect lots of opposition to a cougar relocation program for fear of danger to livestock, pets and people. Arkansans already complain about bears and alligators, and state officials say they would expect more nuisance calls if the mountain lion population increased.

However, mountain lions may be on their way to Arkansas whether state officials like it or not. But until hard evidence is found, experts shy away from declaring Arkansas home to wild mountain lions.

Scott will lead Heidt and biologists from the Game and Fish Commission to the spot where the picture was taken sometime in the next few days to look for evidence of a big cat. Asked about the image captured by his camera, Scott said Friday he was surprised as anyone. "I didn't know what to think," he said. "I really didn't expect to get a picture of one there."

Eminence Men Forfeit $2,000 Each in 1994 Cougar Killing Case

Missouri Wildlife, 57(6), December 1996/January 1997
(Published by the Conservation Federation of Missouri)

Eminence, MO—Do "panthers" still prowl the Ozarks? The resolution of a poaching case shows that at least one did as recently as 1994. Was it a wild mountain lion or an animal escaped from captivity? No one will ever know for sure.

Troy Wayne Norris, 32, of Winona, and Brocki Joe Vermillion, 32, of Bourbon, each chose not to contest the case built against them by state and federal wildlife agents and forfeited $2,000 each in connection with the killing of a mountain lion in December of 1994.

Conservation Agent Kevin Dixon opened the case in March of 1995 when he began hearing persistent rumors that someone had killed a mountain lion near Peck Ranch Conservation Area. That interested him for two reasons.

First, if it was true, the law had been broken. Missouri has no mountain lion hunting season, and the state Wildlife Code grants protection to any animal for which no hunting season is specifically established.

Besides that, the mountain lion, *Felis concolor,* has been considered extirpated in Missouri since the 1920s. Although reports of "panther" sightings surface in the Show-Me State from time to time, reliable sightings are rare, and have almost always been found to involve animals that escaped or were released from captivity. Extended, methodical efforts to find wild cougars in the rugged mountains of northern Arkansas, have come up empty. Finding a wild mountain lion in Missouri would be akin to locating a flock of passenger pigeons.

So Dixon and Conservation Agent Tom May pursued the rumors, eventually enlisting the help of the U.S. Fish and Wildlife Service. Together, they identified a handful of people who had first-hand knowledge about the killing of a 100- to 125-pound adult female mountain lion.

Agents finally obtained a photo of the dead cat on the tailgate of a pickup truck and confronted the two men who were rumored to have been present when it was killed. Vermillion and Norris subsequently admitted killing the cougar and transporting it through part of the Mark Twain National Forest, which violated the federal Lacey Act.

Special Agent Larry Keck said Norris and Vermillion were hunting raccoons with a third man when one of their hounds treed the mountain lion. According to Keck, Vermillion said he told Norris they had to kill the mountain lion, and Norris killed it with a .22 caliber rifle. Killing the cat violated state law. But Keck says that killing, possessing or aiding and abetting the possession of the mountain lion also violated the federal Lacey Act.

Agents had photographs of the dead mountain lion and statements from Vermillion, Norris and others describing how the animal was killed but the agents were not able to recover any of the animal's remains. The carcass was dumped at Peck Ranch Conservation Area after skinning. Because simply possessing the skin was illegal, it too, eventually was dumped in a rural area.

Gary Cravens, Ozark Region protection supervisor for the Missouri Department of Conservation said witnesses described the cat as sleek, with long, sharp claws and no tattoos or other identifying marks that captive cats usually carry. If it had been an escaped cat without experience catching its own food, it probably wouldn't have been so well fed. "We would have loved to know if it was a wild, native mountain lion," said Cravens. "Now we'll never know."

Kansas City Cougar Probably Was Wild, from the West; Body Condition and Stomach Contents Point to a Free-Ranging Life

by Jim Low
All Outdoors (issued by the Missouri Department of Conservation), March 28, 2003

Kansas City, MO—A mountain lion killed by a motorist in Kansas City area last fall probably came from a Western state. That's the conclusion of Wildlife Research Biologist Dave Hamilton, the Conservation Department's furbearer specialist.

The 2½-to-3-year-old male cougar died after being struck by a car while crossing I-35 near Parvin Road at 1:45 A.M. Oct. 14. It weighed 125 pounds and measured more than 7 feet from nose to tip of tail.

At the time, Hamilton noted the lack of unusual wear on the cat's claws and paw pads. Such wear is normally seen in captive animals that have been kept in concrete-floored enclosures. This, together with the lack of tattoos, tags or other signs of captivity, led Hamilton to speculate that the cougar might have been a wild specimen that wandered here from another state. He reserved judgment, however, until receiving test results on the animal's DNA and stomach contents.

The DNA tests showed it was a North American cougar. This is significant, since many captive mountain lions come from South American stock. "The stomach contents included white-tailed deer and raccoon," said Hamilton, "so it probably was feeding in the wild, rather than being fed by humans. There was no tartar buildup on its teeth, and it wasn't obese, which are other telltale signs of a captive lifestyle. Judging by all these things, I think it's pretty likely this animal wandered into Missouri from somewhere to the west, however it could have been a captive animal. We just don't know."

Hamilton said the animal's age and sex are consistent with this theory. "Young males often wander long distances looking for areas not already occupied by adult male lions," he said. "Colorado has a thriving, self-sustaining cougar population. The fact that this cat turned up in western Missouri probably is more than just a coincidence."

Hamilton said the Conservation Department receives hundreds of reports of mountain lion sightings each year. Most sightings remain unverified due to a lack of physical evidence such as tracks, droppings, photographs, or video tape recordings. In about a third of the cases, physical evidence clearly shows that other animals—often dogs or bobcats— were involved.

However, Hamilton said the Conservation Department's Mountain Lion Task Force investigates all credible reports of mountain lion sightings. He said people who think they have seen a mountain lion should call the nearest conservation agent or Conservation Department office.

As this book went to press, David Hamilton of the Missouri State Department of Conservation had confirmed six cougars living wild in a state where the last confirmed cougar had been killed in 1927. Hamilton said that "it's only a matter of time until we have a breeding population." The next paper describes an apparently wild cougar killed in southern Illinois just twenty miles from the Mississippi River. This raises the question: Can cougars swim the Mississippi River? Cougars are known to swim, and to cross bridges at night.

Record of a North American Cougar *(Puma concolor)* from Southern Illinois

by Edward J. Heist,[1] Jennifer R. Bowles,[2] and Alan Woolf[1]

Transactions of the Illinois State Academy of Science (2001), Volume 94, #4, pp. 227–229

Abstract

A cougar *(Puma concolor)* was recovered in the proximity of railroad tracks in Randolph County, Illinois on July 15, 2000. A necropsy indicated that the cougar died from injuries it received when struck by a train. The animal appeared to be in good health prior to the accident, and no indications of captive rearing were observed. Genetic data were used to verify that the cougar was of North American origin and not an escaped or released cougar of South American origin. This is the first confirmed occurrence of a cougar in Illinois in over 100 years.

Introduction

On July 15, 2000 officials of the Illinois Department of Natural Resources retrieved the carcass of a cougar from Randolph County, Illinois. The native range of cougars stretches from the Yukon to Argentina, and in North America from California to the Maritime Provinces of Canada (Hansen 1992). While cougars were native to Illinois, predator control efforts of the last two centuries and habitat alteration have extirpated cougars from the entire Midwest (Hansen 1992). The last resident cougars were removed from Illinois prior to 1860 (Danz 1999). The closest known cougar populations are in Texas and Colorado. However, there is evidence for the existence of cougars in the Arkansas Ozarks (Witsell et al. 1999) as well as eastern Kentucky and Tennessee (Nowack 1976) and there have been recent unconfirmed cougar sightings in southern Illinois. Some cougars found outside of their current range are escaped or released captive animals, and many of those cougars are of South American origin.

In a recent study of 315 cougars from North and South America including 31 of 32 putative subspecies, Culver et al. (2000) compared partial DNA sequences of several mitochondrial genes. They found that

---

[1]Fisheries and Illinois Aquaculture Center

[2]Cooperative Wildlife Research Laboratory

[1,2]Department of Zoology, Southern Illinois University, Carbondale, IL 62901

cougars from North America are genetically homogeneous and distinct from South American cougars. Only two mtDNA haplotypes were found north of Panama, one of which was restricted to the Olympic Peninsula of the Pacific Northwest. Cougars from Panama and South America are genetically more diverse; however no South American cougar possessed either of the North American mtDNA haplotypes. Thus mtDNA provides a reliable method of determining whether the cougar killed in Randolph County Illinois was of North American origin, and therefore potentially a wild cougar, or of South American origin and an obvious captive release.

Methods

The cougar carcass was frozen by IDNR personnel and shipped to Southern Illinois University, Carbondale where a necropsy was performed. The animal was weighed and measurements taken. The nature of the trauma to both external and internal anatomy were noted. A piece of tongue was taken for genetic analyses.

Whole genomic DNA was extracted from tongue tissue using a commercial DNA extraction kit (Quiagen Inc.). Portions of two mitochondrial genes (ATP-base and ND-5) were amplified using primers described in Johnson et al. (1998). Each 50 µl PCR reaction contained 5 µl IOX buffer (Promega Inc.), 65 ng cougar genomic DNA, 2 mM $MgCl_2$, and 2.5 picomoles of each PCR primer. PCR products were prepared for cloning using a commercial kit (Quiagen Inc.), ligated into a TA cloning vector (Promega Inc.), and cloned into DH5α competent cells. Miniprep plasmid DNA was obtained using a commercial kit (Promega Inc.) and sequenced on an ABI 377 automated DNA sequencer. Sequences were compared to published sequences from Culver et al. (2000).

Results and Discussion

The cougar was a 226 cm long male with a tail length of 72.5 cm and a total weight of 50 kg. Based on a combination of cementum annuli and tooth wear criteria the cougar was estimated to be a 4–6 year old adult. The head was nearly detached from the carcass between the 2nd and 3rd cervical vertebrae, and was connected to the carcass by only a few strands of dorsal skin. Findings were consistent with blunt trauma as a cause of death. There was no indication that the cougar had recently worn a collar, nor was there wear on the foot pads consistent with cage or pen habitation. Stomach contents included partially digested material (skin, hair, bones) from a single white-tailed deer *(Odocoileus virginianus)* fawn. The cougar exhibited well-developed musculature and abundant visceral/ mesenteric fat.

DNA sequences at both mitochondrial genes were identical to those of haplotype "M" reported as the common mtDNA haplotype in North American cougars by Culver et al. (2000). Sequences of the Illinois cougar differed from all South American mtDNA haplotypes by at least one substitution in the ATP-base gene and two substitutions in the ND-5 gene. Thus the cougar killed by the train in Randolph County Illinois was of North American origin and appears to have been successfully foraging in the wild prior to its accidental death.

Literature Cited

Culver, M., W. E. Johnson, J. Pecon-Slattery, and S. J. O'Brien. 2000. Genomic ancestry of the American puma *(Puma concolor)*. *J. Heredity* 91:186–197.

Danz, H. P. 1999. *Cougar!* Ohio University Press, Athens Ohio. 310 pp.

Hansen, K. 1992. *Cougar, the American lion*. Northland Publishing, Flagstaff, AZ. 129 pp.

Johnson, W., C. Culver, J. A. Iriate, E. Eizirik, K. L. Seymour, and S. J. O'Brien. 1998. Tracking the evolution of the elusive Andean mountain cat *(Oreailurus jacobtta)* from mitochondrial DNA. *J. Heredity* 89:227–232.

Nowack, R. M. 1976. *The cougar in the United States and Canada*. U. S. Fish and Wildlife Service, Washington, D. C. and the New York Zoological Society, New York. 189 pp.

Witsell, T., G. A. Heidt, P. L. Dozhier, T. Frothingham, and M. Lynn. 1999. Recent documentation of mountain lion *(Puma concolor)* in Arkansas. *J. Arkansas Acad. of Sci.* 53:157–158.

Iowa Officials to Seek Legislation Protecting Stray Mountain Lions; A State Wildlife Chief Is Asking the Public not to Harm Cougars Unless They Present a Threat

by Chris Clayton
Omaha World-Herald, Omaha, Nebraska, September 30, 2001. Reprinted with permission from the *Omaha World-Herald*.

With confirmation that mountain lions have returned to Iowa, conservation officials will seek legislation next year to protect the animals.

Right now, any mountain lions roaming the state are doing so at their own risk because they have no legal protection in Iowa.

The animals can be killed on sight, although the state's wildlife chief is asking residents to leave them alone.

"They are not protected in Iowa, and somebody can do anything they want to them," said Richard Bishop, chief of the wildlife division at the Iowa Department of Natural Resources.

In August, a full-grown mountain lion was struck by a car and killed in Harlan. It was the first confirmed killing of one of the big cats since 1867.

Sightings continue, particularly north of Council Bluffs. There have been several recent reports of another mountain lion, possibly with cubs, in northern Shelby County or southern Crawford County.

Based on reports, Bishop said he believes there may be as many as three other mountain lions roaming western Iowa.

He plans to ask lawmakers next year for legislation giving the Department of Natural Resources authority to protect mountain lions in the state.

For now, Bishop would like residents to leave the animals alone if the cougars are doing no harm.

"If one is found in Iowa, we are going to discourage anybody from bothering them if the animal is not causing any damage," Bishop said.

Nebraska enacted legislation in 1991 labeling mountain lions as a protected game species after a rancher killed one of the animals.

Kirk Nelson, assistant director of the Nebraska Game and Parks Commission, said the few cougars in Nebraska are migrants or young males trying to establish a territory.

Farmers often are fearful of the animals and their effect on livestock, but Bishop said there is enough wildlife in western Iowa that cougars may not do any harm to livestock.

If farm animals were harmed by a mountain lion, state officials likely would destroy the cat. Any threats to people would elicit the same reaction.

Crawford County Sheriff Tom Hogan said he received a flurry of reports about three weeks ago, but hasn't heard about any large cats since then.

He is fascinated by the idea that cougars have returned to the state and would like to see one.

But in coffee-shop talk around the area, some have expressed reservations about large cougars roaming wild in the area.

"A few people want it destroyed, but others think it needs to be captured and relocated," Hogan said.

Right now, Bishop would prefer not to relocate any animals, but that would depend on the circumstances.

The Mountain Lions of Michigan

by Kirk Johnson[1]
Endangered Species Update 19(2): 27–31, 2002

Abstract

Though the mountain lion *(Puma concolor)* has been considered extirpated in Michigan since the early 1900s, sightings of the big cats have persisted in both the Upper and Lower Peninsulas. Reports of mountain lions increased during the 1990s, and the Michigan Department of Natural Resources (DNR) does acknowledge the existence of this species within the state. However, state officials continue to insist that the majority of these sightings involve former captive animals or misidentification of other species, rather than a wild population of mountain lions. The growing number of mountain lion sightings in recent years—by biologists, hunters, and other citizens—suggests that there may well be a small breeding population of the species in Michigan.

History

In 1984, while hunting on the Patowachie-Hannaville Indian Reservation fifteen miles west of the town of Escanaba in the Upper Peninsula of Michigan, a Native American hunter spotted a mountain lion *(Puma concolor)*—also known as cougar or puma—while trying to spook some deer. The man quickly lifted his rifle and fired, wounding the cat, which responded by leaping ten feet into the air, and then running off with one leg flopping (Zuidema 1999). The hunter discovered bone fragments from the right front paw and proceeded to track the cat in light snow into a bog full of leatherleaf shrubs (Zuidema 1999). He collected the bone fragments and gave them to wildlife officials. Michael Zuidema, a retired Forester from the Michigan Department of Natural Resources (DNR), sent the bone samples to a wildlife lab at Colorado State

[1]International Ecological Partnerships, P.O. Box 40323, Grand Junction CO 81504 USA

University's College of Veterinary Medicine and Biomedical Sciences in Fort Collins, where high resolution electrophoresis determined it was indeed from a mountain lion (Zuidema 1999).

The mountain lion was originally part of Michigan's native fauna, at the top of the food chain with the black bear *(Ursus americanus),* the wolf *(Canis lupus),* and the wolverine *(Gulo gulo).* By the late 1800s, however, only a few of the felids still survived in remote recesses of the Upper Peninsula (UP) (Zuidema 1999). The last recorded cougar killed in Michigan was in the UP in December of 1906, near the Tahquamenon River, in Luce County (Zuidema 1999).

By the early 1900s the species was listed as extirpated in Michigan (Manville 1948). It seems clear, though, that the Tahquamenon cat was not the last of its kind in the UP, or even the Lower Peninsula. Since the 1920s, there has been a steady stream of reports of the big cats, mostly dismissed by DNR officials (Zuidema 2000, pers. comm.). There are several reliable records of people seeing pumas in the late 1930s and early 1940s, including one documented record of a cougar from the Huron Mountains of Marquette County in 1937 (Manville 1948).

Credible sightings of the felids also date from the 1960s to the present. From 1962 to 1992 there were valid reports of cougars from every county in the UP except for Keweenaw (Evers 1994). Many of those reports, though, were not verified by DNR officials (Minzey 2000, pers. comm.).

Frequently, people who claim to have spotted a large felid either inform the DNR too long after a sighting or sign, or the supposed cat turns out to be another large mammal, such as a deer or wolf (Minzey 2000, pers. comm.). In addition, a large number of reported puma sightings are in areas where wolves are known residents (Minzey 2000, pers. comm.).

Recent Sightings in the Upper Peninsula

There is, however, conclusive evidence of mountain lions in Michigan. On Memorial Day in 1998, a puma was photographed on the grounds of Thistledowne, a Bed & Breakfast establishment near the town of Gulliver in southern Schoolcraft County (Hughes 2000, pers. comm.) (Figure 1). Three fuzzy photographs through a plate-glass window were taken of the cougar as it stood outside in the yard by the gazebo along the sand dunes. The animal then ran into the woods on the shore of Seul Choix Point, on Lake Michigan (McCarthy 2001, pers. comm.). Two of the photographs show the unmistakable outline of a large felid's lithe body and rounded head. Seul Choix Point is a sandy spit of land in southern Schoolcraft County stretching out from the bay into Lake Michigan (Figure 1). In 2000, there were several sightings of cougars on the Point (Bowman 2000, pers. comm.). In 1997 or 1998, hunters discovered a dead deer covered up with leaves in the forests on Seul Choix Point, with scrapes approximately five feet long—too long for the reach of bobcat covering its kill (Bowman 2000, pers. comm.). (Typically, cougars and some other large cats, including bobcats, cover their kills with leaves to hide them from scavengers.)

Seul Choix Point is one of the areas where the existence of cougars was irrefutably demonstrated in the UP, through the efforts of an independent organization not affiliated with the Michigan DNR (Rusz 2001, pers. comm.). Dr. Patrick Rusz, the Director of Wildlife Programs for the Michigan Wildlife Habitat Foundation, a non-profit research organization, conducted field studies in areas of the state where there have been multiple reliable sightings of cougars (Rusz 2001, pers. comm.). Once a week between May 5, 2001, and June 1, 2001, Dr. Rusz and his team conducted research along a 33-mile-long stretch of Lake Michigan shoreline, including the sand dunes of Seul Choix Point (MWHF 2001a). The team discovered cougar tracks in the eastern half of the study area each week, with most of the tracks confined to a four-mile long strip of dunes (MWHF 2001a).

Where the tracks were most numerous, the crew found six distinct locations where deer had been killed and dragged away. In each case, the deer were killed within 40 feet of a dune crest with no sign of a chase (MWHF 2001a). There was suggestive evidence of nine cougar-killed deer dragged up the dunes, but only six deer carcasses were conclusively identified (Rusz 2001, pers. comm.). The sand dunes and beaches along the lake shoreline also turned out to be a gigantic natural litter box where it was unexpectedly easy to find cougar droppings (Rusz 2001, pers. comm.). Rusz and his team collected dozens of scat samples in the shoreline dunes covered in a manner typical of pumas (MWHF 2001a).

Eight feces samples were sent to Wyoming's Department of Game and Fish forensics laboratory in Laramie. The results arrived in late September 2001, and the lab concluded there was DNA evidence confirming the existence of at least two cougars in the Seul Choix area (Rusz 2001, pers. comm.).

In early 2001, the Foundation team also received a one-year-old, 10.5 inch scat from a woman in the town of Hancock, on Lake Superior's Keweenaw Peninsula in Houghton County. This sample was also sent to the Wyoming lab and confirmed to be from a puma (MWHF 2001a). Rusz's team also verified mountain lion tracks on the Stonington Peninsula of Delta County along Lake Michigan, plus several possible cougar scats (MWHF 2001a). By the late fall of 2001, the Foundation confirmed the presence of at least seven pumas through the verification of scat, tracks and deer kills at six sites scattered over the Upper and Lower Peninsulas (Rusz 2001, pers. comm.). Such an abundance of evidence confirms that the Seul Choix cats are not just transients passing through the area, but represent a handful of resident, reproducing cougars indigenous to the UP.

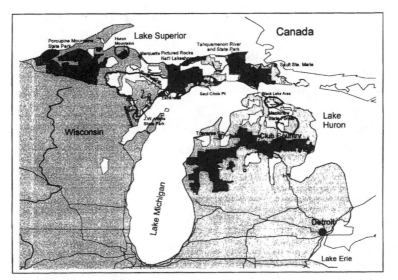

Figure 1. Areas circled indicate locations of frequent puma reports in the Upper Peninsula (UP) and upper Lower Peninsula of Michigan. The known puma range is near Gulliver in the UP.

Although most cougar reports come from the south central Upper Peninsula where deer densities are the highest, sightings have been reported from virtually every county in the UP (Zuidema 2000, pers. comm.). Three elderly trappers living in Delta and Menominee Counties insisted they saw cougars occasionally in the central UP over the past fifty years (Zuidema 2000, pers. comm.). One trapper reported trapping and shooting a female cougar in 1964, describing it as being a rack of bones weighing about 60 pounds which appeared to have been nursing (Zuidema 1999).

Another trapper allegedly caught a cougar in a trap five miles south of Escanaba, but the cat pulled the stake out and escaped (Zuidema 2000, pers. comm.). Zuidema collected over 600 reports of sightings or signs of mountain lions, dating back to the 1930s. Prior to the confirmation of *Puma concolor* in the UP, there were scores of sightings of mother pumas with young, indicating the likelihood of localized breeding populations (Zuidema 2000, pers. comm.).

There has also been an increase of puma reports filed with the DNR in recent decades, especially in the 1990s. On average, the DNR receives approximately one hundred cougar reports a year, but these do not include verified sightings or signs (Wagner 2000). In spite of Rusz' confirmation of some wild pumas in the UP, some DNR biologists remain skeptical that very many of the big cats reside as wild residents in the state (Robinson 2000, pers. comm.). Of the approximately 750,000 licensed hunters in Michigan, few have reported seeing the cats. There have not been any identifiable prints, road kills, or legitimate plaster casts of tracks (Robinson 2000, pers. comm.).

In August and September 2001, the Michigan Wildlife Habitat Foundation team searched Stonington Peninsula in Delta County of the UP on three occasions and discovered additional tracks that were verified to be cougar. The team also discovered some old scats on the peninsula that are still awaiting conclusive DNA analysis (MWHF 2001a).

The 60,000-acre Porcupine Mountains State Park, bordering Lake Superior in Ontonagon County, is another area of the UP where there has been some evidence of pumas over the past few decades. The Park was spared the logger's ax and contains the largest stand of old-growth forests between the Mississippi River and the Adirondacks. Some of the maples in the Park measure three feet in diameter.

Sightings of cougars within or near the Park have been recorded in past years. In 1997 a group of deer hunters found a deer carcass cached in a tree (Sprague 2001, pers. comm.). (The Park does allow white-tailed deer hunting.) There are also earlier records of pumas in the Porcupine Mountains. In 1970, a former assistant park manager discovered cougar tracks embedded in a clay hiking trail in the Park, which had been recently soaked by rain (LaPointe 1977).

Another area with persistent mountain lion sightings is the Huron Mountains of Marquette County east of Porcupine Mountains State Park. Like the Porcupine Mountains, the Huron hills have significant stands of old-growth cedar forests and high deer densities (Rusz 2001, pers. comm.). There have been persistent sightings in or along a 56,000-acre area within the mountains that includes the Huron Mountain Club and adjacent private property (Rusz 2001, pers. comm.). Access to the 28,000-acre Club is very restricted, and Club members have reported seeing cougars in the last few years. Moose and wolves, supposedly extirpated from the state in the early 1900s, were also reported there in every decade of the 1900s (Rusz 2001, pers. comm.).

South and east of the Huron Mountains lies the Ottawa National Forest, containing over 1.7 million acres of spruce, aspen, and isolated stands of old-growth white pine and hemlock. Ottawa contains three wilderness areas totaling over 50,000 acres, and one area, the Sturgeon River Gorge Wilderness, covers 14,193 acres with steep rugged gorges up to 300 feet deep and nearly a mile wide (USFS 2000). There have also been several puma reports within the 18,327-acre Sylvania Wilderness, lying within eastern Gogebic County and bordering northern Wisconsin.

In fact, northern Wisconsin and the UP represent one continuous ecosystem, with the UP containing more unsettled wilderness. Any lions in this region would need to be managed as one population. Abundant deer, wolves, black bears and fishers already inhabit these rugged outcroppings of the Canadian Shield, and undoubtedly, some pumas are also present.

The U.S. Forest Service typically receives two or three reports of cougars a year in the Ottawa National Forest of Gogebic County (Edde 2000, pers. comm.). Three recent records have been deemed as credible (Edde 2000, pers. comm.). The first report was on November 16, 1998, when a hunter saw a mountain lion feeding on a deer gut pile not far from the town of Ironwood. The second incident which took place on April 16, 2000, involved a man who reported seeing a cougar chasing a rabbit through his yard, five miles south and east of the town of Wakefield. In the third incident on June 6, 2000, a man from Ironwood spotted a puma crossing Fisher Road (Edde 2000, pers. comm.). A trapper who catches a lot of bobcats is convinced cougars are in the Bessemer area (Edde 2000, pers. comm.).

Recent Sightings in the Lower Peninsula

Reports are even coming from the Lower Peninsula. On one occasion, while setting up baits for black bears in Huron National Forest in Alcona County 25 miles west of Lake Huron, a DNR wildlife biologist reported a puma walking on a narrow forest path (Robinson 2000, pers. comm.). He was approximately 60 yards away from the cat, and discovered tracks after it disappeared. It was unclear, however, whether this cat was actually a wild puma or an escaped/released captive.

Based on the density of reports, there is growing evidence of a resident cougar population in northeastern Lower Michigan between the towns of Mio and Rogers City and north to Cheboygan; in Emmet County near Cross Village; and between Cadillac and Traverse City in the northwest (MWHF 2001a). Two "hotspots" for puma reports are the Black Lake region of Presque Isle and Cheboygan counties and the Deadstream Swamp region of northern Missaukee County (Rusz 2001). The Deadstream Swamp is one of the most remote areas in the Lower Peninsula and is largely roadless. DNR foresters have found tracks that appeared to be cougar in the Deadstream (Rusz 2001).

The DNR also has filed some credible reports from the Lower Peninsula. In southern Missaukee County, not far from Cadillac, there was a report of tracks in late 1999. A conservation officer went out to investigate, and reportedly saw the big cat during deer season (Perez 2000, pers. comm.). There are also several other unconfirmed sightings by DNR biologists of pumas in the area (Perez 2000, pers. comm.). Part of southern Missaukee County lies within the Pere Marquette State Forest, which connects to the much larger Manistee National Forest in the county's southwest corner. Such intact habitat could provide a forested peninsula for juvenile cougars leaving their mothers' home ranges and entering new territories, assuming that there is a very small breeding population.

Oscoda County to the west consists of state or federal owned wood-lands, locally called the Club Country (Robinson 2000, pers. comm.). Nearly all the old-growth trees on the rather poor, unproductive soils of the Club Country were clear-cut by the early 1900s including northern red oak (Robinson 2000, pers. comm.). Much of the remaining private land in the region was bought in the 1940s by wealthy landowners who created large exclusive hunting reserves, but who do not live in the area (Robinson 2000, pers. comm.). On September 13, 1997, the *Detroit Free Press* newspaper published a photograph of a cougar reportedly about 10 miles from where Robinson saw his cat in Alcona County. The photo clearly showed a cougar lying in ferns and grass.

Further north on the Lower Peninsula, Rusz's research team also appears to have verified the existence of mountain lions. In July 2001, the Foundation team documented a 3.5 inch cougar track on Dale Willey's horse ranch just north of the town of Tower in the Black River Swamp region of Mackinaw State Forest (MWHF 2001a). Willey also claimed to have seen a cougar in early July 2001, and found evidence that a puma had dragged off a newborn colt a couple days later (MWHF 2001a).

On Rusz's suggestion, Willey agreed to bulldoze a half-mile long road along the north edge of his 70-acre pasture, and check it from [sic] tracks every other day. On the fourteenth day, he found a suspected set of cat tracks, which were photographed three days later and confirmed to be cougar by retired biologist Harley Shaw, a cougar researcher from Arizona (MWHF 2001a).

In actual fact, the existence of cougars in the wilds of the Lower Peninsula had already been confirmed. In February 1997, Christi Hillaker captured a puma on videotape as it walked through woods at the edge of her yard near the town of Mesick, in Wexford County. Her video clearly showed all the distinguishing characteristics of mountain lions, including the long tail (MWHF 2001b). A few hours after the incident, her husband measured the tracks at an enormous four and a half inches in diameter. Rusz later reviewed the videotape, measuring the cat's size by a tree it passed in the background, and determined that it reached at least 28 inches at the shoulders: clearly cougar-sized. He also confirmed the tracks to be those of a puma (MWHF 2001b).

Mesick sits on the northern boundary of Manistee National Forest, and in 2000–2001 there were several reports of lions along the Big

Manistee River northeast of Mesick in southern Kalkaska County (Rusz 2001, pers. comm.). Another credible report from January 1996 came from near the town of Meauwataka, about five miles from Mesick. Wildlife Biologist Marci Johnson, who previously had worked on a cougar project in Colorado, saw a puma near town and recorded a great number of tracks in the snow (MWHF 2001a).

Future Protection in Michigan

The Michigan mountain lion was listed as a state protected species in the 1980s, off-limits to hunting (Zuidema 2000, pers. comm.). Such protection has undoubtedly allowed the state's residual resident pumas to stage a very modest comeback. In fact, finding evidence of cougars was considered the easy part—after only two days in the field the researchers found deer carcasses, scat, and tracks (Rusz 2001, pers. comm.). It has been difficult, however, to build a case for wild *Puma concolor,* as skeptics have believed that any confirmed sightings were of former captive animals (Rusz 2001, pers. comm.).

The question now is this: Will the DNR now seek to embrace the few attested cougars as natives, or will it continue to write them off as exotics? The lessons gained from Florida's experience with the Florida panther are instructive. Until the 1970s, that state dismissed recurring reports, and even isolated mortalities, of that remnant cougar population as being escaped captives or descendants of captives (Rusz 2001, pers. comm.). As in Michigan, it took the persistent efforts of independent researchers and hunters to uncover a genuine endemic population of native cougars in Florida. If Michigan's Department of Natural Resources follows Florida's example and embraces this top predator as part of the state's native fauna along with black bears and wolves, this most adaptable of all wild cats in the Western Hemisphere just might find the state's rugged wilderness an inviting home again.

Literature Cited

Bowman, G. 2000. Private businessman and eyewitness, Gulliver, MI: pers. comm.

Detroit Free Press. September 13, 1997. Cougar photograph.

Edde, J. 2000. Wildlife Biologist, Ottawa National Forest, U.S. Department of Agriculture, U.S. Forest Service, Bessemer, MI: pers. comm.

Evers, D. C., ed. 1994. *Endangered and Threatened Wildlife of Michigan.* University of Michigan Press, Ann Arbor.

Hughes, B. 2000. Owner, Thistledowne Bed N-Breakfast, Gulliver MI: pers. comm.

LaPointe, D. 1977. The Cat That Isn't. *Michigan Natural Resources Magazine* November/December.

Manville, R. H. 1948. The Vertebrate Fauna of the Huron Mountains, Michigan. *American Midland Naturalist* 39(3): 615–640.

McCarthy, J. 2001. Retired police officer and eyewitness with photographs, Ann Arbor, MI: pers. comm.

Michigan Wildlife Habitat Foundation (MWHF). 2001a. Foundation Study Confirms Cougar in Michigan. *The Wildlife Volunteer,* November/December: 4–5.

Michigan Wildlife Habitat Foundation (MWHG). 2001b. Cougar Caught on Video. *The Wildlife Volunteer,* September/October: 3.

Minzey, T. 2000. Wildlife Supervisor, Michigan Department of Natural Resources, Cadillac, MI: pers. comm.

Ottawa National Forest. 2000. U.S. Department of Agriculture, U.S. Forest Service, www.fs.fed.us/r9/ottawa

Perez, R. 2000. Management Units Supervisor, Michigan Department of Natural Resources, Saginaw Bay, MI: pers. comm.

Robinson, L. 2000. Wildlife Biologist, Michigan Department of Natural Resources, Mio, MI: pers. comm.

Rusz, P. 2001. Director of Wildlife Programs, Michigan Wildlife Habitat Foundation, Bath, MI: pers. comm.

Rusz, P. 2001. *The Cougar in Michigan: Sightings and Related Information.* Bengal Wildlife Center Technical Publication, February, 63 pp. Michigan Wildlife Habitat Foundation, Bath.

Sprague, B. 2001. Park Naturalist, Porcupine Mountain State Park, White Pine, MI: pers. comm.

Zuidema, M. 2000. Retired silviculturist, Michigan Department of Natural Resources, Escanaba, MI: pers. comm.

The private, nonprofit Michigan Wildlife Habitat Foundation cited in the above paper changed its name to the Michigan Wildlife Conservancy and became the focus of intense and often personal controversy by 2003. The Michigan Chapter of The Wildlife Society (MITWS) became interested in the situation.

Conservation Review Update

Newsletter of the Michigan Chapter of The Wildlife Society, Fall 2003

In April, a MITWS member requested that the Conservation Review Committee consider involving MITWS in the current debate over the population status of mountain lions in Michigan. This issue fell squarely within the category of "issues where MITWS can positively contribute professional expertise to an uninformed or value-laden debate," one of two areas considered suitable for conservation review. During the past several months, various media sources have reported on the Michigan Wildlife Conservancy's cougar research. The Conservation Review Committee discussed the idea that MITWS, as an organization that sets ethical standards for wildlife biologists, offer to critique the science behind the cougar research and evaluate the credibility of evidence that there is a viable cougar population in Michigan. As a result of this process, Gary Roloff, the acting Committee Chair, drafted a letter from MITWS to the Michigan Wildlife Conservancy for the Executive Board to review. The Board voted in favor of having President Roloff mail the letter . . . to the Michigan Wildlife Conservancy. The Michigan Wildlife Conservancy promptly responded to our letter by contacting President Roloff. President Roloff discussed the content of the letter, the history of the mountain lion issue, and potential follow-up activities with Dr. Patrick Rusz. Dr. Rusz noted that the Michigan Wildlife Conservancy would gladly review their information on mountain lions with anyone who is interested and that those informal reviews can be initiated with a phone call to Dr. Rusz. The Michigan Wildlife Conservancy is initially hesitant to accept our Chapter's offer for a formal review for a couple of reasons. First, the Michigan Wildlife Conservancy would like more clarity on who would participate on the review team from the Chapter. Second, the Michigan Wildlife Conservancy would like a clear understanding of how the review would be used and disseminated and an explicit statement as to the motives of our Chapter for offering to conduct the review. Last, and most importantly, timing of a formal review is less than optimal pending completion of a manuscript to be submitted in a peer-reviewed journal (expected completion date is the end of 2003). As a means to initiate an exchange between the Michigan Chapter of the Wildlife Society and the Michigan Wildlife Conservancy on this issue, Dr. Rusz offered to give a formal presentation of the mountain lion program at our fall meeting in Grayling. Dr. Rusz's formal presentation will last approximately 1 hour and he has graciously offered to stay as long as we wanted for questions and discussion. The Michigan Wildlife Conservancy has also extended an invitation to President Roloff to visit their offices in Bath to learn more about this issue.

No presentation took place, and the spring 2004 issue of the MITWS newsletter stated that "Without a firm response to our offer, and given that several months have passed, MITWS sent a second letter renewing our offer." There were no further developments as this book went to press.

The presence of cougars in eastern Canada has been as controversial as in the United States. Below are articles that document cougars in Ontario, Quebec, and New Brunswick. For another case in Ontario that represents the first confirmed cougar attack in eastern North America since at least the nineteenth century, see Chapter 3.

Cougar, *Felis concolor,* Sightings in Ontario

by Helen B. Gerson[1]
The Canadian Field-Naturalist 102(3): 419–424, July–September 1988

Three hundred and eighteen sightings of Cougars, *Felis concolor,* were reported in Ontario for the period 1935 to 1983, and were evaluated by Ontario Ministry of Natural Resources staff. Most sightings were made in wilderness areas. About half of the sightings were reported from areas outside the deer range. None of the sightings was confirmed by positively identified Cougar tracks or other sign. Six areas in Ontario, relatively free from human disturbance and with good tracking conditions and repeated Cougar sightings, have been recommended as areas in which systematic searches for Cougar sign should be initiated.

Key Words
Cougar, *Felis concolor,* Ontario, sightings.

More than 300 sightings in Ontario from 1935 to 1983 and evidence from bordering Minnesota (W. Berg, Minnesota Department of Natural Resources, personal communication) and Manitoba (Nero and Wrigley 1977) suggest that Ontario might support a resident Cougar, *Felis concolor,* population.

The Cougar once ranged coast to coast from the Canadian Yukon to the southern tip of South America (Young and Goldman 1946; Hall 1981). In North America, European settlers persecuted the Cougar until it disappeared from most of its eastern North American range. The eastern subspecies, *Felis concolor couguar,* was considered extinct by the late 1800s (Young and Goldman 1946). Since then, however, increasing num-

---

[1]Wildlife Branch, Ontario Ministry of Natural Resources, Whitney Block, Queen's Park, Toronto, Ontario M7A 1W3

bers of people have reported seeing Cougars throughout the eastern United States and eastern Canada (e.g. Cram 1925; Wright 1948; Bue and Stenlund 1953; Dear 1955; Wright 1961; Goertz and Abegg 1966; Clarke 1969; Thomson 1974; Lawrence 1983).

The earliest Cougar sighting in Ontario on record in the Ontario Ministry of Natural Resources (OMNR) files dates from 1935. However, earlier records of the Cougar's presence in Ontario are reported in the historical literature (Brodie 1894; Calcutt 1894; Orr 1911). Since the 1950s the number of sightings reported in each decade has increased substantially as follows: 1950 to 1959—28; 1960 to 1969—44; 1970 to 1979—138; 1980 to 1983—103 [H. Gerson. 1985. The status of the Cougar (*Felis concolor* Linnaeus) in Ontario, with an overview of the status in Canada. Ontario Ministry of Natural Resources, Toronto. Manuscript].

There is evidence that Minnesota supports a small resident or transient Cougar population. Photographs of tracks in north-central Minnesota have been tentatively identified as those of a Cougar by M. Hornocker, a western Cougar authority. A Minnesota Department of Natural Resources wildlife biologist and other natural resource professionals have observed Cougars in the state (W. Berg, personal communication). Recent sightings of Cougars with kittens and of mating Cougars suggest a breeding population. Almost all the sightings in Minnesota are in the northern half of the state near the Ontario border (W. Berg, personal communication).

More than 260 sightings in Manitoba from 1930 to 1975 and a specimen collected in 1973 suggest that the species might be resident in the province. The animal was killed only 82 km from the Ontario border (Nero and Wrigley 1977; Wrigley and Nero 1982).

In this paper I describe the Cougar's distribution, habitat and behaviour in Ontario based on the records of sightings on file at the Wildlife Branch, Ontario Ministry of Natural Resources. These sighting records are not meant to serve as a basis for evaluating Cougar status or describing actual distribution. Publication of the Ontario sightings is meant to stimulate interest in alternate methods of determining the status of the Cougar in Ontario. Locations where Cougar sightings have been reported repeatedly over the last four decades are recommended as areas that should be searched systematically for Cougar sign. Since the probability of obtaining a photograph or specimen of a Cougar is low, the discovery of cougar tracks identified by an authority is necessary to verify the presence of Cougars in Ontario.

Methods

Reports of Cougar sightings were investigated and recorded by staff of the Ontario Ministry of Natural Resources. Data collected for each record include, where possible, date, time, location, number of animals seen, observer(s), distance from animal(s), observation conditions, colour, estimated body length and shoulder height, presence of tail, estimated tail length, description of other features, behaviour, presence of tracks and habitat. I converted all estimated body measurements to metric units.

Sightings were divided into two categories—probable sightings and possible evidence. Sightings in the first group consisted of complete and accurate descriptions of Cougars or their sign. Sightings in the latter group consisted of reports of tracks, scats and vocalizations, incomplete descriptions of cougars, and second-hand information. Sightings in the latter group were sometimes used as supporting evidence for some "probable" records.

Results and Discussion

Cougar Sightings. From 1935 to 1983, OMNR staff collected records of 318 sightings (189 probable, 129 possible). Through conversations with field staff, trappers and hunters, I learned that many Cougar sightings, especially those from earlier years, have not been documented.

A high proportion of cougar sightings are not valid (R. H. Brocke. 1981. Reintroduction of the cougar *Felis concolor* in Adirondack Park: a problem analysis and recommendations. New York State Department of Environmental Conservation. Manuscript). Van Dyke and Brocke (1987a) have concluded that compilation of sighting reports seems to be an unreliable method of assessing Cougar presence. Nevertheless, compilation of sighting reports is a necessary step in the investigation of the Cougar in Ontario.

Description of Cougars. Descriptions generally consisted of a tan or brown animal with a long tail and cat-like features, and sometimes included details such as a white chin, chest and throat, black markings on the face, ear tips and tail tip, and a lighter colour ventrally. Some observers described the tail as rope-like, drooping down and turned up at the tip.

Observers often reported that the hind legs were larger than the forelegs. Of 137 observations of the animal's colour, 35% were brown (often light brown or reddish brown), 15% were tan, 14% were tawny, 9% were black, 8% were fawn, 5% were beige and 4% were yellow. The remaining 10% were grey, gold, sandy or rusty.

Estimated mean body measurements are as follows: body length from snout to base of tail—136 cm±44 cm (S. D.) (N = 46); shoulder height—67 cm±19 cm (S. D.) (N = 67); tail length—75 cm±19 cm (S. D.) (N = 28). Observer estimates were consistent with body measurements reported in the literature (Banfield 1974, Hall 1981).

Behaviour and Vocalization. The activities of Cougars noted in 121 sightings were as follows: 30% walking, 26% running, 17% leaping, 10% standing, 5.5% lying down, 5.5% sitting, 4% eating or chasing prey, 1% drinking and 1% swimming. Movement of the tail from side to side was described in eight reports. The Cougar's apparent indifference to being observed or approached as pointed out by Nero and Wrigley (1977) is mentioned in 13 of our reports. Two observers claim to have approached a Cougar to within a distance of about 8 m before it walked away.

Vocalizations of Cougars described as snarls, screams, screeches, yowls, roars, shrieks, hisses and growls were reported on 18 occasions. Cougars that were approached closely by observers sometimes snarled or hissed. The other vocalizations usually were heard at night or when Cougars were not in sight, and therefore could not be attributed definitely to Cougars. Cougars are generally silent (Seidensticker et al. 1973), although they can call loudly and probably do so during mating time (Wright 1959).

Season and Time of Sightings. Cougars were seen in every month. Of 289 sightings in which the season was recorded, 48% were made in summer (June to August), 28% in autumn (September to November), 11% in winter (December to January), and 13% in spring (March to May). These results, which are similar to those reported by Nero and Wrigley (1977), probably reflect the amount of time people spend outdoors in the different seasons. Most sightings were made during daylight hours. Peak periods were between 0700 and 1300 hrs (44%, N = 95), between 1500 and 1700 hrs (17%), and between 2000 and 2100 hrs (9%).

Sightings of Pairs and Young. There were twelve sightings of two or more Cougars seen together, including seven of an adult with one or more kittens. The Cougar is generally a solitary animal. Adult males and females become established on "home areas" or territories before they breed, although "transient" males may occasionally breed (Seidensticker et al. 1973). For this reason, sightings of two or more Cougars (adults and young or breeding adults) may provide evidence of a resident Cougar population.

Prey and Distribution. In Ontario, there are 18 reports of Cougars said to be chasing or eating prey, or implicated in the injury, death or removal of domestic livestock. The prey species in these records consist of deer (2), Red Fox *(Vulpes vulpes)* (1), Snowshoe Hare *(Lepus americanus)* (1), Woodchuck *(Marmota monax)* (1), Beaver *(Castor canadensis)* (2), Porcupine *(Erethizon darsatum)* (1), pig (2), horse (1), sheep (2), cattle (4) and bait (1).

In Manitoba and New Brunswick, the distribution of Cougars (based on sighting records) is similar to that of deer, the major prey species (Wright 1972; Nero and Wrigley 1977; van Zyll de Jong and van Ingen 1978). In Ontario, the northern limit of the White-tailed Deer *(Odocoileus virginianus)* range is much farther south at present than that indicated in Peterson (1966) and Banfield (1974) [Smith and Verkruysse 1983].

About half of the Ontario Cougar sightings were reported from areas outside the present White-tailed Deer range (Smith and Verkruysse 1983), although other prey, including Moose *(Alces alces),* Woodland Caribou *(Rangifer tarandus),* Porcupine and Beaver are available in those areas. Spalding and Lesowski (1971) found that Cougars do prey on Moose in areas where Moose are common. Smaller prey species, such as Porcupine, Snowshoe Hare and Beaver may be locally important (Young and Goldman 1946; Robinette et al. 1959; Toweill 1977).

Although historical records indicate that the Cougar occupied only southern Ontario (Brodie 1894; Calcutt 1894; Orr 1908, 1909a, b, 1911), some accounts of its former distribution describe a much wider range, as far north as Hudson Bay (Fountain 1902; Ingersoll 1906). Lett (1887) believed that the Cougar "abounded, at one time, in the Valley of the Ottawa, in considerable numbers" and that "the panther was found in every part of Ontario and Quebec." Seton (1925) described a Hudson's Bay Company record of a Cougar that had killed a Caribou and was shot by an Indian hunter in northern Ontario, 15 miles north of Lake Temiscamingue [Timiskaming].

If the historical accounts of the wide range of the Cougar are accurate, the present distribution of sighting records in Ontario coincides with a liberal interpretation of the historical range. However, Cougar sightings are rarely reported in the heavily populated and cleared areas of southern Ontario.

Habitat. I have used Nero and Wrigley's (1977) habitat descriptions to group the Ontario Cougar sightings by habitat. The results are as follows: 64% "wilderness" (areas with few hard-surfaced roads or towns); 23% "mixed land" (agricultural land and towns interspersed with large forest tracts); and 13% "farmland" (agricultural land with forest cover restricted to woodlots and river valleys). These results differ from those of Nero and Wrigley (1977), who reported 40%, 30%, and 30% in the respective categories above. According to Van Dyke et al. (1986a), dispersing Cougars in Utah and Arizona tend to select areas for residence that are characterized by absence of recent logging, relatively low road densities, and few or no sites of human disturbance.

Systematic Search Techniques for Cougar Sign. There are two convenient ways to investigate the presence or absence of Cougars in an area. The first is to search the area in the immediate vicinity of a sighting for tracks as soon as possible after the sighting and to conduct such a search for as many sightings as possible. The second method is to search along dirt roads in areas where sightings are common.

The first technique, briefly outlined here, is described in detail by Van Dyke and Brocke (1987b). For each sighting, the investigators searched the perimeters of five concentric squares of increasing size, centered on the sighting location. They determined the dimensions of each square by pacing (lengths of sides of squares are 43, 86, 129, 172 and 215 m). The results of their study of this search technique suggest that the probability of finding at least one track or other physical evidence of Cougar on bare soil or snow is 80% for up to nine days after a valid sighting, if the site has not been disturbed by precipitation or high winds.

Van Dyke and Brocke (1987b) proposed that sighting reports that meet the following criteria be investigated preferentially: (1) the observer can identify the exact location of the sighting; (2) the substrate at the sighting location is snow or bare soil; (3) the site can be searched within nine days of the sighting; (4) the site is not disturbed by high winds, precipitation or other disturbance after the sighting. When a site meets all of the above criteria, but does not yield conclusive evidence of Cougar presence, the validity of the sighting report is extremely suspect (Van Dyke and Brocke 1987b).

In the east, sightings are reported frequently in areas that seldom experience the conditions identified in points 2 and 4 above. The results from the Utah study suggest that even disturbed sites would reveal tracks or other physical evidence of a Cougar 33% of the time, assuming all sightings were valid (Van Dyke and Brocke 1987b).

Systematic searches of dirt roads in areas where Cougar populations were present indicated that less than 90 km of dirt roads need to be searched in an area of 500 km² under ideal tracking conditions to find the track of any Cougar remaining in the area during the search period. The maximum search effort that should be necessary under less than ideal tracking conditions is 360 km of road searched per 500 km² of area (Van Dyke et al. 1986b). Searches may be conducted on roads with snow or dirt substrates, although snow lowers track persistence because of freezing, thawing, drifting and successive snowfalls (Van Dyke et al. 1986b). Also, Cougars tend to restrict movement after heavy snowfalls (Seidensticker et al. 1973), and therefore may cross roads less frequently (Van Dyke et al. 1986b).

Experienced Cougar hunters use other highly effective, but more subjective, methods to determine Cougar presence, usually involving intensive off-road searches in areas with specific terrain features. The services of such individuals should be engaged whenever possible to assess Cougar presence in an area (F. Van Dyke, personal communication).

Recommended Areas to Search for Cougar Sign. Resident Cougars studied in Arizona and Utah were rarely found in or near sites logged within the past six years and they selected home areas with relatively low road densities and little human disturbance (Van Dyke 1983; Van Dyke et al. 1986a). Transient Cougars were found in logged areas more often, but did not usually remain there (Van Dyke et al. 1986a). Cougars crossed improved dirt roads and hard-surfaced roads less often than unimproved dirt roads and were less likely to have hard-surfaced roads and improved dirt roads in their home areas than unimproved dirt roads, suggesting avoidance (Van Dyke et al. 1986b).

Based on this information, I have recommended six areas in Ontario that should be searched preferentially for Cougar sign. Within these areas . . . (The OMNR administrative districts and areas within the districts are 1 = Thunder Bay District—west of Thunder Bay; 2 = Nipigon District—south and east of Lake Nipigon and Limestone Lake area; 3 = Wawa District—northwest of White River, north of Highway 17; south and east of White Lake; between Highway 17 and Pokei Lake, south of White River; and Obatanga Provincial Park; 4 = Hearst District—Oba south to Irving Township; 5 = Cochrane District—south, north and west of Cochrane; 6 = North Bay District—Marten River area), there are sites that meet all of the following criteria: 1) not closer than one km to sites being logged at present or logged within the past six years; 2) few or no sites of human residence; 3) no major permanent human disturbance, habitat alteration or human presence; 4) low road densities (i.e. 50 km of road/100 km^2), but enough passable dirt roads to conduct a search of at least 90 km of roads per 500 km^2; 5) mainly sand or clay unimproved dirt roads and few improved dirt roads and hard-surfaced roads (many other areas meet all criteria except this one, since logging roads in Ontario are often covered with gravel); 6) repeated Cougar sightings over many years or sightings of two or more Cougars or Cougars with young.

Acknowledgments

The Wildlife Branch of the Ontario Ministry of Natural Resources (OMNR) kindly allowed me to use the data in the Cougar sighting reports as a continuation of my work for the Ministry on the status of the Cougar. The Ministry Cougar sighting file was initially developed by G. McKeating, now of the Canadian Wildlife Service, with assistance from D. Chamberlain. I would like acknowledge the many people who reported observations to the OMNR and the OMNR biologists and conservation officers who forwarded the observations to me.

Discussions with R. E. Wrigley, Manitoba Museum of Man and Nature, and R. W. Nero, Manitoba Department of Natural Resources, were helpful in preparing this publication. I thank W. F. Berg, Minnesota Department of Natural Resources, for the information he provided on the Cougar in Minnesota, F. Van Dyke, then at the Fort Wayne Bible College, Indiana, but now with the Montana Department of Fish, Wildlife and Parks, for the information on survey techniques, and F. Van Dyke, I. Bowman, OMNR, C. D. MacInnes, OMNR and C. Wedeles, OMNR, for reviewing the manuscript. Finally, I am grateful to I. Bowman, who made this work possible.

Literature Cited

Banfield, A. W. F. 1974. *The mammals of Canada.* University of Toronto Press, Toronto. 43R pp.

Bue, G. T., and M. H. Stenlund. 1953. Recent records of the mountain lion *(Felis concolor)* in Minnesota. *Journal of Mammalogy* 34(3): 390–391.

Brodie, Wm. 1894. The panther in Ontario. *The Biological Review of Ontario* 1(2): 27–28.

Calcutt, J. 1894. American panther. *The Biological Review of Ontario* 1(2): 23–26.

Clarke, C. H. D. 1969. The puma in Ontario. *Ontario Fish and Wildlife Review* 8(4): 7–12.

Cram, W. E. 1925. Notes on some New England carnivores. *Journal of Mammalogy* 6: 199.

Dear, L. S. 1955. Cougar or mountain lion reported in northwestern Ontario. *Canadian Field-Naturalist* 69: 26.

Fountain, P. 1902. *The great mountains and forests of South America.* Longmans, Green, and Co., London. 306 pp.

Goertz, J. W., and R. Abegg. 1966. Pumas in Louisiana. *Journal of Mammalogy* 47(4): 727.

Hall, E. R. 1981. *The mammals of North America.* Second edition. John Wiley and Sons, New York. Two volumes. 1081 pp. + 90 pp.

Ingersoll, E. 1906. *The life of animals. The mammals.* New York. 555 pp.

Lawrence, R. D. 1983. *The ghost walker.* Holt, Rinehart and Winston, New York.

Lett, W. P. 1887. The cougar or panther. *Ottawa Naturalist* 1(9): 127–132.

Nero, R. W., and R. E. Wrigley. 1977. Status and habits of the cougar in Manitoba. *Canadian Field-Naturalist* 91(1): 28–40.

Orr, J. E. 1908. The last panther. *Rod and Gun and Motor Sports in Canada* 10(3): 266.

Orr, J. E. 1909a. Some old time reminiscences of old Ontario. *Rod and Gun and Motor Sports in Canada* 10(9): 840–842.

Orr, J. E. 1909b. Old time stories of old Ontario. *Rod and Gun and Motor Sports in Canada* 11(3): 259–261.

Orr, J. E. 1911. Old time stories of old Ontario. *Rod and Gun and Motor Sports in Canada* 12(11): 1439–1446.

Peterson, R. L. 1966. *The mammals of eastern Canada.* Oxford University Press, Toronto. 465 pp.

Robinette, W. L., J. S. Gashwiler, and O. W. Morris. 1959: Food habits of the cougar in Utah and Nevada. *Journal of Wildlife Management* 23: 261–273.

Seidensticker, J. C., IV, M. G. Hornocker, W. V. Wiles, and J. P. Messick. 1973. *Mountain lion social organization in the Idaho primitive area.* Wildlife Monographs 35. 60 pp.

Seton, E. T. 1925. *Lives of game animals. Volume 1(1), Cats, wolves and foxes.* Charles T. Branford Company, Boston. 337 pp.

Smith, H. L., and P. L. Verkruysse. 1983. *The White-tailed Deer in Ontario: its ecology and management.* Ontario Ministry of Natural Resources. 35 pp.

Spalding, D. J., and J. Lesowski. 1971. Winter food of the cougar in south-central British Columbia. *Journal of Wildlife Management* 35(2): 378–381.

Thomson, S. C. 1974. Sight record of a cougar in northern Ontario. *Canadian Field-Naturalist* 88(1): 87.

Toweill, D. E. 1977. Food habits of cougars in Oregon. *Journal of Wildlife Management* 41(3): 576–578.

Van Dyke, F. G. 1983. A western study of cougar track surveys and environmental disturbances affecting cougars related to the status of the eastern cougar *Felis concolor couguar.* Ph.D. thesis, State University of New York, Syracuse, New York. 245 pp.

Van Dyke, F. G., and R. H. Brocke. 1987a. Sighting and track reports as indices of mountain lion presence. *Wildlife Society Bulletin* 15(2): 251–256.

Van Dyke, F. G., and R. H. Brocke. 1987b. Searching technique for mountain lion sign at specific locations. *Wildlife Society Bulletin* 15(2): 256–259.

Van Dyke, F. G., R. H. Brocke, H. G. Shaw, B. B. Ackerman, T. P. Hemker, and F. G. Lindzey. 1986a. Reactions of mountain lions to logging and human activity. *Journal of Wildlife Management* 50: 95–102.

Van Dyke, F. G., R. H. Brocke, and H. G. Shaw. 1986b. Use of road track counts as indices of mountain lion presence. *Journal of Wildlife Management* 50: 102–109.

van Zyll de Jong, C. G., and E. van Ingen. 1978. *Status of the Eastern Cougar* (Felis concolor couguar) *in Canada*. Committee on the Status of Endangered Wildlife in Canada (COSEWIC). Available from Canadian Nature Federation, Ottawa.

Wright, B. S. 1948. Survival of the northeastern panther *(Felis concolor)* in New Brunswick. *Journal of Mammalogy* 29: 235–246.

Wright, B. S. 1959. *The ghost of North America: the story of the Eastern Panther.* Vantage Press, New York. 140 pp.

Wright, B. S. 1961. The latest specimen of the eastern puma. *Journal of Mammalogy* 42(2): 278–279.

Wright, B. S. 1972. *The Eastern Panther: a question of survival.* Clarke, Irwin and Company Limited, Toronto. 180 pp.

Wrigley, R. E., and R. W. Nero. 1982. *Manitoba's big cat: the story of the Cougar in Manitoba.* Manitoba Museum of Man and Nature, Winnipeg. 68 pp.

Young, S. P., and E. A. Goldman. 1946. *The Puma, mysterious American cat.* The American Wildlife Institute, Washington, D.C. 358 pp.

The Cougar Leaves a Calling Card

by Ray Ford
The Globe and Mail, Toronto, Ontario, June 19, 1999

Kenora.—Claiming to have seen a cougar in Ontario was once akin to confessing to drinking bouts with an invisible rabbit. Now, with a simple stoop-and-scoop manoeuvre, Lil Anderson has changed all that. Ms. Anderson, a resource management technician with Ontario's Ministry of Natural Resources, has the poop on the big cat. Found on a trapline near Kenora last year, the fecal matter "is the first solid or semi-solid piece of proof we've had for the cougar's existence," says wildlife biologist Neil Dawson.

Listed as an endangered species and protected against hunting, the eastern cougar was supposed to have been driven out of the province during the past century. "There are still a lot of cougar skeptics out there," Mr. Dawson concedes. "But with Lil's finding, I think the tide is turning."

Cougars, also called pumas, mountain lions and panthers, once roamed throughout much of North America. Nearly two metres long and weighing as much as 60 kilograms, the big tan-coloured cats became increasingly scarce as forests gave way to farms and they were persecuted as livestock killers. Ontario's last known cougar was shot near Creemore, north of Toronto, in 1884.

Since then, at least 1,000 cougar sightings have been reported in the province, all without definite proof of the animal's existence—until last year, when Ms. Anderson found herself hot on the trail of the mysterious cat. Responding to a call about possible cougar tracks northeast of Kenora, Ms. Anderson and Natural Resources technician Rob Moorley found another set of tracks. "They were so fresh, we were expecting a close encounter of the furred kind," Ms. Anderson says.

They soon found the crucial evidence, still unfrozen despite the −15° C temperature. Ms. Anderson scooped up the deposit—technically known as scat—and shipped it to the Edmonton forensic laboratory of Alberta's Natural Resources Service. There, forensic biologist Tom Packer subjected the stool to thin-layer chromatography, a process that separates the chemicals found in an animal's bile salts into a pattern specific to individual species. He compared the results with scat obtained from an Alberta cougar. The patterns matched.

On the surface, the finding is good news. Top predators are a sign of a healthy environment, and should indicate the existence of both good habitat and abundant prey. On the other hand, as loggers, hunters and campers push into previously untracked wilderness, there may simply be more pressure on the cougar's habitat, and greater opportunities to catch sight of the beast.

Reliable cougar sightings have ranged from Manitoba to Quebec borders, and from Hearst in the north to Bracebridge and Pembroke in the south.

For Ms. Anderson's part, she is still on the case. The next time cougar scat falls in the forest, she hopes someone will notice and call the ministry. "My big goal is to see and photograph a cougar," she says.

Cougar Believed Extinct May Be Roaming Quebec; Eastern Canada Sightings: DNA Tests on Strand of Hair Could Solve Mystery

by Kate Jaimet

National Post, Don Mills, Ontario, October 15, 2002

(Reprinted with permission of the National Post Company, a CanWest
   Partnership)

Ottawa.—The mysterious eastern cougar—missing and presumed extinct since 1938—may be prowling in the Gaspe region of Quebec. The discovery lies in the DNA molecules in a strand of hair in Virginia Stroeher's microbiology lab at Bishop's University in Quebec. Dr. Stroeher and her colleague Marc Gauthier are clutching at a few tawny hairs, caught this summer in a hair trap on the rugged Quebec peninsula.

"When we started this project two years ago, we laughed about this being the Sasquatch of the East. But now we have some really hard evidence that we've got something more tangible," Dr. Stroeher said in an interview from her university lab in Lennoxville, Que., near Sherbrooke. "It's very exciting."

Once widespread across North America, cougars were hunted during European colonization and driven into three last strongholds: the Rocky Mountains, the Olympic Peninsula in Washington State, and the Florida Everglades. The last known eastern cougar was shot near the Quebec-Maine border in 1938. Since then, thousands of cougar sightings have tantalized Ontario, Quebec, the Maritimes and the New England states, but hard evidence of the cats has remained elusive.

On July 23, 1953, two employees of the Great Lakes Paper Company reported a tawny, 5½-foot-long cat standing at the side of the Trans-Canada Highway about 50 kilometres west of Thunder Bay, Ont.

On April 13, 1954, an engineer and a fireman traveling on the Canadian National Railway between Thunder Bay and Atikokan, Ont., said they saw a cougar cut across the tracks in front of the train and leap on to a rocky promontory.

In the spring of 1990, Roger Noble of Waasis, near Fredericton, attempted to capture on videotape an animal he believed to be a cougar, but the fuzzy images allowed no independent identification.

There was hope of solving the mystery of the cat's existence when a cougar was shot on May 27, 1992, in front of a house in Saint-Lambert-de-Desmeloizes, in the Abitibi region of Quebec. But that turned out to be a South American cougar that had escaped after being brought north as an exotic pet.

Cougar tracks and scat found near Deersdale, N.B., in 1992 were tantalizing, but offered no evidence whether this was a wild cougar or another escaped pet.

Then, in 2000, a truck driver contacted Dr. Gauthier, a wildlife biologist at the small research company Envirotel 3000 in Sherbrooke, saying he had hit a cougar with his rig near East Hereford, in Quebec's Eastern Townships. He asked whether the scientist could identify the animal's origins: Was it another escaped zoo animal or a true eastern cougar?

To solve the puzzle, Dr. Stroeher began looking for molecular markers that uniquely characterize the DNA of cougars.

Meanwhile, Dr. Gauthier began setting up poles, scented with cougar urine, in the Gaspe region, the Eastern Townships and the Mont Tremblant area of Quebec to attract the cats. The poles were covered with velcro to catch the animals' hairs. If any cougars were out there, he hoped to capture evidence of their existence. The breakthrough came in August, when a hair sample collected by Dr. Gauthier in the Gaspe came up positive in Dr. Stroeher's lab.

"My student came in. He's a very serious student. He always has a furrow in his brow. He looks at me and he says: 'I've got an interesting result,'" Dr. Stroeher recalled. "He said: 'I've worked this up, I've done the reactions three times, and I keep getting a cougar.' We re-did the whole procedure from the hairs on, and sure enough. We definitely have a cougar."

Where did the Gaspe cougar come from? There are only three possible explanations, Dr. Stroeher said.

The first is that it escaped from a zoo or from an owner who kept it as an exotic pet.

The second is that cougars from elsewhere in North America are returning to colonize their old habitat in the East.

The third explanation is that the secretive eastern cougar never really died out. "It's possible they just hunkered in, somewhere north of here, and because we have such an expansion in prey, they're coming down again."

As she refines her molecular analysis techniques, Dr. Stroeher hopes she will eventually be able to tell the difference between cougars native to the Rocky Mountains, South America, the Florida Peninsula and eastern North America, based only on their DNA samples. That, together with Dr. Gauthier's research, could provide evidence about how many cougars are roaming through Eastern Canada and where they came from.

Recent Confirmation of a Cougar, *Felis concolor*, in New Brunswick

by Roderick E. Cumberland and Jeffrey A. Dempsey
Department of Natural Resources and Energy, Fish and Wildlife Branch, P.O. Box 6000, Fredericton, New Brunswick E3B 5H1
The Canadian Field-Naturalist 108(2): 224–226, 1994

The presence of Cougar *(Felis concolor)* in the northeast, specifically New Brunswick, has been a controversial topic for decades, due primarily to an abundance of reports and sightings confounded by a lack of physical evidence. However, on 16 November, 1992, characteristics and measurements of tracks and identification of hair from a scat found near Deersdale New Brunswick were determined to be that of a Cougar. Confirmation of the endangered subspecies, the eastern Cougar *(Felis concolor couguar)* is not possible with the collected data.

Key Words
Cougar, *Felis concolor,* Eastern Cougar, *F.c. couguar,* New Brunswick.

The existence of the Eastern Cougar *(Felis concolor couguar)* has long been a controversial topic of discussion in eastern Canada and the United States. Allen (1894), and Boardman (1899) felt that the presence of the Cougar was well authenticated, while Gesner (1847) and Ganong (1903) suggested that there was no authentic evidence of the Cougar's existence in New Brunswick. Another advocate of the Eastern Cougar throughout the mid 1900s was the late Bruce Wright (1948, 1953, 1959, 1961, 1965, 1972), who compiled accounts and reports that he felt substantiated the animal's existence. Despite his conclusions, Van Zyll de Jong and van Ingen (Status of the Eastern Cougar in Canada, National Museum of Natural Sciences, Ottawa, Canada, Unpublished Report 1978) reviewed data on the eastern subspecies in the Maritimes over this same time period and concluded that no reliable estimates of the number of Cougar could be made.

In the spring of 1990, a tawny cat was taped on home video at the edge of a field near Fredericton, New Brunswick. Tischendorf (1990) investigated the poor quality videotape and concluded that it was a young Cougar, although not all officials shared his conclusion. Rainer Brocke, a professor at the State University of New York in Syracuse, states that there is no viable breeding population of Cougars in the northeast. He believes that only 5% of sightings are reliable and these may only be of escaped captive animals (Hansen 1992).

Although sightings of the animal in New Brunswick are frequent, actual physical evidence of animals has been lacking for over 50 years, since the last reported Cougar was killed at the Maine, USA/ Quebec/New Brunswick border in 1938. This specimen is now in the collections of the New Brunswick Museum Catalogue Number NBM 5678. The only other catalogued evidence of a Cougar in New Brunswick was a 1932 photograph of a skin from a Cougar shot in Kent County (Wright 1972).

The Eastern Cougar is listed as a nationally endangered species by the Committee on the Status of Endangered Wildlife in Canada (COSEWIC). In New Brunswick, the Eastern Cougar has been protected under the Endangered Species Act since the Act was proclaimed in 1976. However, lack of concrete evidence of a viable population has made it difficult to validate its status as endangered. The Canada Lynx *(Lynx canadensis)* is also listed as endangered in New Brunswick and are occasionally trapped incidentally during the Coyote *(Canis latrans)* and Bobcat *(Lynx rufus)* seasons (four incidental Lynx were reported in the 1992–1993 fur harvesting season alone). In comparison, Cougar have never been reported to be trapped, shot or found dead in New Brunswick over the last 50 years. This note reports on field observations and laboratory analysis that confirm the first indisputable evidence of the presence of a Cougar in New Brunswick.

Materials and Methods

Data were gathered approximately 5 km north of McKiel Lake, west-central New Brunswick (43'22" N and 67'00" W). The area, a one million acre tract of land belonging to J. D. Irving Woodlands (Deersdale Division), is high, cool temperate forest characterized by a predominance of Balsam Fir *(Abies balsamea)* and spruce *(Picea* spp.) in lowlands and dominant hardwoods on more upland sites. It is classified as Miramichi highlands with elevations up to 800 m, annual snowfall over 400 cm and mean annual precipitation over 1200 mm (S. L. Lusk, 1990, Wildlife Management Zones. Unpublished New Brunswick Department of Natural Resources and Energy Report). Timber harvesting has produced a mosaic of clearcuts and conifer plantations of various ages interspersed with hardwood, mixed wood and softwood stands.

On 16 November 1992, Tom O'Blenis of the J. D. Irving Woodland's Deersdale Division reported large cat-like tracks along a woods road on their freehold land. Tracks were visible in snow that had fallen one day prior to the report, resulting in a light, fluffy snow accumulation of 10 cm. Daily maximum temperatures at the Juniper, New Brunswick weather office did not exceed $-2°$ Celsius before we investigated the tracks, reducing the likelihood of enlarged or distorted tracks.

We followed the tracks for over 2.5 km along a skidder trail, then into hardwood saplings which led to a dominant hardwood stand. From here the tracks meandered down a ridge and passed through balsam fir thickets. Stride was measured where the same foot touched the ground twice, measuring from the front of both tracks. Stride, plus length and width of the tracks, were measured in the shade and through all habitat types encountered along the trail. Careful observation was made of every tree/branch that the animal might have contacted. Only one sample of hair was collected along the animal's trail and identified by the observers using cuticular scale patterns (Adorjan and Kolenosky 1969; Carter and Dilworth 1971).

Scat was found approximately 400 meters along the trail in association with the tracks. The scat was on top of a rock and not covered by debris, a characteristic of the cat family. The size of the scat suggested its origin could have been Bobcat, Lynx, Coyote or Red Fox *(Vulpes vulpes)*. Hairs from the scat were analyzed by Dr. C. G. Van Zyll de Jong then at the Canadian Museum of Nature in Ottawa, by using reference specimens with respect to pigmentation, shape, length and width dimensions, cuticular scale patterns and nature of the medulla.

Results and Discussion

A total of 30 stride measurements were recorded along the length of the trail and resulted in an average stride of 109.4 cm (43.8 inches). Eighteen individual measurements of track length and width resulted in average dimensions of 9.72 cm wide by 9.62 cm long (3.9 by 3.8 inches). In addition, we measured a 15.9 cm straddle (width from outside of left foot to outside of right foot), a leap 5.25 m long and 1 m high over balsam fir saplings without disturbing snow on top of the saplings, tracks along two logs for over 3 m and measurements where the animal had sat on its haunches (34.4 cm long including heel impression).

The tracks revealed strong feline characteristics, including width equal to or greater than the length, deeper impression of the front of the plantar pad, tear-drop shaped toes, non-symmetrical pattern to the toes and lack of claw marks. Balance required to walk along logs several feet above the ground over a considerable distance is also typical of felines and not indicative of canines.

Stride changed little throughout the different forest cover types. The 110 cm average stride is double the typical Bobcat and Lynx stride (Murie 1974; Dixon 1982).

Microscopic analysis of the hair sample found on a Balsam Fir sapling along the track trail was identified as underfur from a Coyote. All characteristics of the hair found in the scat were consistent with that of Cougar.

There have been over 100 credible sightings of "Cougar" over the last 16 years in the Maritimes (R. F. Stocek, personal communication, 24 September 1990. Eastern Cougar sightings in the Maritime provinces, Atlantic Society of Fish and Wildlife Biologists Annual Meeting, Mill River, Prince Edward Island). Tracks reported from previous Cougar sightings have been identified as Coyote, Fisher *(Marten pennati),* Bobcat, housecats *(Felis* spp.) or occasionally Lynx. Robert Downing, after five years of tracking Cougar in the eastern United States, found that sighting reports were generally unreliable (Hansen 1992).

Although we present indisputable evidence of a Cougar in New Brunswick, we cannot distinguish subspecies from these data. Therefore, these data lend little support to the existence of a remnant Eastern Cougar population. It is possible that the animal responsible for the tracks could have been an escaped or released animal. Photographs of the tracks, slides of the hair from the scat as well as a portion of the scat itself are on collection with the New Brunswick Museum in Saint John, New Brunswick.

Acknowledgments

We acknowledge L. Stone, JDI Woodlands Division, for notifying our Department about the tracks, L. Grant for accompanying us, C. G. Van Zyll de Jong for his scat analysis, and R. Stocek, D. McAlpine, and G. Redmond for their review of this manuscript.

Literature Cited

Adorjan, A. S., and G. B. Kolenosky. 1969. *A manual for the identification of hairs of selected Ontario mammals.* Department of Lands and Forests, Ontario. Research Report (Wildlife) number 90.

Allen, J. A. 1894. Remarks on the second collection of mammals from New Brunswick. *Bulletin of the American Museum of Natural History* 6: 359–364.

Boardman, G. A. 1899. St. Croix mammals. *Calais Times,* Calais, Me. Nov 22. Reprint in *The Naturalist of the St. Croix.* S.C. Boardman. Bangor, Me. 1903. pages 319–321.

Carter, B. C., and T. G. Dilworth. 1971. A simple technique for revealing the surface pattern of hair. *American Midland Naturalist* 85(1): 260–262.

Dixon, K. R. 1982. *Mountain lion in Wild mammals of North America.* Edited by J. A. Chapman and G. A. Feldhammer. John Hopkins Press. London. 1139 pages.

Ganong, W. F. 1903. On reported occurrences of the panther *(Felis concolor)* in New Brunswick. *Bulletin of the Natural History Society of New Brunswick* 21: 82–86.

Gesner, A. 1847. *New Brunswick: With notes for immigrants.* Simmonds and Ward. London. 388 pages.

Hansen, K. 1992. *Cougar—The American lion.* Northland Publishing Co. Flagstaff, Arizona. 144 pages.

Murie, O. J. 1974. *A field guide to animal tracks.* Peterson's field guide series. Second Edition. Houghton Mifflin Co. Boston, Massachusetts. 375 pages.

Tischendorf, J. W. 1990. The Eastern Panther on film? Results of an investigation. *Cryptozoology* 9: 74–78.

Wright, B. S. 1948. Survival of the northeastern panther *(Felis concolor)* in New Brunswick. *Journal of Mammalogy* 29(3): 235–246.

Wright, B. S. 1953. Further notes on the panther in the northeast. *Canadian Field-Naturalist* 67(1): 12–28.

Wright, B. S. 1959. *The ghost of North America.* Vantage Press, New York. 140 pages.

Wright, B. S. 1961. The latest specimen of the eastern puma. *Journal of Mammalogy* 42(2): 278–279.

Wright, B. S. 1965. The cougar in eastern Canada. *Canadian Audubon* 27(5): 144–148.

Wright, B. S. 1972. *The eastern panther: A question of survival.* Clark, Irwin and Co. Toronto, Ontario. 180 pages.

Cougar Sighting? Possible Mountain Lion Prints Studied by State Game Officials

by Dwayne Rioux

Central Maine newspapers (*Morning Sentinel* and *Kennebec Journal,* both published in Augusta, Maine), November 19, 2000

State game officials have taken plaster casts of paw prints thought to be those of a mountain lion sighted in Monmouth. The evidence was gathered at a spot where a Monmouth man said he saw two cougar-like animals in mid-September.

The animals, believed to be a mountain lion and her cub, were reported seen in mid-September by Roddy Glover, 39, in a heavily wooded area divided by railroad tracks between routes 132 and 135 near the Monmouth municipal transfer station.

"It was a week before bow hunting season and I was scouting for deer," Glover said. "Actually, I had broken my ankle shortly before and was looking for a good area to set up a ground blind when this occurred." Glover was standing in a ditch just off a railroad trestle and leaning up against a metal fence when he heard the clicking sounds of something stepping on crushed stone. "I moved out to take a look, thinking it might be a deer," he said. "At first, I thought it was a large bobcat walking toward me about 150 yards away. It was taking its sweet time walking down the tracks—not a care in the world. But it looked too weird to be a bobcat."

The large feline turned broadside, and Grover [*sic*] realized it was not alone. He believes it was a mountain lion with a smaller cub trailing behind. He froze and felt his heart sink deep down into his chest as fear gripped him.

He focused on the larger cat. He doesn't recall paying much attention to the smaller animal.

"I wasn't sure if it would attack to protect its young. I didn't know what they would do," he said. "I couldn't run because of my ankle. I just lay down behind some ferns."

Grover [*sic*], a taxidermist who has mounted a fair number of bobcats for display, said he once tanned a mountain lion hide for a client, so he is familiar with their appearance.

He said the cats were in an area literally infested with deer.

A mountain lion will usually attack a deer by grasping the shoulders and neck with the front paws, claws extended, digging its hind claws into the deer's flanks. The cat then bites the back of the deer's neck, breaking its spinal cord and killing it.

Mountain lions often drag their prey to a sheltered area, covering the kill with soil, leaves, grass and other debris and returning later to feed.

Grover [*sic*] said he watched both cats unnoticed for more than 20 minutes. At one point, they came within 50 yards of him before moving off into the woods.

"I distinctly remember the wind being in my favor so they couldn't smell me," he said.

Glover said the cougars were reddish-brown in color. The larger animal was about the size of an adult Labrador retriever, and the smaller cat itself could have weighed 40 to 50 pounds.

"I had a very good view, and they definitely had a long tail," he said. "There's no question in my mind I was looking at two mountain lions. They can say I'm crazy. I don't care. I just wish I'd had my camera along with me."

He immediately called district game warden Kevin Anderson to report the sighting.

Anderson, in turn, contacted assistant regional wildlife biologist Keel Kemper at his Sidney office. Kemper, along with 20-year warden veteran and investigator Philip A. Dugus Jr. met with Glover within an hour of the sighting.

Dugus said he was reluctant to believe Glover at first and went along just to observe. He changed his mind when he saw the cats' prints in mud at the scene.

"The tracks were too big to have been made by bobcat, even a big one," he said. "There were a couple hundred tracks within the area. There was a three-to-four-foot distance between paw strides. I can tell you they weren't made by a coyote, wolf, or lynx. I believe Mr. Glover. You can't discount every sighting before you start adding a little credibility to the evidence."

Kemper, who agreed, made several plaster molds of the large tracks, both front and rear paws, found well-formed in mud.

"I'm confident it's a very large cat track," he said. "We have fairly solid physical evidence given to us by a credible witness that the tracks were made by a large cat, possibly a mountain lion. Mr. Glover's findings are the most solid piece of cougar evidence we've ever had." Kemper said the front paw prints measure 4 inches in length and 3 inches across. Dugus questioned whether the creature is a wild feline or one domestically raised and released into the wild to fend for itself.

"If it is a mountain lion, where did it come from?" he asked. "It's illegal to introduce any exotic species in Maine without a permit sanctioned by our department. At this time I know of six domesticated cougars within striking distance."

Glover believes the cats are wild.

"My question is, if there was a female cat with a cub, there's got to be a male around as well. I can't believe someone would purposely release two cougars, especially getting rid of a kitten."

Having written about other possible cougar sightings, we thought this might be just another unconfirmed report. Not so. At DIF&W headquarters in Sidney on Thursday, we showed several of the paw casts to Warden Sgt. Christopher Simmons of Morrill and District Warden Daniel G. Murray, of Belgrade.

Both men were unaware of Glover's sighting.

"It's one heck of a big cat track," said Simmons. "What is it?" Murray was equally surprised.

"It's a big cat track," he said. "One of the biggest I've ever seen. It's not a coyote track, that's for sure."

Mountain lions, or cougars, are currently on the Federal Endangered Species list. Anyone injuring or killing a mountain lion would be subject to the same penalty as someone harming a bald eagle.

In April 1994, agents of the Vermont Fish and Wildlife Department responded immediately to a resident near Craftsbury who called with a convincing sighting of three large cats. The men collected a fresh scat, and the following letter describes the first analysis of that evidence.

National Fish and Wildlife Forensics Laboratory Response to Vermont Cougar Evidence

United States Department of the Interior
Fish and Wildlife Service
Division of Law Enforcement
National Fish and Wildlife Forensics Laboratory
1490 East Main Street
Ashland, Oregon 97520
(503) 482-4191

In Reply Refer To: FWS/LE LAB
September 12, 1994

Cedric Alexander
Dept. of Fish and Wildlife
184 Portland St.
St. Johnsbury, VT 05819

Dear Mr. Alexander:

As we discussed today, I am sending this letter report concerning the identification of hairs from a scat you sent earlier this summer. Initial samplings of hairs from the dried scat proved unsatisfactory as far as obtaining complete, undamaged hairs. I rehydrated a small fragment of the scat and was able to secure a larger sample.

I have searched the samples and have confirmed the presence of cougar *(Felis concolor)* hairs in that scat. There appear to be additional animals represented (skunk, bovid [goat or cow]) and some synthetic fiber and frass. The hairs are very degraded (cleared, broken, compressed etc.), but I managed to identify a foot hair definitively as cougar.

Foot hairs of most mammals are very different from dorsal guard hairs, which constitute the basis for most hair collections. We maintain a collection of hairs from at least seven body areas of those mammals that we process here in the Lab. For the North American cats, our collection is now quite complete. Should you happen to procure more scat from this sighting area, I would be pleased to examine them.

Sincerely,
Bonnie C. Yates
Sr. Forensic Scientist (Mammals)
Morphology Section

Three days after receiving this letter, the Vermont Department of Fish and Wildlife issued a press release headlined "Cougar Evidence Confirmed in Crafts-bury." But confusion arose in 1997 when the department sought to apply the newly emerging technology of DNA analysis to the scat. Vermont District Wildlife Biologist Cedric Alexander retrieved the scat from the Wildlife Forensics Laboratory (it's unclear exactly when). He noted that it looked significantly smaller in diameter than the sample he had sent in, even accounting for the fact that it had been dried by both himself and Ms. Yates.

Mr. Alexander sent the scat to Holly Ernest, then a Ph.D. candidate at the Veterinary Genetics Laboratory of the School of Veterinary Medicine at the University of California–Davis. Because the results of that test were apparently conveyed by phone, with no official report available, editor Chris Bolgiano asked Dr. Ernest to summarize her test and its results for this anthology.

Summary of DNA Analysis of Vermont Cougar Scat

Email from Holly Ernest, January 19, 2004

A scat (fecal sample) was submitted to me for DNA analysis in 1997 by Cedric Alexander of the Vermont Fish and Wildlife Department. I extracted DNA from multiple sections of the scat, and tested the DNA extract using a panel of fluorescently-labeled felid-specific nuclear microsatellite markers by employing PCR (polymerase chain reaction). Following multiple tests, no felid markers amplified. Next, I tested the DNA extract with unlabeled canid-specific microsatellite markers— which did amplify in the appropriate size ranges for dogs. The work was confirmed by dog geneticists at the UC Davis Veterinary Genetics Laboratory, who ran a more extensive panel of fluorescently-labeled canine microsatellite markers (10). The results of this panel were consistent with dog genetic type, but do not preclude the possibility that the DNA that amplified was that from another canid. Although I sampled multiple sections of the scat, it is theoretically possible (but not likely), that the scat was not deposited by a canine animal but by another animal and that my DNA results came from canine animal that was eaten. Felids can defecate material that they eat very rapidly after ingestion, therefore there can be relatively undigested whole chunks of prey in feces. Theoretically undigested prey in feces might supply DNA that does not represent the feces depositor.

Holly Ernest DVM PhD
Wildlife and Ecology Unit
Veterinary Genetics Laboratory
School of Veterinary Medicine
University of California
One Shields Avenue
Davis, CA 95616–8744 USA

Ms. Bonnie Yates was then contacted. Concerned by the possibility that the scat returned to Vermont might have been one of two coyote scats sent to her from New York and Maine, she explained that non-forensic items could not be included in her normally precise work flow and had to be handled differently: She had to request special permission to work on such items, had to keep them in a small space within a lab dedicated to other procedures, and depended on interns for unpacking, drying, repacking, and record-keeping, although she did the microscope work herself.

"I found only a very few, very degraded cougar hairs among many other types of hair," she said, "but I went back and reconfirmed my findings from slides I made then, and I stand by them. There is not necessarily a discrepancy in the two sets of findings. I never believed the scat was from a cougar and I never stated that it was. Months passed before the scat was returned to Cedric Alexander, time for any remaining felid DNA that might have been present to degrade even further. Hairs in the scat could be from the depositor or from the prey, that is, what was eaten. What I found were signs of a scavenger. The cougar hairs I found probably indicate a cougar carcass scavenged by another animal."

Cedric Alexander's reports indicate that the cougar trackers on that April morning in Vermont believed that the fresh scat they collected was deposited by one of the three animals they were following. But whether the original scat was deposited by a cougar or by a canid that had fed on a cougar carcass, there was at least one cougar in Vermont.

The Quabbin Reservoir in central Massachusetts has been a hotbed of cougar sightings for many years. In 1997, John McCarter, an authority on animal signs who has taught workshops for the U.S. Fish and Wildlife Service, among other groups, found several large, covered scats next to some covered beaver remains while hiking in the reservoir. At that time, McCarter was working as senior staff instructor in the Nature School run by natural history writer and photographer Paul Rezendes in Athol, Massachusetts. Below is John McCarter's statement.

John McCarter's Own Account of the Scat Sample Found in the Quabbin Reservoir

by John McCarter
Written in September 1999 and posted on Paul Rezendes' New England
    Mountain Lion Web Pages until 2003

In April of 1997 I was in the northern Quabbin Reservation preparing for a program I was to teach for Paul Rezendes. Stepping from a dense stand of young hemlocks into a small clearing by the reservoir, I found a low mound of leaf litter which covered a scat that was deposited in a prepared scrape. The scat was ⅞ of an inch in diameter and of larger volume than any of the known bobcat scats I'd seen. Less than two feet away was a second covered scat. It was 1 1/16 inches in diameter with one piece eleven inches long and a second piece 3 ½ inches long. This scat was similar in size to feline scats I had seen in Florida and believed to have been from cougar.

The upper and lower sections of a beaver jaw were lying in the open about eight feet away. They were well chewed and appeared to have been from a recent kill. Perhaps 30 feet into the woods, beneath a canopy of white pines and hemlocks lay a dead hemlock and under it was a large mound of coniferous leaf litter. This mound turned out to be a cache. Limited exploration of its interior only revealed bits of beaver fur and what appeared to be the contents of a beaver's entrails. There were also tufts of beaver fur next to the cache and the beaver's lower incisors nearby. The cache was irregular in shape and measured 9 feet by 8 feet. It seemed larger than it needed to be to conceal the remains of an animal the size of a beaver. I failed to find any coyote sign in the vicinity and the cache showed no signs of having been raided. There were scrapes made by the pawing inward of leaf litter while the cat was covering the beaver remains. Some of these measured: 21, 21, 19, 23, 13, 15, 12, and 15 inches. The shorter measurements appeared to have been influenced by a branch.

Thirty feet away from the cache, on the opposite side from where the first and second scats were located, was a third scat. This one was 1 inch in diameter and was partially covered by a volcano shaped mound (i.e. open at the top). A fourth scat, fully covered and also 1 inch in diameter was an additional 6 feet away.

Eleven feet east of the cache was a mound of pine needles over a scrape with no scat in it and no smell of urine on it. The lengths of the inward pawing scrapes radiating around this mound were 21, 20, 18, 16, 20, and 24 ½ inches.

I collected one of the scats that day to show to Paul Rezendes. A couple of days later I returned to the site with Mark Elbroch so that he could take some photographs and so that I could collect a second fecal sample. During that visit to the site we discovered a fresh scat deposited on top of the cache exactly where I had opened and closed the leaf mound with my hands on the first day. This scat was 1 ¼ inches in diameter but lacked clear feline characteristics.

The Massachusetts Department of Fisheries and Wildlife expressed an interest in having the scats analyzed to discover their origin. A forensics lab in Oregon undertook to answer that question by identifying the hairs in one of the scats.

More than a year later we were told by Massachusetts Fish & Wildlife that the scat contained beaver fur, but that no coyote or cougar hair was found. Paul Rezendes then sent the second sample to the Science Resource Center at the Wildlife Conservation Society in New York where George Amato quickly determined by DNA testing that it was in fact cougar scat. We are currently trying to locate the appropriate lab to send the remaining sample to for a second analysis.

In July of 2000, feline geneticist Dr. Melanie Culver reconfirmed Dr. Amato's DNA analysis and stated further that the Quabbin Reservoir scat was of the North American type. The Massachusetts Department of Fisheries, Wildlife, and Environmental Law Enforcement responded three months later with a press release.

Cougar Questions

Massachusetts Department of Fisheries, Wildlife, and Environmental Law
    Enforcement
November 2000 press releases,
    www.state.ma.us/dfwele/press/Prs0011.htm#upland
Released November 16, 2000

Cougar, mountain-lion, catamount, panther; the mere mention of these names conjures up images of big cats poised on high ledges in the Rockies, ready to pounce on an unsuspecting mule deer. While populations of mountain lions in the western states are stable or increasing, the only known population in the eastern United States, the Florida Panther of the Everglades region, is collapsing as mortality of adults annually exceeds the recruitment of young. Opinions on whether mountain lions exist elsewhere in the eastern U.S., and in Massachusetts specifically, vary widely. Biologists at MassWildlife field numerous calls from people who believe they have sighted a mountain lion crossing a road or walking along a field edge. Follow-up conversations, site visits and review of physical evidence (photographs, video, tracks, etc.) either point to a misidentified house cat, bobcat, coyote or dog or are inconclusive. Some 26 historic specimens of the eastern mountain lion (12 mounts, 1 partial mount, 11 skulls and 2 skins) exist in museums or other collections representing 7 states and one Canadian Province where cougars once roamed. The last known record of the eastern mountain lion in Massachusetts was from Hampshire County ca. 1858. The tremendous increase in human population, habitat development and fragmentation, major highway construction and other landscape changes throughout the east would seem to preclude the possibility of a relict wild population surviving for the past 150 years. But what about individual animals? Could lone cougars be wandering through Massachusetts from distant populations? According to recent research the answer is, "Probably not." The closest cougar concentrations are found in Florida and Manitoba and dispersal distances measured for western cats averaged less than 50 miles. A more likely scenario for the presence of a mountain lion in Massachusetts would be the escape or release of a captive animal. While the possession of a cougar as a pet in Massachusetts is prohibited, cougars and other exotic cats are easily available from out-of-state sources and via the internet. Cougars, servals, tigers and African lions have been seized from persons keeping them illegally in the Commonwealth. In six eastern states a total of 8 free-ranging cougars have been killed since 1967. In each instance the animals displayed behavior or physical characteristics indicative of captive origin.

Massachusetts' most compelling evidence for the presence of an individual mountain lion was discovered by animal track and sign enthusiast John McCarter. In April of 1997 McCarter found scat (feces) that appeared to have been deposited by a large cat near the Quabbin Reservoir. DNA sequence lab tests done by George Amato of the Wildlife Conservation Society in New York and confirmed by Dr. Melanie Culver of Virginia Polytechnic Institute and State University identified the sample as cougar scat.

"The lab tests tell us one thing, that the scat sample came from a mountain lion," states MassWildlife biologist Susan Langlois. "John McCarter's notes and observations and my site visit suggest that the scat was deposited by a free-ranging animal and not placed there as part of some elaborate hoax. Since there has been no additional hard evidence collected in the ensuing 3 years the escape or release theory looms large. One could speculate that a captive cougar escaped or was released in the area and survived long enough to feed on a beaver and leave this tangible evidence of its presence." Langlois and other MassWildlife biologists will rigorously investigate any promising leads where hard evidence is available. "We need additional data to answer the questions that the presence of this scat raises," continues Langlois. "We need photos, tracks or a road-killed cougar to help us understand what may be happening out there. A concentration of reported sightings might point to a particular area for further investigation but sightings by themselves aren't evidence. It's too easy to misidentify wildlife, particularly if it's a species the person has never seen before."

Panther Killed

The Pocahontas Times, Marlinton, West Virginia, Volume 94, October 1976

"If only Cal Price were alive" is what everyone has been saying since Sunday afternoon at 2:15 when a panther was killed in the Jacox-Lobelia area by Kessler Pritt. Pritt was working on his truck outside his home and saw an animal in his flock of sheep about 50 yards away. At first he thought it was a dog but then realized it was a cat animal. It picked up a lamb in his mouth and went over a rail fence down the hill a little ways and started eating on the back leg of the lamb. Pritt got his gun and came after it. He shot and the bullet from the 3.08 went through the lamb and exploded in the shoulder-chest area of the panther; when he saw what it was he called a conservation officer. Within 15 minutes several were there.

Conservation Officer Larry Guthrie, of Durbin, took the animal to the Department of Natural Resources Office in Elkins [WV].

He stopped off in Marlinton where a big crowd quickly gathered.

The big cat weighed an even hundred pounds. He was a young male, 1 to 2 years old, 68 inches long from nose to tail (tail was 25 inches long).

The dictionary says cougar, puma, panther, catamount and mountain lion are all interchangeable.

We couldn't put our hands on any panther facts—or even "unfacts"—but remembered the story of Francis McCoy, who probably killed the last panther killed in Pocahontas before the turn of the century. We checked with his granddaughter, Mrs. Lee Barlow. Theodore Roosevelt records in his "Winning of the West" that Col. Cecil Clay and Francis McCoy killed a panther but I can't find the date. Col. Clay was a friend and frequent hunting visitor of McCoy on Day's Run of Williams River. Clay had lost an arm in the Civil War. One hunting trip they treed a panther. Clay steadied his gun on McCoy's shoulder and shot. The wounded panther fell among the dogs and started mauling them, McCoy rushed in and with bare hands saved the dogs.

As if there wasn't already enough excitement, Tuesday evening the report came that another panther was on Bruffey's Creek. It was bedded down against a fence beneath a rocky ledge on the farm of Norman Walker. The night before his cattle and sheep had tried to push through the fence and now he knew why. The DNR was called and soon officers arrived to observe the animal and to keep it from being disturbed.

THE POCAHONTAS TIMES

West Virginia state conservation officer Larry Guthrie holds a cougar killed in Pocahontas County in 1976. Another cougar was captured.

Federal authorities were also notified as eastern cougars are an endangered species and protected by federal law.

Some who saw it thought this one was bigger than the other one and, by the way it acted, a female about ready to give birth. The tail looked about half as long.

At 1 A.M. the big cat was shot with a tranquilizer gun, ran about 80 yards and collapsed. The men got her in a box and took her to the French Creek Game Farm. A call from Pete Zurbuch Wednesday said a veterinarian verified it was a pregnant female, 65 to 75 pounds. But they question the wildness of the animals because they don't seem to fear humans and this one didn't mind the cage.

In 1998, Todd Lester, the West Virginia resident who established the Eastern Cougar Foundation in that same year (see his essay in Chapter 3), invoked the Freedom of Information Act to obtain U.S. Fish and Wildlife Service correspondence concerning the fate of the pregnant female. The file letters he unearthed ultimately don't answer the question but do show the difficulties of interpreting the Endangered Species Act in this situation.

[File Memoranda on the Fate of the Pregnant Female]

Official Correspondence Regarding Captured West Virginia Cougar

TO: The File
FROM: Deputy Regional director [U.S. Fish and Wildlife Service]
SUBJECT: Eastern Cougar (?)
DATE: April 14, 1976

On April 14, 1976 I received a call from Regional Director Larsen (in Washington) who said we had a problem regarding a cougar in West Virginia. I said we were aware of the situation, that Endangered Species Specialist Paul Nickerson had briefed me on the matter earlier this morning, and that we had advised Washington (Schreiner's Office) of the situation.

At any rate, I was told that we should advise the State officials to release the animal as near as possible to the capture site. Otherwise, they would be in violation of the Endangered Species Act. I pointed out that we were not even sure it was an "endangered" eastern cougar, or that it might be a released "game farm" animal. These points were being checked out.

Keith Schreiner, who was with Mr. Larsen, said that there are no experts who can identify eastern from western cougars, and we should get the State people to release the animal. O.K. [Includes several sets of initials]

Memorandum

TO: Regional Director, Boston, Mass.
FROM: Deputy Regional Director
SUBJECT: Eastern Cougar (?)
DATE: April 15, 1976

After my discussion with you on Wednesday morning, April 14, I called the Chief of the West Virginia Wildlife Resources Division, Dan Cantner, but he was not in, so I talked to Jim Ruckle who was apparently handling the cougar matter for the State.

From my conversation with Jim, it appears that the State has handled the matter quite well. When the male cougar was killed by local residents in a small community east of Droop, West Virginia, the State officials got to the scene rather quickly and prevented them from killing the female. They have the animal, which appears to be a pregnant female cougar, at a facility in French Creek, West Virginia. It is in good shape, and they know how to handle cats such as this.

Upon capturing the animal, they talked to Agent Leo Badger and then called the office of Endangered Species to talk to Ron Skoog and later to Tom Steigler in our Central Office Law Enforcement organization. The State was advised by Dr. Skoog to hold on to the animal. Under these instructions, they had proposed to hold on to the female while the dead male was positively identified as an eastern cougar. This appeared to be a sound approach under the circumstances.

However, I told Mr. Ruckle that we were advised by our Washington Office to urge the State to release the animal as soon as possible somewhere in the vicinity of its capture. Jim Ruckle took this literally and said that if it was released in the area of its capture it would be immediately killed by some of the local residents. He suggested a possible release in the Cranberry Williams Wilderness Study Area [now Cranberry Wilderness] of the Monongahela National Forest, about 20 to 25 miles west of the capture site. It is an extremely wild area with no bear hunting and very few people, and on the surface it seems ideal for the release of such a wild animal (if it is, indeed, wild).

Since this sounded good to me, I volunteered to call Ralph Mumme, Forest Supervisor of the Mononhagela National Forest, and coordinate the release of the female cougar on Forest Service land. I talked to Ralph Mumme, who concurs in the proposal and thought the Wilderness Study Area would be a good release site. He and his staff will cooperate fully.

However, before they release the animal, and for reasons understandable to me, Jim Ruckle wants a written statement from us to release what he calls "your" cougar. Jim was promised full cooperation unless, for some reason or other, someone above him might object. [Signature illegible]

Memorandum

TO: The Files
FROM: Endangered Species Program Specialist
SUBJECT: West Virginia's Cougar
DATE: April 20, 1976

Last Friday, April 16, after talking with Service lion expert Maurice Hornocker, I advised Ralph Mumme of the U. S. Forest Service that the cougar being held by West Virginia Department of Natural Resources was not to be released. The reasons for doing this were: If the cat is tame, and Dr. Hornocker believes it is, releasing it could pose a real danger because these tame cougar home in on young children. If the cat is not tame, its behavior when captured was atypical; therefore, it should be observed for possible rabies infection and examined for other wildlife diseases.

I believe we should have the cat examined by a competent zoologist, versed in captive lion care. If he or she verifies our suspicion that the cat is tame, we should make provisions for its continuing to remain in captivity.

Paul R. Nickerson [Signature]

[No letterhead]
[Stamped] FILE COPY APR 22 1976

Mr. Dan E. Cantner, Chief
Wildlife Resources Division
Charleston, WV 25305

Dear Dan:

As you know, we have decided for now at least, that the controversial cougar at French Creek should not be released to the wild. We made that decision based upon discussions with Service lion expert, Maurice Hornocker. He believes the cat is a tame one because of its behavior when captured, its sagging belly and its shortened tail, and he told us that these animals are dangerous when turned loose in the wild because they home in on small children.

We would like to have the cat examined by a competent zoologist versed in lion care and get a formal opinion on whether the cat is tame. Once we establish that, we can make provisions for its continuing to remain in captivity.

Please let us know if you agree with this approach and also if you would like to keep the cat at French Creek once its degree of domestication is established.

Sincerely yours,
[Signature illegible]
Regional Director

[Letterhead] State of West Virginia
Department of Natural Resources
Charleston 25305

May 7, 1976
Mr. Howard N. Larsen, Regional Director
U.S. Department of the Interior
Fish and Wildlife Service
Post Office and Courthouse Building
Boston, Massachusetts 02109

Dear Mr. Larsen:

In reply to your April 22, 1976, correspondence concerning the captive cougar, we suggest the following. Since the disposition of this animal is governed by the Federal Endangered Species Act, West Virginia will do everything possible to assist your organization in the proper disposition of the subject cat. Should you wish to have the cat examined by a competent zoologist to determine if it is tame, we will assist you in this endeavor.

Two mountain lions are being maintained at the French Creek Game Farm and we have no desire to keep this animal. Since this is the Service's cat, you should feel free to make whatever disposition of it you deem necessary. We would, however, like some indication as to when you will pick up the animal.

Should you have any questions concerning this matter, do not hesitate to contact me.

Sincerely,
[Signature]
Dan E. Cantner, Chief
Division of Wildlife Resources

Several people who have tracked eastern cougar incidents over many decades told editor Chris Bolgiano that the Southeastern Cooperative Wildlife Disease Study Center in the College of Veterinary Medicine at the University of Georgia in Athens had examined the two West Virginia cougars and found parasites that could only have been obtained south of Athens, and it was therefore concluded that the cougars were former pets. When contacted for confirmation, however, Jeanenne Brewton, senior secretary at the center, said that the center "did not do a clinical case" on this incident, and no one at the center responded to repeated requests for further information.

In 1996, Todd Lester made plaster casts of several sets of tracks he found near his home in Wyoming County, West Virginia. Two years later he established an online cougar discussion group through which he met Dr. Lee Fitzhugh, who agreed to review scanned photos of the casts.

Todd Lester holds the plaster casts he made of tracks in Wyoming County, West Virginia, in 1996. They were confirmed as cougar tracks.

Interpretation of Track Casts Made in West Virginia

From: E. Lee Fitzhugh
To: Todd Lester
Date: Tuesday, September 01, 1998
Subject: Re: Tracks

Todd,

I looked carefully at the pictures, downloaded, enlarged, printed, measured, etc. I think I sent you my paper on telling dog tracks from cougar tracks. These were a little difficult, but if you follow along with the paper in hand I think you'll be able to see why I made each determination.

Picture 1: heel pad is concave at rear (a dog sign); front of heel pad seems to be rounded (a dog sign); a line drawn tangential to the bottom of the heel pad (accuracy of this is not important), intersecting with lines drawn through the long axis of the outer toes, form two angles. In each cast, the toe on the right was somewhat obscure, so I drew two lines for each one of those, one that I thought was correct, and the other that would be "possible" toward the inner side of the track (making it more cougar-like). Measuring the angles with a protractor, and subtracting the acute from the obtuse angle provides a number represented in the paper. In this case, both figures from the top cast were strongly in the "dog" camp, and one of the figures from the bottom cast was also. The other one was 15, meaning it could be either one, but more like "dog." Other clues: the size of the toes with respect to the heel pad, the closeness together of the toes. Second toe width divided by heel pad width = 0.5, far into the "dog" camp. My conclusion: these casts are most likely from a dog. Also, it appears that there may be a hint of blunt claw marks on the two center toes.

Picture 2: Following the same reasoning, top cast on the left side is definitely a cougar (unless, of course, it might be leopard, jaguar, etc.).

E. Lee Fitzhugh, Ph.D.
Extension Wildlife Specialist
Department of Wildlife, Fish, and Conservation Biology
University of California
One Shields Avenue
Davis, CA 95616-8751
530/752-1496; FAX 752-4154
elfitzhugh@ucdavis.edu

Evidence Mounting that Elusive Cougars Are Back in Smokies Park

by Morgan Simmons
News-Sentinel, Knoxville, Tennessee, September 22, 2002

Wytheville, VA.—At first glance the two photographs on Don Linzey's desk appeared to capture nothing but underbrush and shadow.

With his finger Linzey, a biology professor at Wytheville Community College, traced the outline of a cat-like animal that was approximately 30 feet from the camera, but camouflaged behind the summer foliage. In the first photo a tree blocked the head, but part of the body and a long tail could be detected in the center of the frame.

The second photo showed the animal running away, and here the back of the head and most of the body were more visible. Linzey explained that the two photos were taken in July from a rental cabin near the boundary of the Great Smoky Mountains National Park.

Linzey said the vacationing couple that shot the photos believe they saw a cougar, and he thinks they might be right.

"There's really not another animal in the park that has that basic body shape and size," Linzey said.

Twenty-four years ago Linzey began tracking down cougar reports in Virginia. Four years ago he expanded his investigation to include the 800 square miles of the Great Smoky Mountains National Park.

Linzey is the author of two guidebooks, "Mammals of Great Smoky Mountains National Park," and "The Mammals of Virginia." He is also the lead mammalogist for the All-Taxa Biodiversity Inventory under way in the Smokies.

While the prevailing wisdom holds that wild cougars were eliminated throughout the East (except for southern Florida) by the 1940s, sightings of these elusive predators have persisted, particularly in the Smokies, 20 percent of which have never been logged and remain an undisturbed refuge.

Linzey said cougar sightings inside the park have increased "astronomically" over the last eight to 10 years.

He said that up to 1995 the National Park Service had received about 50 reports of cougars inside the Smokies park and that this summer alone there were seven sightings during an eight-week period between May 14 and July 17.

"Nobody put a lot of confidence in these reports in the past," Linzey said. "The Park Service simply does not have time to check them all out."

In order for Linzey to investigate a cougar sighting, it has to carry weight. He looks for sightings that involve more than one observer, and he takes into account the observer's experience with animals and the outdoors.

Once a sighting inside the Smokies passes the credibility test, Linzey marks its location on a map with a color-coded pin. The oldest sighting on the map—marked by an orange pin—dates back to 1946 when a female cougar and cubs were spotted near the Chimneys Campground.

According to Park Service records, there have been four cougar sightings in Cades Cove this summer, the first occurring in June on the north side of the Loop Road near Tater Branch.

The observer, a man from Ohio, took a long-range picture of the cougar out in a field that failed to produce an identifiable image. According to the report, the man wanted to get closer, but his wife wouldn't let him.

The next day another sighting occurred at the same location, and this time the observer saw what looked like a cougar catch a deer fawn.

Of the two other Cades Cove sightings this summer, one occurred on July 14 near the Cooper Road Trail close to Abrams Creek, while the other occurred July 16 a half-mile east of the Cades Cove entrance at Laurel Creek Road.

Linzey said another cougar sighting occurred the first week of June when a man and his wife spotted what appeared to be a cougar while driving on U.S. Highway 441 just north of the Sugarlands Visitor Center. According to the report, the animal was fawn-colored, weighed about 75 pounds and crouched at the edge of the road before walking slowly in to the woods.

Linzey said that in this case the observer was a veterinarian who had treated cougars as part of his practice.

"How can you tell somebody like that they didn't see what they saw?" he asked.

One of the most credible sightings recently reported in the park occurred on May 14 along Little River Road about one mile west of the Sugarlands Visitor Center. The observer was Rebecca Shiflett, a professional nature photographer from Knoxville who has documented the park's elk reintroduction and is employed by Discover Life in America as the official photographer for the All-Taxa Biodiversity Inventory.

Shiflett said the sighting occurred at 6:25 A.M. while she was driving to an early morning wildflower shoot.

"It was a 40-mile-per-hour zone, but I was driving below that because I knew I was approaching a game trail where I see deer, turkey, and coyotes all the time," Shiflett said.

"So I'm coming around the curve and watching my speed when I see this cougar about 75 to 100 meters in front of me standing 5 feet off the pavement and on the left side of the road where they had mowed. He's looking right at me, and when he heard my car, he walks to the tree line; he doesn't run."

Shiflett described the cougar as weighing about 75 pounds with round ears, short thick legs, tawny highlights, and a long tail. She said at first she was hesitant to report the sighting to park officials even though she was sure of what she saw.

"I didn't have a photograph, and there was nobody with me," she said. "But I felt somewhat vindicated after I learned there have been several other cougars seen and photographed in the park this summer. From now on, I'll keep a backup camera with a telephoto lens."

Park officials say that two months after Shiflett's sighting, another cougar was reported at the same location at 8:45 P.M.

In 1973 the growing number of cougar sightings throughout the East prompted the U.S. Fish and Wildlife Service to include the eastern cougar on the Endangered Species List.

But during the early 1980s a comprehensive field survey of the Southern Appalachians by the U.S. Fish and Wildlife Service failed to produce hard evidence of cougars, although possible deer kills, scat and scrapes were identified.

So what are people seeing? Kim DeLozier, wildlife biologist for Great Smoky Mountains National Park, said the number of cougar sightings in the park over the last 20 years has him asking a slightly different question.

"I think people are seeing big cats. The question is where did they come from?" DeLozier said. "Most states believe these are captive cats that are released after they grow up and get too hard to handle. Is there a remnant wild population out there that has been hidden for decades and is starting to re-surface? I think that's a possibility, but not a big possibility. More likely, I believe these are captive cats."

Linzey said as far as the question of where the cougars are coming from goes, he wouldn't go out on a limb.

"My goal," he said, "is to obtain positive evidence that cougars are in the park and, ideally, to prove they're breeding there."

Linzey said his best photographic evidence so far comes from video camera footage taken in January 2001 by a couple from Florida who, while hiking along a creek bed in the park's Greenbrier section, saw what appeared to be a cougar staring out of a rocky cave at close range.

"As far as I'm concerned, that's the first picture image ever taken of a cougar in the park," he said.

With the help of park volunteers, Linzey has set out 30 "hair snare" devices in areas where the most reliable cougar sightings have occurred. Consisting of roofing nails attached to patch of carpet, the snares are placed about 2 feet off the ground and smeared with a special cougar-attracting paste developed in Montana.

Hairs caught in the nails are sent off to a laboratory in British Columbia for DNA analysis. Linzey said he is running into the expected problem of black bears ripping the snares off the trees, and that out of the eight samples he sent off three weeks ago, one was positively identified as belonging to a bear.

He said that while most of the hair samples couldn't be identified through DNA analysis because they were too damp and moldy, one sample of cream-colored hair taken at Davenport Gap was described as looking like it came from a cat.

In addition to the hair snares, Linzey and the Park Service also have mounted automatic infrared cameras along select game trails in an attempt to photograph a cougar.

"With an animal as rare as the cougar, you don't go about searching haphazardly. I hope if I'm ever fortunate enough to see one, I have someone with me."

The following letter was written to editor Chris Bolgiano in response to a request for information on a cougar kitten killed by a vehicle in eastern Kentucky in 2001. It documents the first cougar kitten known to have been growing up wild in the East since the 1800s, as well as the genetic mixing that is probably occurring.

Kentucky Department of Fish & Wildlife Resources
Letter Discussing Killed Cougar Kitten

Commonwealth of Kentucky
Department of Fish and Wildlife Resources
C. Thomas Bennett, Commissioner

April 20, 2001

Dear Chris,

Here is the information you requested on the Kentucky puma kitten. Sometime after dark in June 1997 a 19-year-old man, alone in his pickup truck, was heading south on KY highway 850 and going down "Hippo Hill" (just north of the town of Hippo, KY in western Floyd county, which lies in rural eastern Kentucky) when he hit and killed a puma kitten. He stopped the truck, picked up the kitten, put it into the back of his truck, and went to his house. The next day he reported it to one of our Conservation Officers, who in turn, told him to call the Department of Fish and Wildlife Resource's (KDFWR) Wildlife Biologist, Jason Plaxico who covered 11 counties in eastern Kentucky, including Floyd. Next, the young man took the kitten to Jason's office and gave it to him. Jason talked to the fellow about the incident and then put the kitten into his freezer. Sometime later Jason gave the specimen to the US Army Corps of Engineers to have it mounted and displayed for educational purposes at the visitor center at nearby Paintsville Lake. However, the taxidermist said he wouldn't mount it because he thought the specimen was "rotten." So, the US Army Corps returned it to Jason. It sat in his freezer until sometime in early 1998 when it was given to David Yancy, the former Nongame Program Coordinator for the KDFWR. David brought the kitten to Frankfort, KY and placed it in a freezer at the KDFWR headquarters.

I was told about the specimen in late August 1998, took a look at it, and decided to have DNA analyses conducted to evaluate its genetic heritage. I had only been with the KDFWR's Nongame Program (now called "Wildlife Diversity Program") for 2 ½ years and didn't know much

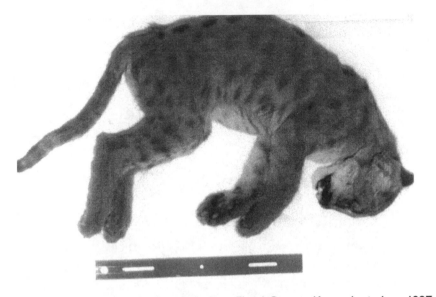

A female puma kitten hit by a vehicle in Floyd County, Kentucky, in June 1997.

about pumas and DNA testing. I sent out two tissue samples on February 15, 1999. One tissue sample went to Dr. Melanie Culver (then finishing up her Ph.D. work on pumas) at the National Institutes of Health/National Cancer Institute in Washington, DC to conduct mitochondrial DNA analysis (to determine if the genetic type of the kitten's mother was compatible with a North American type). The other tissue sample was sent to Dr. Holly Ernest at the University of California, Davis to conduct microsatellite DNA analysis (to determine if the genetic type of both of the kitten's parents was compatible with a North American type).

I received the results of Dr. Culver's analysis on April 15, 1999. She found that the KY kitten's mother had a genetic type that is identical to a genetic type found in South America . . . it only occurs in central Brazil and Peru. Thus I assumed that the kitten was either itself a captive animal that had been released or had escaped, or the offspring of a captive puma.

On December 31, 1999 I received the result of Dr. Ernest's DNA analysis. Her findings confirmed that one of the kitten's parents (the mother, according to Dr. Culver's mitochondrial analysis) was most likely of South American ancestry. She also found that the other parent (the father, by default) was most likely of North American ancestry. The combined results of these analyses indicated that the puma was most likely the results of hybridization with both North and South American ancestry, and was not likely a wild native North American puma. Of course, if these results are correct, it is likely that no one knows where (in captivity or not) this kitten's mother was bred, and the whereabouts of its father.

Here is specific information on the kitten itself. The skull is broken in several places. It is a female, weighs 4 kg (8.8 lbs), is 805 mm long, has a tail of 300 mm, a hind foot of 134 mm, and an ear length of 63 mm. All toe nails are sharp, intact, and there are no visible human markings (e.g., tattoos, tags, collars, etc.). The hair was not "slipping" at the time I took the tissue samples, so the taxidermist probably could have successfully mounted it. I have about a dozen slide photos of the specimen and the specimen is still in the Wildlife Diversity freezer. The fellow who hit it would still like to see it mounted and displayed at Paintsville Lake . . . I'm looking into the feasibility of this. If it is mounted, I would like to at least preserve some internal organs and the skull for possible future analysis.

You probably read the recent Lexington (KY) *Herald* article about this incident (see: http://www.kentuckyconnect.com/heraldleader/news/012001/hstatedocs/20cougars.htm) . . . Wildlife biologist, Jason Plaxico, is quoted as saying "the man who ran over the kitten told him it was following a mature cougar and two other young ones across a road near Martin in rural Floyd County." When I questioned the man again on February 27, 2001, he told me he saw a large shape and then a smaller shape cross the road in front of the kitten he hit. He agreed that it could have been the kitten's mother and a sibling, but he couldn't see well enough to say for sure. It seems most likely that the young kitten was following its mother and sibling(s). Also, the man said that he lives in Martin, KY, not that the kitten was hit near Martin.

I have included two photos of the kitten.

Steve Thomas
Wildlife Biologist
Wildlife Diversity Program
Kentucky Department of Fish and Wildlife Resources
#1 Game Farm Road
Frankfort, KY 40601
1-800-858-1549, ext. 369

The following article about Delaware is out of geographical place because of the strong possibility that the cougars here are released captives.

Cougar Buffs Say Delaware Could Be Big Cat Capital

by Edward L. Kenney
The News Journal, Wilmington, Delaware, June 5, 2003

Wilmington.—When it comes to cougars in the Middle Atlantic region, northern Delaware could be the capital.

Experts said there might be only two or three cougars roaming here. But it turns out that northern Delaware is a regional hotbed for the big cats when compared with the surrounding area, according to the Eastern Cougar Network, a new Web site that tracks cougars in the Eastern United States.

Capt. Robert Hutchins, who is in charge of the state's Division of Fish & Wildlife enforcement for New Castle County, said the Delaware cougars probably were tame at one time. That is because they are so isolated from all other cougar enclaves in the Eastern United States, with the nearest clusters in upstate New York.

Delawareans have heard about cougars slinking around in the state's suburban neighborhoods for years. The cats were thought to be extinct in the Eastern United States outside of Florida. But tell that to people in Brandywine Hundred, Bear, Newark and other places where they have seen and videotaped the cats since they were first sighted in there in 1995.

The Eastern Cougar Network gives Delaware a newfound credibility in the cougar world. What makes it even more legitimate is the Web site places strict criteria on the sightings it posts, shunning the less scientific approach found on other cougar Web sites.

Ken Miller of Concord, Mass., spent the past nine months researching and putting the Web site together with several other cougar buffs. He said they gather information from professionals such as state and federal wildlife officials, and university researchers. It is a forensic approach that relies on solid data such as cougar tracks, killed prey, reliable photographs and videotapes, all of which, except photos, have been used to verify sightings here.

"There hasn't been much science of turning the figures out, the phenomenon of cougars coming east," he said. "We want to take this out of the realm of UFOs and Bigfoot kind of stuff."

Miller said he was surprised Delaware has more cougar sightings than anywhere in the Middle Atlantic region.

"We didn't think this would be a likely place where we would find them," he said.

A Delaware link on the Web site includes a November e-mail to the Eastern Cougar Network from Hutchins. He lists 24 confirmed cougar sightings in the county last year, 20 in 2001, 13 in 2000 and 12 in 1999. Wildlife officials confirm sightings through paw prints and other evidence.

Hutchins said the time and distance between sightings suggest there might be two or more cougars in the Delaware area.

He said the Delaware cougars have not posed a threat to people.

"There have not been any human beings that have been attacked or have been threatened to be attacked," he said. "Or livestock."

Delaware SPCA Executive Director John E. Caldwell said cougars are "rather a timid animal."

"They'd rather slink away than be confronted," Caldwell said. "Even a small dog or a poodle could tree a cougar."

Caldwell said he was the first to officially confirm the existence of at least one cougar in Delaware when he positively identified cougar tracks in December 1995 at St. Edmond's Academy, a Catholic boys school in Brandywine Hundred.

Hutchins said he doubts the cougars ever will be caught because their domain is so urbanized.

"It makes it almost impossible to hunt these cougar down with dogs," he said. "There's too many accesses and avenues of escape."

Cougars have a life expectancy of 15 to 17 years, he said, so Delaware's cougars might not rule the Middle Atlantic region for long—unless they are breeding.

Caldwell said he doubts the cats are mating. And he discounted a sighting in April 2002 by a woman on Churchmans Road near Stanton who said she saw a cougar with a couple of cubs.

People often make mistakes, he said, and the new Web site might help weed out some of the false claims.

A booming trade in pet cougars operates, often illegally, within a confusing maze of federal and state laws. The states of Missouri and Arkansas each estimate a minimum of 101 captives, while Florida estimates between one and two thousand, but there is little additional data. Could an escaped or released pet cougar, many of whom are declawed, survive in the wild? There is no definitive answer. Roy McBride, a well-established cougar tracker from Texas who works for the Florida Panther Project, told editor Chris Bolgiano that he personally had witnessed two separate occasions in which declawed pet cougars had escaped and survived on their own for nearly a year.

Because the issue of captive cougars is important to the eastern cougar situation, the editors asked Mark Jenkins, member of the board of the Eastern Cougar Foundation and director of the Cooper's Rock Mountain Lion Sanctuary in Bruceton Mills, West Virginia, to end this chapter with an essay describing his experience with abused and neglected cougar pets. In light of the ignorance and irresponsibility that Jenkins has seen in many cougar owners, it seems entirely possible that some owners simply drive to the nearest woods and open a cage door to rid themselves of a pet that has grown annoying and dangerous.

The Pet Trade Is Devastating to Cougars

by Mark Jenkins
Director of the Cooper's Rock Mountain Lion Sanctuary, Bruceton Mills,
      West Virginia

This scenario happens all too often in America today: The cougar kittens have spent only three weeks with their mother and have barely opened their eyes when the human snatches them up while the mother is being distracted. The mother cougar will call and search for her stolen cubs for several days. These cubs will become the next members of the captive cougar pet trade, while the mother will be forced into heat and continue her unhealthy role as a breeding machine.

I first started working with cougars in 1992 as a volunteer at a large animal park in South Carolina. I remember my first experience in a pen with a full-grown cougar. I was helping Dave, the head of animal staff, clean out the pen of a large male cougar named Milo. I turned my back on Milo. He then stood on his hind legs, drooped his paws over my shoulder, and sank his teeth into my back. Fortunately, Dave was able to force

Milo to release his jaws and let me go. Keep in mind that this cougar had been hand-raised.

Working at the park gave me valuable hands-on experience with almost all the big cats of the world. It was a private facility that did a large business in commercials and cinematography, and I hand-raised and helped train many of the cats for appearances in films with movie stars, commercials for huge corporations, and even onstage theatrical productions. Once, a hand-raised tiger cub we were using in the ballet "Aladdin" gave me a vicious bite on the chin. Even trained exotic cats are unpredictable.

While getting my start working with these great cats, I was able to meet many knowledgeable people and organizations that dealt with eastern North America's largest native cat, the cougar. I fell in love with the cougar while spending hours observing cougar behavior. I also became aware of the plight of cougars and many other big cats in the exotic pet trade. In the early nineties a quarterly magazine called the *Animal Finders' Guide,* through which you could buy or sell just about any exotic animal from tigers to chimps, was probably the main avenue, other than exotic animal auctions, to acquire cougars. However, today you can buy all these animals over the Internet. Ownership of cougars is not legal in all states. Currently nineteen states ban the practice.

During the several years I worked at the animal park, we would frequently have to nurse a cougar cub back to health after someone unsuccessfully tried to make a pet out of it. One particular cub I remember was named Skeeter. His owners brought him to us when he was about five months old and said he wasn't acting right. We quickly found out they had been feeding him meat without the bones. Eating the bones of its prey is one way a cougar gets the calcium necessary for bone growth. It turned out that Skeeter had a severe calcium deficiency and we had to immobilize him for a month so his bones could heal. Immobilizing a young cougar cub full of energy is disheartening to say the least. The cub wants to play but must be confined to a small space so he doesn't risk fracturing his weak bones.

Skeeter is only one story, and a mild one at that, among the many devastating situations I have witnessed as a result of the cougar pet trade. After seeing numerous disasters of people trying to make pets out of cougars, I dreamed of starting a sanctuary where we could rescue these captives and educate the public about their plight. I had already read every book I could find on cougars and quickly learned about the people and organizations that had any kind of connection with them. One national organization I joined, and then became a board member of, was the Long Island Ocelot Club–Feline Conservation Federation. I soon resigned when the group rejected all the proposals I made to make sure no one owned a cougar without the proper knowledge to care for it. But over the years I have met a number of people around the East who share my concerns about the pet trade and provide sanctuaries for big cats, including Craig Cylke in Georgia and Joe Taft in Indiana.

Finally, in 1998, the pieces came together and my wife, Sheila, and I founded the Cooper's Rock Mountain Lion Sanctuary in the heart of the Appalachian Mountains near Morgantown, West Virginia. We acquired the proper license and permits and applied for nonprofit status. A board of directors was required along with a supporting veterinarian. Space for enclosures, time, manpower, food supply, and food storage and mainte- nance money are just a few of the many resources needed to provide a home for just one captive cougar. It didn't take long to start growing our sanctuary. The pet trade in big cats is prolific in the U.S.; in fact, there are now more tigers kept as so-called pets in this country alone than live in the wild. Since we began in 1998, we have turned down at least seventy- five needy cougars. There just aren't enough sanctuaries to meet the demand.

By the summer of 2000 we were already rescuing our fourth cougar. Sheila and I drove to an older residential section of a large eastern city to pick up a cougar that had been kept in a ten-foot-by-ten-foot cage in a backyard. A female cougar had lived in this cage without veterinary care and with an improper diet for approximately twelve years. On our trip back, we noticed that she was mostly deaf, among other obvious health problems. When our veterinarian, Dr. George Seiler, performed oral sur- gery on her, he first had to remove large chunks of hardened tartar that had completely encased many of her teeth. There was pus, blood, and infection under the tartar. George commented that this cat must have been in excruciating pain daily.

Another one of our cases was the all-too-typical pet cougar story. The well-meaning family purchased the cute little spotted cub from a breeder but had no idea how to properly care for it. The cub grew up, lost its spots, and the novelty of having a pet cougar wore off. The family decided it would rather have a dog. The cougar arrived at our facility extremely malnourished.

We host hundreds of students annually from elementary to college age who come to Cooper's Rock eager to learn about cougars. We have noticed through the years that our sanctuary doesn't just help the animals. Many people who visit or become involved with our facility are affected in a positive way. We've had people who have found a needed purpose and cause toward which to devote their energies. Young people, especially, have often had life-changing experiences by spending time with the cats. Abused and neglected youth groups, which can obviously relate to the former "pets" at our sanctuary, seem to receive the biggest impact.

In many cases, a huge burden is lifted off the owner or caretaker of the cougar involved. I've found over the last decade that many, although not all, of the owners of captive cougars are well-meaning people that let their emotions cloud their judgment of what's best for the animal. The vast majority of pet cougars come from breeders, not from the wild. These breeders' first concern is moving their product. To do that quickly, they often declaw (all four paws) the kittens. If the breeder doesn't declaw, he/she recommends that the buyer have it done. Even if a declawed cougar can survive for a while, how long can it last, and how will it defend itself against dogs and other threats if it can't climb trees?

Buyers are usually given some "token" instructions on how to care for the animal and quickly find out they have bitten off more than they can chew. The cute little kitten requires nearly as much time (feeding, cleaning, exercise, and so on), knowledge (nutrition), and money (medical care) as a child. If the cub ever reaches maturity (sixteen to twenty months of age), it will be a one hundred- to one hundred fifty-pound carnivore that needs approximately five pounds of raw meat and bones a day to survive for the next twenty years. It also is designed to travel a two hundred-square-mile territory—but an owner tries to keep it happy in a backyard cage!

A cougar is a wild animal even when bred in captivity. To keep one as a so-called pet is to create a situation in which both the owner and the cougar suffer. Even in the very rare cases where the owner has the ability (finances, knowledge, vet care, and so on) to care for the physical needs of the animal, he/she can never supply all of the needs that living in the wild can. There are hundreds of big-cat sanctuaries in the U.S., but only a few that specialize in cougars. All these sanctuaries combined cannot meet the needs of cats victimized by the captive industry. Our sanctuary turns down at least a dozen cougars a year for lack of facilities. If no sanctuary will take them, the cats are often euthanized.

The problem is continuing to grow. Congress is now considering a bill banning the interstate sale and transport of big cats to curtail the trade. I can only hope that it becomes law and will make a difference in the devastating trade in cougars.

Potential Cougar Habitat in Eastern North America

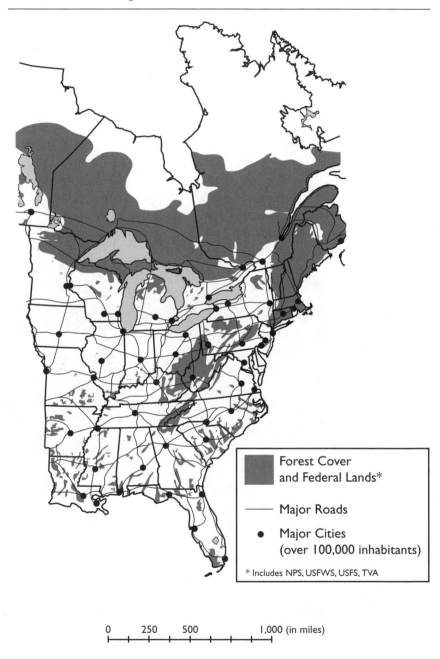

Forest Cover
and Federal Lands*

— Major Roads

● Major Cities
(over 100,000 inhabitants)

* Includes NPS, USFWS, USFS, TVA

0   250   500   1,000 (in miles)

3

Outlook:
Can They Come Back?

The last chapter presented evidence of several dozen cougars living wild across the East and Midwest, with a few cases suggesting reproduction. Unassisted recolonization by a large predator is extremely unusual. Can cougars successfully reestablish viable, long-term populations in the East? The answer is tangled in a knot of legal, biological, and social issues. This chapter contains documents that address those concerns.

LEGAL STATUS
The legal status of the eastern cougar as a protected subspecies was established in 1973 by passage of the Endangered Species Act. (The cat was then listed as Felis concolor couguar, *now known as* Puma c.c.) *The required recovery plan was written by Robert L. Downing, the USF&WS biologist who was searching the Southern Appalachians for cougars even as he wrote. The plan, excerpted below, was never implemented.*

Eastern Cougar Recovery Plan

prepared by
Robert L. Downing
Wildlife Research Biologist
Denver Wildlife Research Center
U.S. Fish and Wildlife Service
Clemson, SC 29631
August 1981

Approved: Robert A. Jantzen [Signature], Director, U.S. Fish and Wildlife
Service
Date: 8/2/82

This is the complete Eastern Cougar recovery plan. It has been approved by the U.S. Fish and Wildlife Service. It does not necessarily represent official positions or approvals of cooperating agencies. This plan is subject to modification as dictated by new findings and changes in species status and completion of tasks described in the plan. Goals and objectives will be attained and funds expended contingent upon appropriations, priorities, and other budgetary constraints.

Literature Citations Should Read as Follows:
U.S. Fish and Wildlife Service. 1982. Eastern Cougar Recovery Plan. U.S. Fish and Wildlife Service, Atlanta, Georgia. 17 pp.

Part I: Introduction

At one time, the cougar *(Felis concolor)* occurred in all the provinces of southern Canada, throughout the United States, and in most of Central and South America. The animal is known in the United States by several names, especially panther, painter, and catamount in the East; and puma, cougar, and mountain lion in the West. Today, sizeable populations are found in the United States only in the western mountains.

The eastern cougar *(F. c. couguar),* one of 27 subspecies presently recognized (Young and Goldman 1946; Charles O. Handley, Jr., pers. comm., April 28, 1981) originally occurred within South Carolina, Tennessee, Kentucky, Indiana, and all states to the north and east. The exact range is unknown because only eight *F. c. couguar* skulls were available to Young and Goldman (1946), all from West Virginia, Pennsylvania, and New York. To the south, only 17 Florida panther *(F. c. coryi)* specimens were available for study, 14 from southern Florida and 3 from northeastern Louisiana. To the west, the subspecies, *F. c. schorgeri,* was named based on three specimens from Wisconsin, Minnesota, and Kansas (Jackson 1955). The almost total lack of reference specimens from near the lines of separation between subspecies leaves those lines both unsupported and unchallenged.

The eastern cougar was first called *Cougar de Pensilvanie* by Buffon in 1776. Kerr (1792) renamed it *Felis couguar* based on Buffon's description. True (1884) reassigned it to *Felis concolor* and Nelson and Goldman (1929) first used the present subspecific designation *Felis concolor couguar.* This subspecies was the first described among all North American subspecies and the name has always been reserved for specimens from the Northeastern United States and Eastern Canada. Stoner (1950), Wright (1972), and Lazell (pers. comm., January 4, 1981, August 6, 1981) list several additional specimens that have not been thoroughly examined by taxonomists, but they are also from the Northeastern United States or Eastern Canada. No specimens are known from the southern and western portions of *F. c. couguar's* accepted range.

The lack of reference specimens from a substantial portion of *F. c. couguar's* range could cause some taxonomic confusion as to the subspecific identity of any cougar found within the accepted range of *F. c. couguar.* It is uncertain how animals from the southern and western portions of the eastern cougar's range would differ morphologically from those of the northeast. In addition, it is likely that there would be some hybridization in areas where two subspecies overlap. Western cougars, held in captivity in the East, and then released or escaped to the wild would add confusion to the taxonomic issue, especially if breeding with natural populations of eastern cougars occurred. Even if natural populations of eastern cougars remained "pure," recent inbreeding due to isolation of populations may cause certain morphological characteristics to be modified. The proper subspecific identification of any cougar found in the east may be difficult.

Before considering the present status of the cougar, let us first consider why it became endangered. The earliest settlers feared cougars and vigorously resisted the occasional depredations of this animal on their livestock. Cougars were frequently persecuted and many States offered bounties to persons who killed them. There is no doubt that cougars were virtually eliminated from each region soon after it became settled by European immigrants.

Nevertheless, cougars may have survived in a few localities because of their rugged terrain and lack of access, or because local hunters lacked the skills, dogs, or time needed to hunt them effectively. An example of the importance of special skills can be found by closely examining the records of cougar bounty payments for New York (Brocke, Rainer H., Senior Research Associate, Adirondack Research Center, in 1978 research proposal to the U.S. Fish and Wildlife Service). In the western Adirondacks in the late 1800's only one man, a George Muir, was a successful cougar hunter. In the eight years between May 1879 and February 1887, Muir claimed 67 cougar bounties (the number killed may have been less than 67, with several bounties claimed for the same animals), while in those same years all the remaining citizens of New York claimed only four.

One way to judge the remoteness of an area and the persistence and skills of its hunters is to observe whether or not bear and deer were able to survive. The Jefferson–George Washington–Monongahela National Forests in Virginia and West Virginia, respectively, continuously supported deer, bear, or both, and although there are no verified kills of cougars there this century, seemingly reliable sighting reports have persisted and recent evidence of track and scat (July 1981), although not certain, suggests that at least one cougar lives in the area today. Pennsylvania, the New England States and several Canadian Provinces have continuously supported deer and bear; and there is considerable evidence that cougars survived too, since many individuals have been reported killed (most cannot be confirmed) in the region since 1900 (Downing 1981) and the frequency of seemingly reliable reports is impressive (Helen McGinnis, pers. comm., August 12–14, 1981).

Deer and bear became quite scarce in the Appalachians of North Carolina by the late 1800's, but responded to protection on the Vanderbilt Estate (later becoming the Pisgah Game Preserve and Pisgah National Forest). This herd became large enough to experience a dieoff by 1908 (Ruff 1938) and was estimated to contain 1,000 deer by 1916. Large-scale purchases of land under the Weeks Act to form the National Forests began in 1914, and it is conceivable that the increasing solitude and deer populations allowed one or more small cougar populations to exist without experiencing fatal encounters with man. Several cougars were recorded killed (most records are unconfirmed) in the mountains of North Carolina and adjoining States during this century including some in the last decade (Downing 1981), suggesting that cougars were not extirpated. Seemingly reliable reports of cougar sightings have been increasingly frequent and widespread.

Cougar habitat is not necessarily synonymous with mountains, as attested by the Coastal Plain swamp habitat that comprises the last major stronghold of the Florida panther. Extensive swamps, some of which are called pocosins, are present in North Carolina in particular, and many of these were never devoid of deer or bear, and many do not have vehicular access to this day. There are fewer reports from the Coastal Plain than from the mountains, but the likelihood of cougars being present may not be directly related to the frequency with which they are reported, since man seldom penetrates these swamps.

The Federal Government has responded to the rising interest in cougars by sponsoring several research and survey projects. Fish and Wildlife Service (FWS) Federal Assistance projects have been conducted in North Carolina and Virginia for *F. c. couguar;* and in Georgia, Florida, Mississippi, and Arkansas for *F. c. coryi.* The FWS Office of Endangered Species and World Wildlife Fund are sponsoring a project in New York and other northeastern States to define the most likely habitat and to interpret cougar sighting reports in the vicinity of each. Another project at Clemson, South Carolina, solicits reports and other evidence, investigates as many of these as possible, trains observers, and conducts searches for tracks and other sign in the vicinity of the most promising reports. This project is support by the Forest Service, the Fish and Wildlife Service, and the National Park Service.

At least one small population of *F. c. coryi* is well known in South Florida. As many as four small populations are strongly suspected in southern and western Arkansas (Sealander 1979), northern Louisiana (Lowery 1974), and eastern Oklahoma based on seven kills and numerous sightings and tracks in the last 33 years. A small cougar population may also occur in Minnesota (Wm. E. Berg, pers. comm., December 5, 1980).

No breeding cougar populations have been substantiated within the former range of *F. c. couguar* since the 1920's, but investigations have begun in the North Carolina and West Virginia areas to determine if there are viable populations there. Sighting reports continue to be received from many public lands, especially those in mountainous regions. Many of these sightings are accompanied by requests to the responsible agencies to protect the cougars from the people or vice versa. Managers of lands where cougars have been seen but not confirmed have the awkward choice of committing resources to an animal that has not been proven to occur or ignoring the reports and possibly managing in a manner detrimental to the species.

The decision to manage for or ignore cougars requires supporting information. The logical approach is to conduct thorough searches of each area where the animal has been reported before any management plans are formulated. But what constitutes a thorough search? What do we look for? Where do we look? How much effort does it take? Researchers and professional hunters in the West often are able to find cougar tracks within a couple of days where dusty roads bisect the area and often can find "scratch hills" and scats rather easily away from roads, especially where populations are high and stable. But cougar activity may be much more difficult to confirm in the East, especially in the mountains, because there are few sandy roads, populations are small, and territories may be poorly defined. Because there is such a large and diverse area to be searched, we must be prepared to train a large number of workers to perform these searches in the most efficient possible manner. Basic research to describe the abundance, distribution, persistence, and observability of sign is badly needed to guide search planning. Such information can only be collected in areas known to contain cougars, such as Florida, the West, and perhaps Arkansas, Minnesota, North Carolina, and West Virginia. Searchers not only need to know where to look to find cougar sign, they need to know when to stop looking in one area and move to another. By quantifying the frequency and variability of observing positive sign, the level of searching effort necessary to say within acceptable confidence limits that cougars do not exist in an area could be determined.

Hopefully, eastern cougars still survive in the Eastern United States. Even with improved conditions, the cougar may not be recoverable according to the definition that follows in Part II. This recovery plan spells out, in as much detail as is possible considering our present limited knowledge, what needs to be done to speed the recovery and remove the threat of extinction to the eastern cougar.

Part II: Recovery
A. Recovery Objective.

Recovery of the eastern cougar will have been satisfactorily accomplished when at least three self-sustaining populations have been found or established in the United States. Each population (which may consist of two or more separate but interbreeding nuclei) will be considered self-sustaining if it contains a minimum of 50 breeding adults, and if losses of these adults are being replaced through reproduction and/or immigration from nearby populations. Trends in ownership and management of the habitat and in behavior of the human population must be such that the minimum numbers above are expected to be sustained indefinitely. One population with a minimum of 50 breeding adults would allow consideration of downlisting of the cougar to Threatened. Reaching even this stage may be difficult. Suitable habitat is minimal and where such habitat does exist the cougar's use of it may be in conflict with man's utilization of the habitat. In all probability, the cougar will always be Endangered. The number of breeding adults, 50, is based on inbreeding research on other species. This is the minimum number thought necessary to prevent reduced fecundity and survivorship and to ensure fitness for at least short-term survival. Little is known about cougar population dynamics and this number may or may not be applicable to the cougar. It is, however, the best estimate presently available. Therefore, it will be used until new information requires its modification.

B. Step-down Outline.

Step I.   Find and delineate cougar populations.

    I.1   Research and training.

        I.11   Perform research needed to quantify frequency and variability of observing positive sign under a variety of eastern conditions.

        I.12   Develop search techniques of sufficient intensity to say within acceptable confidence limits that, if no evidence is found, cougars are not present.

        I.13   Train personnel to recognize sign and to adapt search procedures to their particular areas.

    I.2   Perform systematic searches in likely places throughout former range.

        I.21   Analyze habitat characteristics and reported sightings, map potential cougar habitat, and assign priorities for searches.

        I.22   Conduct systematic searches.

            I.221 If cougars are found, go to Step II.

            I.222 If no cougars are found, consider declaring *F. c. couguar* extinct.

Step II.   Study and provide interim protection for cougars that are found.

    II.1   Organize advisory committee at each location.

    II.2   Provide interim protection, habitat management, and public education.

    II.3   Study cougars to determine population dynamics and behavior.

        II.31   Determine productivity and mortality patterns.

        II.32   Track movements of each individual.

        II.33   Study behavior.

    II.4   Salvage specimens for subspecific identification (Step III).

    II.5   Refine search techniques (Step I).

Step III. Taxonomic evaluations.

    III.1 Taxonomy of available specimens of *F. c. couguar.*

        III.11   Measure 18th and 19th Century specimens and define parameters of variation using modern statistical techniques.

        III.12   Develop techniques for identifying live cougars to subspecies. Apply in Step III.2.

    III.2 Taxonomic identification of existing populations of eastern cougars.

        III.21 If population is assignable to *F. c. couguar,* go to Step IV.

        III.22 If population is assignable to *F. c. coryi,* apply Florida Panther Recovery Plan.

        III.23 If population is assignable to any other subspecies, consider removing if other populations representing true *F. c. couguar* are present elsewhere.

III.24 If no true *F. c. couguar* are found, protect and manage those assignable to other subspecies in case *F. c. couguar* genes are present but are not detectable morphologically.

Step IV. Develop and implement a permanent management plan.

IV.1 Provide protection, habitat management, and public education.

IV.2 Continue studies (Step II.3) to determine requirements (including critical habitat) and most efficient means of supplying these needs.

IV.3 Determine whether each population is self-sustaining or if trend is in that direction. If neither, consider Step V.

Step V. Capture *F. c. couguar* from the wild as required for management purposes such as restoration, augmentation of small populations, and/or captive propagation.

Step VI. When one self-sustaining population of 50 breeding adults is found or established, consider downlisting to Threatened. When three such populations are reached consider delisting.

C. Recovery Narrative.

The recovery plan is summarized by the step-down outline. At the present time all the effort must be concentrated on Step I, "Find and delineate cougar populations."

Research to determine the frequency and variability of observing positive cougar sign (Step I.11) must first be done in areas where a confirmed *F. concolor* population occurs, such as in Florida, Canada, or the Western United States. Then, by quantifying the frequency and variability of observing positive sign, the level of search effort necessary to say within acceptable confidence limits that cougars do or do not exist in a particular area can be determined (Step I.12). Information and techniques from these areas must then be adapted for use in areas within *F. c. couguar's* range and taught to private, State, and Federal personnel (Step I.13) so that they can systematically search likely places within their jurisdictions (Step I.2). Searches should be performed on a priority basis, taking into account habitat characteristics and recently reported sightings (Step I.21). Searching should continue until all areas have been searched adequately. If cougars are found during these searches (Step I.221), interim protection (Step II) will be immediately provided. Representatives of the landowners and resource management agencies in the vicinity of each population will be organized into an advisory committee (Step II.1) to plan interim protection, habitat management, and public education programs (Step II.2). This committee will also suggest studies needed to determine population dynamics and behavior (Step II.3) and will assist the Service in selecting and overseeing the research team doing the work. This information will be used to aid in management and also to aid in Step I.1. By performing the same studies on actual *F. c. couguar* populations, data obtained using other subspecies can be more accurately interpreted (Step II.5).

Specimens should be used for the taxonomic work necessary to insure correct subspecific identification (Step II.4). Only live animals or those found dead should be used for this purpose. No animal should be sacrificed. If no cougars are found after all likely areas in the United States (and probably Canada) have been thoroughly searched, then it will be necessary to confront the painful task of declaring *F. c. couguar* extinct (Step I.222).

Before the permanent management plan (Step IV) can be put into effect, each population must be assignable to *F. c. couguar*. The required taxonomic evaluation (Step III) will entail a detailed study of all available 18th and 19th Century specimens (Step III.11) and the development of techniques for recognizing the most distinctive features in live cougars, so that none will have to be killed (Step III.12).

To accurately identify the subspecies *F. c. couguar,* a set of discriminating criteria based upon morphological and physiological variations should be established for use on live animals. Such criteria could be determined using radiological and electrophoretic techniques. Such a list of criteria is presently used for the red wolf.

Considerable time may pass, perhaps a decade or more, before enough wild contemporary specimens can be examined to establish population means for any characteristic (Step III.2). Some tough decisions are anticipated since there may be differences of opinion about how to interpret certain morphological differences and likenesses in view of the small number and limited distribution of 18th and 19th Century specimens. The presence of two or more populations may further complicate the decisions. The range of alternatives is spelled out in the outline. If more than one cougar population is found, such decisions cannot be made by the local advisory committees because they may not have a national or international perspective. Therefore, a national or international committee must be formed to decide all issues encountered in Steps III, IV, V, and VI. At least one representative of each local advisory committee will serve on the national or international committee.

The permanent management plan (Step IV) will be a long-range plan designed to enable the cougar to survive and increase its numbers. However, continued research (Step IV.2) may be necessary to better define their needs and behavior to ensure that the proper management is prescribed. It will also be necessary to monitor population size and structure regularly (Step IV.3) so that calamitous events will not go unnoticed and so that downlisting or delisting, if either becomes appropriate, can proceed without undue delay. If population monitoring reveals that there are surplus animals, these may be captured (Step V) for restocking uninhabited areas, for enriching the gene pool in other populations, or for captive propagation. Capture of an entire wild population for captive propagation may also be appropriate (another tough decision) if only a few animals are left and these appear unlikely to survive in the wild.

Step VI, to consider downlisting or delisting when appropriate is self-explanatory. Hopefully, the eastern cougar will recover to such an extent that either decision will be an easy one.

Literature Cited

Buffon, G. L. L. 1776. *Histoirie naturelle.* Suppl. Vol. 3:222–223

Downing, R. L. 1981. Current status of the cougar in the Southern Appalachians. *Proc. 2nd Ann. Nongame and Endangered Wildlife Symposium,* Athens, Georgia. August 13–14. (In press).

Hall, E. R. 1981. *The Mammals of North America.* John Wiley and Sons, New York. Volume 2: 1181 pp.

Jackson, H. H. T. 1961. *The Mammals of Wisconsin.* Univ. of Wisconsin Press. 504 pp.

Kerr, R. 1792. *The animal kingdom.* 644 pp.

Nelson, E. W., and E. A. Goldman. 1929. List of the pumas, with 3 described as new. *J. Mammal.* 10(4):345–350.

Ruff, F. J. 1938. The white-tailed deer of the Pisgah National Game Preserve. USDA Forest Serv. Mimeo Rpt. 249 pp.

Sealander, J. A. 1979. *A guide to Arkansas mammals.* River Road Press. Conway, Arkansas. 313 pp.

Stoner, D. 1950. Extant New York State specimens of the Adirondack cougar. New York State Museum. Circular 25. 34 pp.

True, F. W. 1884. *Proc. U.S. Nat. Mus.* 7:610.

Wright, B. S. 1972. *The eastern panther: a question of survival.* Clark, Irwin, and Co., Toronto. 180 pp.

Young, S. P., and E. A. Goldman. 1946. *The puma, mysterious American cat.* Dover Publications, N. Y. 358 pp.

The difficulty of determining subspecies status that Downing described was com-pounded in 1999 by Melanie Culver's doctoral dissertation, "Molecular Genetic Variation, Population Structure, and Natural History of Free-ranging Pumas (Puma concolor)," completed at the University of Maryland. The original essay below, written for this book, summarizes her work and its implications.

Genetic Variation, Gene Flow, and Population Identification for North American Pumas

by Melanie Culver

In the early 1900s, the puma *(Puma concolor)* was described as having 32 distinct subspecies, fairly evenly distributed throughout North and South America (Young and Goldman 1946; Jackson 1955; Cabrera 1963). These subspecies descriptions were based on several morphological fea-tures (coat color, pelage, skull and skeletal measurements); however, not all specimens compared were full adults, and many of the subspecies were described based on one or a few individuals. Molecular genetic tools provide an alternate method to describe subdivisions within a species, and to examine the accuracy of the traditional 32 subdivisions for pumas.

Utilizing molecular genetic markers to resolve subspecies divisions relies on the assumption that the non-deleterious genetic changes accu-mulate in a predictable manner over time. If populations do not inter-breed, these changes will be able to distinguish those populations, given enough time. Morphological methods provide an important tool for tax-onomy, as do genetic methods, yet if the incorrect marker or trait is selected, both can lead to anomalous results. The advantage of using molecular markers over morphometrics is that molecular markers allow us to select markers that are neutral (having no effect on physical character-istics and thus not under selection pressure) and independent (not on the same chromosome). Neutral markers are important because they give us an indication of the amount of time that non–interbreeding populations have been separated; independent markers are important because they allow us to acquire several separate lines of evidence toward our conclu-sion. If most of the markers provide the same result we can be confident that our conclusion is not guided by a single anomalous marker.

For my research on pumas, I used two classes of molecular genetic markers: 1) DNA sequence variation for mitochondrial genes (DNA outside the nucleus of the cell) and 2) DNA fragment length variation for ten nuclear microsatellite DNA loci. Mitochondrial sequence variation is widely used as a genetic marker to resolve species or subspecies-level taxonomy, population subdivision, gene flow, and maternal lineage assessment. Highly polymorphic nuclear microsatellite markers can distinguish among all individuals of a species (similar to DNA fingerprinting used in forensics), and are also useful to estimate relatedness among individuals, population subdivisions, and gene flow as well as subspecies-level taxonomy. Together, these markers provided 11 independent lines of evidence to examine subspecies designations in pumas (Culver et al. 2000).

With all 11 markers in agreement from more than 300 puma samples throughout North and South America, these molecular data indicated that South American pumas contain high levels of genetic diversity for both mitochondrial DNA and microsatellite markers. In contrast, pumas throughout Central and North America (north of Nicaragua) had no mitochondrial variation (except one mutation observed in the Olympic peninsula) and only moderate levels of microsatellite variation. This pattern of variation formed the basis for establishing one puma subdivision north of Nicaragua. The genetic variation observed in South America resulted in recognizing 5 puma subdivisions south of Nicaragua. Furthermore, the presumed boundaries for these 6 groups of pumas incorporated major geographical features. From north to south, the first boundary occurs in Nicaragua, potentially the "lake region" which was the original location chosen for what is now the Panama Canal. In South America the boundaries incorporate several major rivers (Amazon River, Rio Parana, Rio Negro, Paraguay River).

Molecular markers that are neutral (not under the influence of selection) can estimate time elapsed since populations were founded or since they became isolated. If we estimate timing for puma populations, several conclusions can be made: North America is the most recently founded population, the population inhabiting Brazil and Paraguay (specifically the Brazilian Highlands) is the oldest, and pumas as a species are only 390,000 years old (Culver et al. 2000). A more traditional estimator of timing for species existence is the fossil record. In the case of pumas, the fossil record is approximately 300,000 years old (Kurten 1976; Kurten and Anderson 1980; Savage and Russell 1983; Werdlin 1989), remarkably similar to the molecular data. However, the fossil record does not indicate that North American pumas are a more recent lineage (puma fossils on both continents are equally old).

The disagreement between the North American fossil record and the molecular data that indicates North American to be more recent than South American pumas leads to the conclusion that pumas were extirpated in North America more recently than 300,000 years ago. Pumas in North America today, therefore, are probably the result of a relatively recent re-colonization event. The most likely timing of the extirpation would be 9,000 to 12,000 years ago to coincide with other well-known Pleistocene extinctions. If this is accurate, the North American puma lineage may be only a few thousand years old. This young age for North American pumas is directly related to the lack of genetic diversity and differentiation observed in current North American pumas. Given the young age of North American pumas, it is no surprise that genetic analyses indicate only one subspecies throughout North America.

Another advantage of molecular markers to resolve subdivisions within a species is that genetic tools have a range of resolving power from subspecies level to population level. Up until now I have described subspecies-level differentiation in pumas. However, beginning in 2000 there has been a wave of population-level genetic studies of North American pumas. Within a species, we can further subdivide individuals into broad subspecies groups or higher resolution populations, where each subspecies would be comprised of many populations. If we want to learn how North American pumas are subdivided at the higher resolution population level, what is required is a very large number of samples from each region of focus. Six recent population-level studies have done this for many western U.S. states (Arizona, New Mexico, Utah, Colorado, Texas, Wyoming, South Dakota, California, and Idaho). Optimal sampling density was more than 300 samples per U.S. state versus that same number of samples for two entire continents in my previously described subspecies-level study. These higher resolution studies have found large regions with little or no genetic structure, such as Colorado/Utah (McRae 2004; Sinclair et al. 2001), Wyoming/South Dakota (Anderson 2003), as well as areas with significant population-level subdivision within a single state, such as Arizona and New Mexico (McRae 2004), California (Ernest et al. 2003), and Idaho (Loxterman 2001). When population-level subdivision was found, the population boundaries corresponded to barriers such as low desert, semi-desert grasslands, urban development, and possibly the Grand Canyon in Arizona and New Mexico (McRae 2004), the Central Valley, San Francisco Bay and Delta, Los Angeles Basin, Mojave Desert, and Sonoran Desert in California (Ernest et al. 2003), or the Snake River Plain and associated human development in Idaho (Loxterman 2001).

The results from both the subspecies-level and the population-level studies are relevant to eastern pumas. At the subspecies level the eastern puma is not genetically unique; instead, it is part of the large North American subspecies which, under the custom of using the oldest existing subspecies name when combining subspecies, is given the name of *Puma concolor couguar,* the name traditionally ascribed to the eastern cougar subspecies. Within such a large subspecies, populations occupying a unique (and often disjunct) geographical area are considered "distinct population segments" (DPS). A perfect DPS example is the Florida panther, which clearly occupies a unique geographic location relative to other North American pumas. Considering the landscape features that were found to be barriers to pumas in the western U.S., if similar high resolution studies could be performed east of the Rocky Mountains it would not be surprising if historical genetic structure for pumas in the eastern U.S. was found to be shaped by similar landscape features (i.e., major rivers, interstates, and valleys devoid of puma habitat).

Unfortunately, this question is unlikely to be answered through genetic methods because of the need for a large sample size. The historic eastern U.S. puma occupies a very large geographic area from Ontario and Quebec to Kentucky and the Carolinas and from Indiana and Kentucky to the Atlantic Ocean, an area roughly equal to the area of the combined western U.S. puma genetic studies. Because of this large area approximately one thousand samples that yield PCR (Polymerase Chain Reaction) amplifiable DNA would be needed to achieve the desired resolution. Based on my searches to acquire eastern puma specimens to include in my subspecies-level study, I do not believe this density of voucher (i.e., verified) eastern U.S. puma samples exists. The specimens I am aware of for such a study include only 8 scientifically documented specimens for *P. c. couguar* (described by Young and Goldman 1946), and the very occasional specimen to be found in small town museums and schools (the samples need be 100 years old or older to adequately represent the historical eastern U.S. population). And, a proportion of historical specimens collected will not yield PCR amplifiable DNA. Possible reasons are that the DNA is too degraded to PCR amplify, or chemical treatments on the hides can inhibit the PCR enzyme or render the DNA unusable in some way. A further complication is that high resolution studies that can demonstrate population level genetic diversity depend on nuclear microsatellite markers, which sometimes do not amplify even in samples that contain PCR amplifiable DNA. A possible reason is that PCR amplifiable DNA from historical specimens may be mitochondrial in origin (present at thousands of copies per cell), rather than nuclear (present in one copy per cell) where microsatellites reside. Because of these technical difficulties, in order to obtain successful data from 1,000 samples, one may need to start with 2,000 to 3,000 specimens.

Based on the findings of these various puma genetic studies, several conclusions can be made regarding puma subdivision and population genetics: 1) Pumas originated in the Brazilian Highlands approximately 300,000 years ago. 2) A possible extirpation and re-colonization occurred in North America, the potential timing of which is subsequent to the most recent ice age that ended approximately 10,000 years ago. 3) Molecular data does not support the traditional 32 subspecies divisions for pumas, but rather six subspecies. 4) Within these six groups pumas are fairly panmictic (freely interbreeding because of having no barriers to movement). 5) Recent puma studies have found some genetic structure and barriers to gene flow within the broadly defined North American group. Such a study is not likely possible for eastern cougars given the high number of samples needed for the higher resolution analyses. However, these studies clearly demonstrate that broad-scale maps of puma habitat can be used to predict where significant barriers to movement and gene flow are likely to occur.

These conclusions have several implications relative to puma conservation. 1) Managers should strive to maintain habitat connectivity within the six large groups defined by this data set. 2) Management for the three North American threatened or endangered puma populations (Florida panther, Eastern cougar, Yuma puma) should take into account the revised subspecies designations suggested by this data set. In Florida, managers have done exactly that with the introduction of neighboring Texas pumas to ameliorate the effects of inbreeding. Based on these genetic results,

The six phylogeographic cougar groups defined by Melanie Culver's DNA analysis. These are the basis for her proposed new subspecies taxonomy.

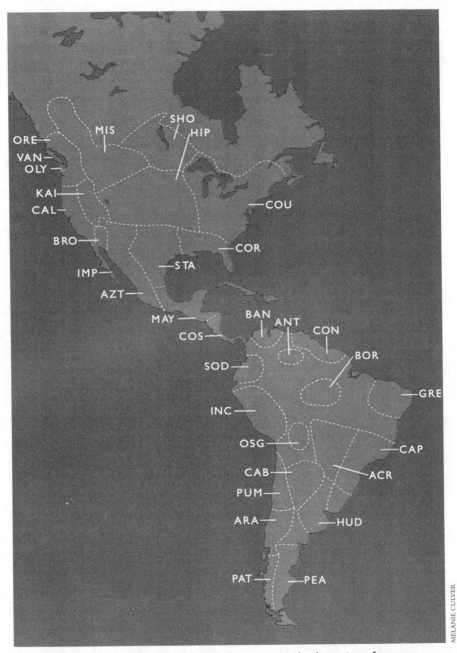

Geographic ranges of the 32 traditionally recognized subspecies of cougar, labeled with three-letter codes.

this action in Florida resulted in a mixing of two populations of the same subspecies, rather than a mixing of subspecies as originally thought. If it is determined by agency managers, nongovernmental organizations, and the general public that a naturally breeding free-ranging population of cougars in the East is a desirable objective, the introduction of pumas from a neighboring region to the west would be worth exploring.

Literature Cited

Anderson C. R. (2003) Cougar ecology, management, and population genetics in Wyoming. Ph.D. Dissertation, University of Wyoming, Laramie, Wyoming.

Cabrera A. (1963) Los felidos vivientes de la Republica Argentina. *Ciencias Zoologicas,* VI (5).

Culver M., Johnson W. E., Pecon-Slattery J., O'Brien S. J. (2000) Genomic ancestry of the American puma. *Journal of Heredity* 91:186–197.

Ernest H. B., Boyce W. M., Bleich V. C., May B., Stiver S. J., Torres S. G. (2003) Genetic structure of mountain lion *(Puma concolor)* populations in California. *Conservation Genetics* 4:353–366.

Jackson H. H. T. (1955) The Wisconsin puma. *Proceedings of the Biological Society of Washington* 68:149–150.

Kurten B. (1976) Fossil puma (Mammalia: Felidae) in North America. *Netherlands Journal of Zoology* 26:502–534.

Kurten B., Anderson E. (1980) *Pleistocene Mammals of North America.* Columbia University Press, New York.

Loxterman J. L. (2001) The impact of habitat fragmentation on the population genetic structure of pumas *(Puma concolor)* in Idaho. Ph.D. Dissertation, Idaho State University, Pocatello, Idaho.

McRae B. (2004) Effects of habitat discontinuities on genetic structuring among puma populations in the southwestern USA. Ph.D. Dissertation, Northern Arizona University, Flagstaff, Arizona. http://www.for.nau.edu/SOFArchive/GraduateResearch/bhm2/chapters.htm.

Savage D. E., Russell D. E. (1983) *Mammalian Paleofaumas of the World.* Addison-Wesley Publishing Company, Reading, Massachusetts.

Sinclair E. A., Swenson E. L., Wolfe M. L., Choate D. C., Gates B., Crandall K. A. (2001) Gene flow estimates in Utah's cougars imply management beyond Utah. *Animal Conservation* 4:257–264.

Walker C. W., Harveson L. A., Pittman M. T., Tewes M. E., Honeycutt R. L. (2000) Microsatellite variation in two populations of mountain lions *(Puma concolor)* in Texas. *Southwestern Naturalist* 45:196–203.

Werdlin L. (1989) The radiation of felids in South America: when and where did it occur? Fifth International Theriological Congress, Rome, Abstract of Papers and Posters, pp. 290–291.

Young S. P., Goldman E. A. (1946) *The Puma, Mysterious American Cat.* The American Wildlife Institute, Washington, DC.

In light of the new genetic findings, the current position of wildlife agencies that wild cougars in the East must be proven to be the eastern cougar subspecies before being recognized and protected is unsustainable. Culver's 1999 dissertation, plus the accumulating field evidence of cougar presence, prompted the newly formed Eastern Cougar Foundation (described in Chapter 1) to write to the Department of Interior. That letter and the response are given below.

Eastern Cougar Foundation Letter to Department of the Interior and Response

Eastern Cougar Foundation
P.O. Box 74
North Spring, WV 24869

March 20, 2000

Mr. Bruce Babbitt, Secretary
Department of Interior
1849 C Street NW #6156
Washington, D.C. 20240

Dear Mr. Babbitt:

I am writing to you on behalf of a large and growing constituency of citizens concerned with the emerging situation of the eastern cougar. This animal is the same species as the western mountain lion and puma, and is commonly called panther, painter, and catamount in the east. Numerous historical sources confirm that cougars were native throughout the east when European settlers arrived. But by the early twentieth century, the cats had been driven to the remotest reaches of the Appalachian Mountains.

Since then, state and federal wildlife officials have considered the cougar extirpated from the east, and pointed to a lack of field evidence that would prove their presence. In the 1990s, however, more than half a dozen instances of field confirmation, including scat in Vermont and Massachusetts, tracks in Virginia and West Virginia, and videos in Maryland and North Carolina, have been reliably documented by reputable scientists (such as one at the U.S. Fish & Wildlife Service's own Forensics Laboratory in Ashland, OR). Several of these cases include indications that cougars are reproducing. I would be happy to share the details of these confirmations with you and your staff.

In the face of this incontrovertible field evidence that at least a few cougars are living wild in the east, F&W Service officials in Regions 4 and 5 are taking the position that these cats cannot be remnant eastern cougar natives, but must be released or escaped pets born elsewhere. Therefore, these cats are not entitled to the protections of the Endangered Species Act, which lists only the Florida panther *(Felis concolor coryii)* and eastern panther *(Felis concolor couguar)*. Taking their cue from the F&W Service, which bears responsibility for administrating the Endangered Species Act, state officials are also adopting this same stance.

This position is untenable. There is little evidence to support the theory that the cougars currently living wild in the east are not eastern cougars. On the contrary, there is a large body of evidence, including some field proof, for the survival of native eastern cougars in remote areas. Furthermore, studies have found that neither morphological nor genetic analyses are capable of positively identifying a cougar of the eastern subspecies in distinction from other subspecies.

Similar findings from studies conducted on red and gray wolves in recent decades have prompted anti-predator interests to sue for delisting and thus remove the protection afforded those animals under the Endangered Species Act. In another situation, in court proceedings in Florida in 1987, a man who admitted killing a wild cougar was acquitted when the prosecution could not prove that the panther he killed belonged to the Florida subspecies.

We are concerned that the position that F&W personnel have developed toward cougars living wild in the East will leave these animals without protection from harm and harassment such as has been exhibited toward red and gray wolves and Florida panthers. Therefore, we request that you make it the explicit policy of U.S. Fish and Wildlife Service staff to clearly state that all cougars living wild in the east are protected under the Endangered Species Act regardless of origins. In so far as this may be an enforcement problem as occurred in the case of the Florida panther cited above, we request that you apply to cougars living wild in the East the precedent set by the F&W Service in Florida, that is, the Similarity of Appearances rule. As stated in 50 CFR 17.40 (h) (l), "Except as allowed in paragraphs (h)(2), (h) (3), and (h)(4) of this section, no person shall take any free-living mountain lion *(Felis concolor)* in Florida."

This ruling, extended to all states east of the Mississippi River, will clarify the legal status of wild cougars in the East and allow us all to turn our attention to more important matters, such as education and involvement of the public with cougar habitat and management issues. If, aided by the protection of the Endangered Species Act, cougars in the east are able to recolonize on their own, we may not need to pursue an expensive reintroduction program.

Thank you for your consideration, and I look forward to hearing from you.

Sincerely,
Todd Lester, President [Signature]

Endorsing Organizations (partial list): The Wilderness Society, Southern Environmental Law Center, Southern Appalachian Biodiversity Project, Heartwood, Natl. Park Trust, Southern Appalachian Forest Coalition, Wild Earth, Forest Watch, Virginia Wilderness Committee, Natl. Assn. of Environmental Professionals, Alabama Environmental Council, Superior Wilderness Action Network, Northwoods Wilderness Recovery, Appalachian Voices, Wildlife Center of VA, Active Students for a Healthy Environment, Potomac Appalachian Audubon Society, Northeastern Forest Campaign, Greater Laurentian Wildlands Project, MD Native Plant Society, RESTORE: The North Woods, MD Alliance for Greenway Improvement & Conservation, American Lands Alliance, Paul Rezendes Photo and Nature Programs, Allegheny Defense Project, Foresters, Inc., Shenandoah Ecosystems Defense Group.

United States Department of the Interior
Fish and Wildlife Service
Washington, D.C. 20240

In Reply Refer to: FWS/TE/CCU00-00726
Jun 21 2000 [Date Stamp]

Dear Mr. Lester:
Thank you for your March 20, 2000, letter to Secretary Babbitt and the Fish and Wildlife Service requesting protection for the eastern cougar *(Felis concolor couguar)* under the Endangered Species Act throughout the eastern United States. You base your request on reports that cougars are living in the wild in several eastern States.

The Service has been reviewing information on this matter for decades. We acknowledge that occasional sightings of cougars have been reported and that some animals have been recovered, but none of these animals has shown any evidence of belonging to a remnant, wild, breeding population of the eastern cougar. Therefore, the Service's position remains that the eastern cougar is extirpated.

As you noted in your letter, the wild breeding population of cougars in Florida, listed as the subspecies *Felis concolor coryii,* is further protected through listing all free-living cougars in Florida under the Similarity of Appearance provision of the Act. We believe that use of the Similarity of Appearance in Florida is appropriate because of the presence of a wild, breeding population there. Use of the Similarity of Appearance provision for the eastern cougar in the remaining eastern States is neither biologically nor administratively justified at this time.

We appreciate your concern for protecting the eastern cougar and would be glad to consider any information you may have that scientifically documents the presence of a wild, breeding population of this subspecies.

Sincerely,
[Signature]
Jamie R. Clark, Director

One of the few published responses by professional wildlife managers to the eastern cougar situation is presented below.

The Eastern Cougar: A Management Failure?

by James B. Cardoza and Susan A. Langlois
Wildlife Society Bulletin 2002, 30(1): 265–273

Address for James E. Cardoza: Division of Fisheries and Wildlife, Field Headquarters, 1 Rabbit Hill Road, Westborough, MA 01581, USA; e-mail: Jim.Cardoza@state.ma.us. Address for Susan A. Langlois: Division of Fisheries and Wildlife, P.O. Box 408, Westminster, MA 01473, USA.

The eastern cougar *(Puma concolor couguar)* has been called a "ghost" (Wright 1959), "elusory" (Hoagland 1973), and "mystery" cat (Parker

1998). Few other North American species seem to evoke the depths of emotion, controversy, and impassioned debate that surround this animal. We review the history of the eastern cougar, its alleged status, and evidence for its existence, and set forth recommendations for a sound, coordinated investigational approach to determine the animal's status distribution.

Distribution, Taxonomy, and Legal Status

The eastern cougar's range originally extended from Nova Scotia west to eastern Quebec, southwest through central Michigan to western Tennessee, and east to South Carolina (Young and Goldman 1946; Hall 1981). The animal has unquestionably declined in abundance throughout this range over the past 300 years (Nowak 1976; Parker 1998) and may be extinct. However, state and provincial agencies have received reports of thousands of sightings since 1950, most of which are inconclusive or contentious.

Hall (1981) recognized 32 subspecies of cougar, including the eastern cougar. Recently, however, Culver (1999) concluded that all cougars north of Guatemala and Belize constitute a single subspecies. This may have implications for cougar recovery in the East.

The United States Fish and Wildlife Service (USFWS) is the principal management authority for the eastern cougar in the United States; Canada currently lacks any federal endangered species authority for the eastern cougar. The USFWS officially lists the eastern cougar as "endangered" (50 CFR 17.11), although its website (http://ecos.fws.gov, 8 September 2000) reported the animal as "presumed extinct in the wild."

Decline and Disappearance

Human persecution, habitat loss and fragmentation, and depletion of white-tailed deer (Odocoileus virginianus) populations were instrumental in the extirpation of eastern cougars (Nowak 1976; Brocke 1981; Hansen 1992). Cougars purportedly vanished by 1882 in the mid-Atlantic states (Young and Goldman 1946; Linzey 1998), 1886 in the south coastal states (Young and Goldman 1946; Golley 1966), 1900 in the central Appalachians (True 1891; Kellogg 1939; Nowak 1976; McGinnis 1996), 1906 in New England (Merriam 1901; Jackson 1922; Palmer 1937; Stoner 1950), and 1908 in Ontario (Wright 1972). Relic populations have been alleged to persist in the Canadian maritimes (Wright 1972; Cumberland and Dempsey 1994; Stocek 1995), but these reports may reflect escaped captives rather than population remnants (Parker 1998; Scott 1998).

The Onset of Legal Protection

Sightings and other reports continued after the cougar's historical extirpation (Leach 1909; Shoemaker 1917), but the cougar was soon believed to be a vanishing species (Allen 1942; Beard 1942). Hostile attitudes toward predators (Hornaday 1913) produced delays, but the states and provinces gradually afforded the cougar protection after 1965 (Nowak 1976). The Committee on Rare and Endangered Wildlife Species (1968) believed the eastern cougar to be extinct in the United States after 1899. Later, however, the animal was formally listed as endangered under the United States Endangered Species Conservation Act of 1969 on 4 June 1973 (38 FR 14687) and was continued in that listing under the subsequent 1973 Act. In accordance with that Act, an eastern cougar recovery plan (USFWS 1982) was approved in August 1982. In Canada, the eastern cougar was listed as endangered by the Committee on the Status of Endangered Wildlife in Canada in 1978, but reclassified as "indeterminate" in 1998 (Scott 1998).

What Was Accomplished?

The actual status of the eastern cougar remains uncertain. Reputed sightings and other reports engendered by an ill-informed public and sensationalized by the popular media complicate the legitimate question of the animal's actual status. V. Fifield (Massachusetts Eastern Cougar Survey Team, unpublished data) received over 150 reports between 1970 and 1983 alone. D. Lee collected over 300 reports in North Carolina between 1975 and 1979 (Eastern Cougar Newsletter, January 1979, unpublished), and over 600 reports from the Canadian maritime provinces were on file with the Canadian Wildlife Service through 1993 (Stocek 1995). The Eastern Puma Research Network has recorded in excess of 2,200 "well-documented" sightings since July 1983 (Lutz and Lutz 1996). J. Lutz (in Bolgiano 1995:169) estimated there were 1,500 to 2,000 "panthers" in the East. These observations suggest that eastern cougars are widespread but secretive, their existence is bureaucratically concealed, or an impressionable public reports cougars that are in fact something else. Credulity, lack of direction, and absence of scientific rigor contribute to the disarray and distrust that characterize cougar investigations in eastern North America.

Do Many Reports Prove the Question?

Why do people see eastern cougars? Believers will answer "because they are there!" Tischendorf (1996) complained that courts of law accept eye-witness testimony; why doesn't science do the same? Dixon's (1982:712) statement that there was ". . . not sufficient evidence at present to assume that viable [cougar] populations exist in eastern North America . . ." was scorned as a "notion" and skeptics were castigated as obstinate and obstructionist. Cougar enthusiasts point to thousands of sightings throughout virtually all of the states and provinces in the cougar's historic range (Stocek 1995; Greenwell 1996; Lutz and Lutz 1996).

We believe the search for cougars in the East must be conducted as a scientific endeavor (Sinclair 1991; Murphy and Noon 1991). The scientific method is the only self-correcting method of attaining knowledge (Ratti and Garton 1994). Studies must be designed to obtain information in an objective manner, reviewed for bias and flaws, and executed with rigor.

What Are People Seeing?

If so many people see cougars, can they all be wrong? Humans seem to be innately drawn to strange or unlikely events or phenomena. Shermer (1997) proposed that people believe such things because: 1) it is comforting and consoling to do so, 2) it is a simple explanation in a complex and confusing world, 3) there is immediate gratification, and 4) it provides warmth, meaning, and morality as compared to the cold logic of science. Cougars also may fulfill a spiritual need for humans (Bolgiano 1995; Altherr 1996), transcending fact into faith. Yet, do such impassioned yearnings explain all the cougar sightings? Clearly not; most observers are seeing something tangible. However, Downing (1996b) believed that 90 to 95% of reports submitted to him were misidentifications. The human visual system exhibits a strong tendency to complete and fill in missing parts of a visual stimulus (Uttall 1981). When this tendency, or closure, occurs prematurely, the missing parts are constructed incorrectly and the mind is tricked into seeing something that is not there. In our experience in Massachusetts, many people have obviously seen coyotes

(Canis latrans), domestic dogs, house cats, or fisher *(Martes pennanti)*, but were adamant that the animals were cougars.

In other instances, the observer has described the cougar in detail while stating that he or she read about cougar sightings in the newspaper or had seen cougars on a television program. These experiences may create an expectation of results, which colors the response. Brocke (1981) often found a burst of cougar reports after an initial media account. Eyewitness memory research has shown that misidentifications can occur due to a combination of perceived familiarity, contextual recall, and the use of conscious inferential processes, which provide a rationale for selecting the most plausible choice (Read 1994). Although some sightings may be valid, we believe most are weak indicators of the animal's presence. Misidentification, unconscious bias, poor memory, and observer veracity often taint eyewitness accounts (Loftus 1979; Cutler and Penrod 1995). Van Dyke and Brocke (1987b) believed that sightings were less efficient, less systematic, and less reliable than other cougar survey methods and should not serve as a basis for describing the distribution and abundance of cougars. However, structured public sighting information has since been used to investigate coyote habitat use in Washington (Quinn 1995) and mountain lion status in Oklahoma (Pike et al. 1999). Public sighting information may be valuable when other methods are unavailable and when respondents are qualified (Pike et al. 1999), but its reliability depends on identifying sources of bias and research objectives (Quinn 1995).

Observers also commonly report seeing cougars accompanied by kittens (Wright 1972; Lutz and Lutz 1996; Parker 1998). Lutz and Lutz (1996:136) alleged that " . . . since 1983, 174 cubs have been reported accompanying larger adults in 20 states." However, kittens may actually be difficult to detect. In Utah, tracks of <6-month-old kittens were found with those of their mother only 19% of the time; those of 7–12-month-olds were found 43% (Barnhurst and Lindzey 1989). Also, the energetic requirements of cougars indicate that an adult female must kill 1 deer/16.1 days when alone, 1 deer/8.9 days with 3 3-month-old kittens, and 1 deer/3.1 days with 15-month-old kittens (Ackerman et al. 1986). Kills of this magnitude should be reflected within the area of alleged female-kitten sightings if the observers are adequately trained.

Sightings aside, is there discrete evidence of the cougar's presence in the East? Wright (1953:15) showed a photograph of a cougar purportedly killed in New Brunswick in 1932. Parker (1998) believed it was authentic, but also discussed a 1941 "New Brunswick" cougar photo, which was probably taken in western Canada. An alleged photograph from Maine in 1994 also was probably of western origin (Bolgiano 1995; Parker 1998). A photo of a group of hunters with a dead cougar, purportedly killed in Franklin County, Massachusetts, in 1927 has also been observed (J. E. Cardoza, personal observation). Problems with such photos, even when the animal's identity is unquestioned, include the lack of provenance and the absence of photographic details that support the alleged date and location.

Cougar tracks are often cited as "confirmed" or "evidence" that cougars are present at a site (Massachusetts Eastern Cougar Survey Team, unpublished data; Cumberland and Dempsey 1994; Lutz and Lutz 1996). However, conditions rarely present the opportunity for unequivocal tracks, and inexperienced observers can misidentify cougar and dog tracks (Wright 1948; Belden 1978). We recommend caution in track identification because few people in the East have substantial field experience with cougars, and field conditions may preclude a definitive answer. Tracks are best used as a component of a package including gait, stride, and behavior, not as a sole identifier. Additionally, food caches, scrapes, and mounds are typical cougar field sign. These features are obvious where cougars are present (Lindzey 1987; Shaw 1987; Van Dyke and Brocke 1987a), and investigators should be trained to search for them.

Hairs are actual physical evidence that may be associated with a particular species (Foran et al. 1997a). Cougar-like tracks and a scat were found at a site in west central New Brunswick in 1992. Hairs from the scat were analyzed at the National Museum of Canada using gross hair characteristics and a reference set, and reported as those of a cougar (Cumberland and Dempsey 1994; Parker 1998). In 1994, residents of Orleans County, Vermont, found 3 sets of tracks and a scat in the area of a cougar sighting (Parker 1998). Hairs from the scat were identified by the USFWS forensics laboratory as those of cougar. However, subsequent testing of the scat by a California laboratory using molecular techniques, identified it as canid (D. Blodgett, Vermont Fish and Wildlife Department, personal communication), and the animal's identity is equivocal.

Species identification from intestinal epithelial cells in scat, using molecular techniques, can be an unambiguous genetic method when the sample is not switched, contaminated, or degraded (Foran et al. 1997b). A scat collected near a cached beaver *(Castor canadensis)* in Franklin County, Massachusetts, in 1997 was tested by 2 different researchers using mitochondria DNA analyses (G. Amato, Wildlife Conservation Society, personal communication; M. Culver, University of Maryland, personal communication) and identified by both as that of a cougar, although the animal's origin was unknown.

Cougar specimens are presumably the ultimate confirmation. We know of at least 15 animals killed in eastern North America, north of Florida, since 1950. Most are known to be escapes of captive origin (Downing 1996a), and the identity of others is unknown. Nevertheless, lone specimens are indicative of individuals, not populations, and do not answer the question of the cougar's actual status. Where do these cougars come from? There are occasional cougars in the wild in eastern North America. The possibilities for their origin include animals originating within the region (i.e., a relic population), animals originating outside the region (i.e., a source population), and escaped or released captives (McGinnis 1996). Each of these possibilities presents challenges.

The idea of relic populations soothes our guilt at eradicating a native species and bolsters our emotional bond with the animal. It also would be a satisfying explanation for the long series of reports since historical extirpation. However, we cannot posit an unproven explanation for the event and then verify the event by the explanation. Based on unconfirmed reports, Wright (1972) presumed there were only 25 to 50 cougars in New Brunswick and <100 in all of eastern North America. Yet, Brocke (1981) modeled cougar populations of 20 to 100 animals and found extinction to occur in 16 years with a 25% decline in survivorship. This suggests that a small cougar population would not persist.

The known cougar populations in closest proximity to eastern North America occur in Florida, Manitoba, and South Dakota (Nero and Wrigley 1977; Maehr 1997; Johnson 2000). Transients, and some residents, undoubtedly are found in the Great Lakes states and adjacent Canada (Rusz 2001). Occasional vagrants from Florida have occurred in Georgia and Louisiana (Golley 1962; Lowery 1974), suggesting that dispersal from the Great Lakes region to parts of the East is possible.

However, the distances from western populations are great, hazardous encounters with humans are probable, and such extreme movements by cougars appear unlikely (McGinnis 1996). Transient animals also may fail to colonize a new area unless there is an adjacent resident population (Seidensticker et al. 1973). Brocke and Van Dyke (1985) believed that it may be impossible to prove the presence or absence of transients in an area without a resident population because the animals wander and do not leave a critical mass of verifiable sign.

Lutz and Lutz (1996:133) alleged that young cougars are regular long-distance migrants that " . . . roam for hundreds of miles." Known dispersal distances in Nevada averaged 29 km for females and 50 km for males, with extremes of 60 km and 92 km for females and males, respectively (Ashman et al. 1983, cited in Lindzey 1987), up to 215 km in New Mexico (Sweanor et al. 2000), and up to 274 km in Wyoming (Logan et al. 1986).

The occurrence of escaped or released cougars of captive origin is an actuality (Downing 1996a; Parker 1998). Not all jurisdictions prohibit private ownership of cougars, and animals may be kept surreptitiously even where possession is unlawful (Busch 1996). There may well be thousands of captive cougars in the eastern United States (Bolgiano 1995; Downing 1996a). Parker (1998) believed that most confirmed sightings and sign represented former captive cougars or their offspring. McGinnis (1996) suggested that Pennsylvania had a small breeding population derived from nineteenth-century survivors bolstered by occasional escapes and releases. While some captives may be socialized to humans, exhibit abnormal behavior, lack survival skills, and would seem to be unlikely candidates for initiating a wild population (Bogue and Ferrari 1976), captive-bred cougars released in Florida quickly learned to kill wild prey (Belden and McCown 1996, cited in Scott 1998).

Is Eastern North America too Developed to Sustain Cougar Populations?

Can cougars persist in the developed and perturbed habitats that characterize eastern North America (McWilliams et al. 1997)? An adequate prey base is essential to sustain cougar populations (Schortemeyer et al. 1991; Pike et al. 1999). Habitat degradation and fragmentation are also serious threats to mountain lions (Paquet and Hackman 1995). Van Dyke et al.

(1986a, 1986b) found that western cougars avoided areas with traveled roads, and selected home ranges with no recent timber sales and little or no human activity. In Florida, male panthers regularly crossed highways but females avoided them (Maehr 1997). Brocke (1981) calculated road densities of 0.42 km/km^2 in a hypothetical cougar area in the central Adirondack Mountains of New York. He believed this density compared poorly with that in known cougar habitats in Florida and Utah with respect to cougar survival. However, road densities in the Black Hills of South Dakota and Wyoming (which support a remnant cougar population) were about 0.8 km/km^2, less than the 1.0 km/km^2 density that inhibited other large carnivores with small isolated populations (Johnson 2000). These presumed road effects may reflect a behavioral response to hunting rather than an innate intolerance of development and related human activity.

Many cougar reports involve animals crossing roads, traversing back yards, and frequenting suburban developments, suggesting that road effects are not as important as previously believed. Cougars are found regularly in suburbs of west coastal states (Danz 1999). In California, Torres et al. (1996) reported that depredation on pets by cougars may be a useful indication of the animal's proximity to humans and the impacts of development. These depredations may be a manifestation of habitat fragmentation. The protection of large blocks of habitat and corridors appears essential to cougar survival (Beier 1993; Sweanor et al. 2000). Cougar density is believed to be determined by environmental factors other than just prey abundance (Lindzey et al. 1994). Yet, protection and management of prey populations and habitat are a major sustaining factor in cougar populations (Quigley et al. 1990, cited in Paquet and Hackman 1995).

White-tailed deer populations are now more abundant than ever before, especially in the East (McShea et al. 1997; Warren 1997), suggesting that prey availability does not preclude the existence of eastern cougars. Thus, although cougar reports cannot be excluded solely on the basis of proximity to roads and humans, developed areas may increase the potential for adverse conflict (Sweanor et al. 2000). Brocke (1981) suggested that any cougars introduced to the Adirondack Mountains of New York would disappear in <10 years due to human-induced mortality. The translocation of 7 cougars from Texas to Florida failed due to

illegal kills, conflicts with livestock, and movement into unsuitable habitat (Belden and Hagedorn 1993).

Recommendations

We consider current research, management practices, and existing data to
be insufficient to address the question of the eastern cougar's identity, status, and distribution. We recommend the following actions by USFWS,
the wildlife conservation agencies of the several states and provinces, and
individual researchers.

Federal Actions

Listing Status. USFWS must decide how it will treat the eastern
cougar. If the animal is extinct, it should be delisted on the basis of
extinction. But if it is to remain listed as endangered, then USFWS must
assume the leadership responsibilities commensurate with that status. If
the animal does not represent a distinct taxon (Culver 1999), it may
remain listed as a distinct population segment provided that USFWS
determines that any population exists.

Recovery Plan. USFWS recovery plans must set forth site-specific
management actions and provide objective, measurable criteria which,
when met, would result in a determination for delisting of the species.
Agencies have failed to meet the objective of " . . . having found or
established . . . " at least 3 self-sustaining populations in the United States
as set forth in the eastern cougar recovery plan (USFWS 1982:8). Consequently, this plan should be revised if it is to adequately guide eastern
cougar recovery.

Recovery Team. USFWS has not appointed an eastern cougar recovery team. Such a recovery team should be appointed. Lessons from the
Florida panther recovery process should be heeded (Maehr 1997).

Restoration. Despite Brocke's (1981) pessimism, Davis (1996) and
Downing (1996a) suggested restoration of cougars to the East. The prac-
ticality of such restoration should be reassessed and incorporated into a
revised recovery plan. World Conservation Union guidelines on reintroductions (Seddon and Soorae 1999) are germane. Reintroductions of
large carnivores also pose social and biopolitical challenges that must be
overcome (Brocke et al. 1990; Lohr et al. 1996; Phillips and Smith 1998)

through adaptive research management (ARM) and a public involvement process.

General Recommendations

Standards. Much of the controversy surrounding the eastern cougar derives from miscommunication and misunderstanding between wildlife professionals and lay investigators. One faction seeks proof, while the other queries "what more proof is needed?" Clear, mutually acceptable standards of evidence must be developed. These standards must necessarily differ among the questions posed. A standardized data collection protocol should be developed and all investigators urged to use it. Comparison of data among the diverse interest groups is hindered by this lack of reporting standards.

Sampling Protocols. Standard protocols should be developed and adopted to collect, handle, and ship biological samples (Wobeser 1996) to minimize contamination and to protect their integrity. A signed chain of custody document should accompany these samples from the source to the testing site. Biological samples should be tested at more than one laboratory, and blind testing procedures should be followed.

Workshops. The Northeast and Southeast Associations of Fish and Wildlife Resource Agencies should consider periodic eastern cougar workshops similar to the Western Mountain Lion or Eastern Black Bear Workshops. Such workshops would provide important forums for providing structure and guidance and coordinating research and education efforts.

Training. Researchers involved in the field investigation of eastern cougars should receive training in cougar biology and behavior and the detection and identification of cougar sign.

Public Participation. Private interest groups and individuals should not be excluded from the decision-making and investigatory processes. Governmental entities must proactively integrate stakeholder interests and concerns into management decisions (Decker and Enck 1996; Decker et al. 1996). The melding of such human dimensions approaches with traditional wildlife management is intrinsic to program success. Scientists should be " . . . consciously aware of their own biases and strive to keep an open mind to new ideas" (Ratti and Garton 1994:6). Private individuals are typically involved in reporting sightings to wildlife agencies. These sightings are often unsubstantiated (Downing 1996b). The value of this information would be enhanced through education and the use of ARM. ARM is an approach that acknowledges uncertainty and the need to learn by balancing learning and system performance (Lancia et al. 1996). ARM is used to accomplish the dual goals of achieving management objectives and gaining reliable knowledge (Lancia et al. 1993). However, because the present eastern cougar question is solely one of uncertain knowledge, a comprehensive ARM approach is initially inappropriate. Agencies should use the guidelines developed by Van Dyke and Brocke (1987a) to investigate those sightings where physical evidence may be collected. ARM should be incorporated into wildlife agency planning when the animal's status is ascertained and population management is desired.

Captive Cougars. Wildlife conservation agencies should acquire and use the legal authority to restrict the private possession of cougars and to implement standards for the secure housing of those animals that are permitted. All captives should be identified with passive integrated transponders or other indelible markers.

Acknowledgments

We thank G. Amato and M. Culver for their analyses of the Franklin County scat and D. Blodgett for unpublished data. We also thank R. D. Deblinger, T. W. French, and an anonymous panelist for their constructive suggestions on the manuscript and W. C. Byrne for photography.

Literature Cited

Ackerman, B. B., E. G. Lindzey, and T. P. Hemker. 1986. Predictive energetics model for cougars. Pages 333–352 in S. D. Miller and D. D. Everett, editors. *Cats of the world: biology, conservation, and management.* National Wildlife Federation, Washington, D.C., USA.

Allen, G. M. 1942. Extinct and vanishing mammals of the western hemisphere. American Committee for International Wildlife Protection, Special Publication 11, Washington, D.C., USA.

Altherr, T. L. 1996. The catamount in Vermont folklore and culture, 1760–1900. Pages 50–91 in J. W. Tischendorf and S. J. Ropski, editors. *Proceedings of the eastern cougar conference, 3–5 June 1994,* Erie, Pennsylvania, USA. American Ecological Research Institute, Fort Collins, Colorado, USA.

Barnhurst, D. and F. G. Lindzey. 1989. Detecting female mountain lions with kittens. *Northwest Science* 63:35–37.

Beard, D. B. 1942. *Fading trails: the story of endangered American wildlife.* Macmillan, New York, New York, USA.

Beier, P. 1993. Determining minimum habitat areas and habitat corridors for cougars. *Conservation Biology* 7:94–108.

Belden, R. C. 1978. How to recognize panther tracks. *Proceedings of the Annual Conference of the Southeastern Association of Fish and Wildlife Resource Agencies* 32: 112–115.

Belden, R. C. and B. W. Hagedorn. 1993. Feasibility of translocating panthers into northern Florida. *Journal of Wildlife Management* 57:388–397.

Bogue, G. and M. Ferrari. 1976. The predatory "training" of captive-reared cougars. Pages 36–45 in R. L. Eaton, editor. *The world's cats.* Volume 3(1). Contributions to status, management, and conservation. *Proceedings of the third international symposium on the world's cats.* University of Washington, 26–28 April 1974, Seattle, USA.

Bolgiano, C. 1995. *Mountain lion: an unnatural history of pumas and people.* Stackpole, Mechanicsburg, Pennsylvania, USA.

Brocke, R. H. 1981. Reintroduction of the cougar *Felis concolor* in Adirondack Park: a problem analysis and recommendations. Federal Aid Endangered Species Project E-1-3, Final Report. New York State Department of Environmental Conservation, Albany, USA.

Brocke, R. H. and F. G. Van Dyke. 1985. Eastern cougars: the verifiability of the presence of isolated individuals versus populations. *Cryptozoology* 4:31–49.

Brocke, R. H., K. A. Gustafson, and A. R. Major. 1990. Restoration of lynx in New York: biopolitical lessons. *Transactions of the North American Wildlife and Natural Resources Conference* 55:590–598.

Busch, R. H. 1996. *The cougar almanac.* Lyons and Burford, New York, New York, USA.

Committee on Rare and Endangered Wildlife Species. 1968. *Rare and endangered fish and wildlife of the United States.* Revised edition. United States Bureau of Sport Fisheries and Wildlife, Resource Publication 34, Washington, D.C., USA.

Culver, M. 1999. Molecular genetic variation, population structure, and natural history of free-ranging pumas *(Puma concolor).* Dissertation, University of Maryland, College Park, USA.

Cumberland, R. E. and J. A. Dempsey. 1994. Recent confirmation of a cougar, *Felis concolor,* in New Brunswick. *Canadian Field-Naturalist* 108:224–226.

Cutler, B. L. and S. D. Penrod. 1995. *Mistaken identification: the eyewitness, psychology, and the law.* Cambridge University, New York, New York, USA.

Danz, H. P. 1999. *Cougar!* Swallow, Ohio University, Athens, USA.

Davis, R. 1996. Giving the eastern cougar a second chance: a feasibility study of reintroducing the cougar *(Puma concolor)* into Allegheny National Forest. Pages 243–245 in J. W. Tischendorf and S. J. Ropski, editors. *Proceedings of the eastern cougar conference,* 3–5 June 1994, Erie, Pennsylvania, USA. American Ecological Research Institute, Fort Collins, Colorado, USA.

Decker, D. J. and J. W. Enck. 1996. Human dimensions of wildlife: knowledge for agency survival in the 21st century. *Human Dimensions of Wildlife* 1(2):60–71.

Decker, D. J., C. C. Krueger, R. A. Baer, Jr., B. A. Knuth, and M. E. Richmond. 1996. From clients to stakeholders: a philosophical shift for fish and wildlife management. *Human Dimensions of Wildlife* 1(1):70–82.

Dixon, K. R. 1982. Mountain lion. Pages 711–727 in J. A. Chapman and G. A. Feldhamer, editors. *Wild mammals of North America: biology, economics, and management.* Johns Hopkins University, Baltimore, Maryland, USA.

Downing, R. L. 1996a. The cougar in the east. Pages 163–166 in J. W. Tischendorf and S. J. Ropski, editors. *Proceedings of the eastern cougar conference,* 3–5 June 1994, Erie, Pennsylvania, USA. American Ecological Research Institute, Fort Collins, Colorado, USA.

Downing, R. L. 1996b. Investigation to determine the status of the cougar in the southern Appalachians. Pages 46–49 in J. W. Tischendorf and S. J. Ropski, editors. *Proceedings of the eastern cougar conference,* 3–5 June 1994, Erie, Pennsylvania, USA. American Ecological Research Institute, Fort Collins, Colorado, USA.

Foran, D. R., K. R. Crooks, and S. C. Minta. 1997a. DNA-based analysis of hair to identify species and individuals for population research and monitoring. *Wildlife Society Bulletin* 25:840–847.

Foran, D. R., K. R. Crooks, and S. C. Minta. 1997b. Species identification from scat: an unambiguous genetic method. *Wildlife Society Bulletin* 25:835–839.

Golley, F. B. 1962. *Mammals of Georgia.* University of Georgia, Athens, Georgia, USA.

Golley, F. B. 1966. South Carolina mammals. Contribution XV. The Charleston Museum, Charleston, South Carolina, USA.

Greenwell, J. R. 1996. The place of the eastern puma in the natural history of the larger felids. Pages 9–29 in J. W. Tischendorf and S. J. Ropski, editors. *Proceedings of the eastern cougar conference,* 3–5 June 1994, Erie, Pennsylvania, USA. American Ecological Research Institute, Fort Collins, Colorado, USA.

Hall, E. R. 1981. *The mammals of North America.* Second edition. Volume 2. John Wiley and Sons, New York, New York, USA.

Hansen, K. 1992. *Cougar: the American lion.* Northland, Flagstaff, Arizona, USA.

Hoagland, E. 1973. Hailing the elusory mountain lion. Pages 46–68 in *Walking the Dead Diamond River.* Random House, New York, New York, USA.

Hornaday, W. T. 1913. *Our vanishing wild life.* New York Zoological Society, New York, New York, USA.

Jackson, C. E. 1922. Notes on New Hampshire mammals. *Journal of Mammalogy* 3:13–15.

Johnson, K. 2000. The return of the Great Plains puma. *Endangered Species Update* 17:108–114.

Kellogg, R. 1939. Annotated list of Tennessee mammals. *Proceedings of the United States National Museum* 86: 245–303.

Lancia, R. A., T. D. Nudds, and M. L. Morris. 1993. Opening comments: slaying slippery shibboleths. *Transactions of the North American Wildlife and Natural Resources Conference* 58:505–508.

Lancia, R. A., C. E. Braun, M. W. Collopy, R. D. Dueser, J. G. Kie, C. J. Martinka, J. D. Nichols, T. D. Nudds, W. R. Porath, and N. G. Tilghman. 1996. ARM! for the future: adaptive resource management in the wildlife profession. *Wildlife Society Bulletin* 24:436–442.

Leach, N. P. 1909. Panthers in New England. *Forest and Stream* 73:412.

Lindzey, F. G. 1987. Mountain lion. Pages 657–668 in M. Novak, J. A. Baker, M. E. Obbard, and B. Malloch, editors. *Wild furbearer conservation and management in North America.* Ontario Ministry of Natural Resources, Toronto, Canada.

Lindzey, F. G., W. D. Van Sickle, B. B. Ackerman, D. Barnhurst, T. P. Hemker and S. P. Lang. 1994. Cougar population dynamics in southern Utah. *Journal of Wildlife Management* 58: 19–624.

Linzey, D. W. 1998. *The mammals of Virginia.* McDonald and Woodward, Blacksburg, Virginia, USA.

Loftus, E. F. 1979. Eyewitness testimony. Harvard University, Cambridge, Massachusetts, USA.

Logan, K. A., L. L. Irwin, and R. Skinner. 1986. Characteristics of a hunted mountain lion population in Wyoming. *Journal of Wildlife Management* 50:648–654.

Lohr, C., W. B. Ballard, and A. Bath. 1996. Attitudes toward gray wolf reintroductions to New Brunswick. *Wildlife Society Bulletin* 24:414–420.

Lowery, G. H., Jr. 1974. *The mammals of Louisiana and its adjacent waters.* Louisiana State University, Baton Rouge, USA.

Lutz, J. and L. Lutz. 1996. The eastern puma. Pages 127–138 in J. W. Tischendorf and S. J. Ropksi, editors. *Proceedings of the eastern cougar conference,* 3–5 June 1994, Erie, Pennsylvania, USA. American Ecological Research Institute, Fort Collins, Colorado, USA.

Maehr, D. S. 1997. *The Florida panther: life and death of a vanishing carnivore.* Island, Washington, D.C., USA.

McGinnis, H. J. 1996. Reports of pumas in Pennsylvania, 1890–1981. Pages 92–125 in J. W. Tischendorf and S. J. Ropski, editors. *Proceedings of the eastern cougar conference,* 3–5 June 1994, Erie, Pennsylvania, USA. American Ecological Research Institute, Fort Collins, Colorado, USA.

McShea, W. J., H. B. Underwood, and J. H. Rappole, editors. 1997. *The science of overabundance: deer ecology and population management.* Smithsonian Institution, Washington, D.C., USA.

McWilliams, W. H., G. C. Reese, R. C. Conner, V. A. Rudis, and T. L. Schmidt. 1997. Today's eastern forests: what have 350 years of European settlement wrought? *Transactions of the North American Wildlife and Natural Resources Conference* 62:220–235.

Merriam, C. H. 1901. Preliminary revision of the cougars. *Proceedings of the Washington Academy of Science* 3:577–600.

Murphy, D. D. and B. D. Noon. 1991. Coping with uncertainty in wildlife biology. *Journal of Wildlife Management* 55:773–782.

Nero, R. W. and R. E. Wrigley. 1977. Status and habits of the cougar in Manitoba. *Canadian Field-Naturalist* 91:28–40.

Nowak, R. M. 1976. The cougar in the United States and Canada. Report to the New York Zoological Society and the United States Fish and Wildlife Service, Washington, D.C., USA.

Palmer, R. S. 1937. Mammals of Maine. Honor's Thesis, University of Maine, Orono, USA.

Paquet, E. and D. A. Hackman. 1995. *Large carnivore conservation in the Rocky Mountains: a long-term strategy for maintaining free-ranging and self-sustaining populations of carnivores.* World Wildlife Fund Canada, Toronto, Ontario, Canada, and World Wildlife Fund, United States, Washington, D.C., USA.

Parker, G. 1998. *The eastern panther: mystery cat of the Appalachians.* Nimbus, Halifax, Nova Scotia, Canada.

Phillips, M. K. and D. W. Smith. 1998. Gray wolves and private landowners in the Greater Yellowstone Area. *Transactions of the North American Wildlife and Natural Resources Conference* 63:443–450.

Pike, J. R., J. H. Shaw, D. M. Leslie, Jr., and M. G. Shaw. 1999. A geographic analysis of the status of mountain lions in Oklahoma. *Wildlife Society Bulletin* 27:4–11.

Quinn, T. 1995. Using public sighting information to investigate coyote use of urban habitat. *Journal of Wildlife Management* 59:238–245.

Ratti, J. T. and E. O. Garton. 1994. Research and experimental design. Pages 1–23 in T. A. Bookhout, editor. *Research and management techniques for wildlife and habitat.* Fifth edition. The Wildlife Society, Bethesda, Maryland, USA.

Read, J. D. 1994. Understanding bystander misidentifications: the role of familiarity and contextual knowledge. Pages 56–79 in D. F. Ross, J. D. Read, and M. P. Toglia, editors. *Adult eyewitness testimony: current trends and developments.* Cambridge University, New York, New York, USA.

Rusz, P. J. 2001. *The cougar in Michigan: sightings and related information.* Technical Publication, Bengel Wildlife Center, Bath, Michigan, USA.

Schortemeyer, J. L., D. S. Maehr, J. W. McCowen, E. D. Land, and P. D. Manor. 1991. Prey management for the Florida panther: a unique role for wildlife managers. *Transactions of the North American Wildlife and Natural Resources Conference* 56:512–526.

Scott, F. W. 1998. Update COSEWIC status report on cougar *(Felis concolor couguar)*, eastern population. Committee on the Status of Endangered Wildlife in Canada, Environment Canada, Ottawa, Ontario, Canada.

Seddon, P. J., and P. S. Soorae. 1999. Guidelines for subspecific substitutions in wildlife restoration projects. *Conservation Biology* 13:177–194.

Seidensticker, J. C., IV, M. G. Hornocker, W. V. Wiles, and J. P. Messick. 1973. *Mountain lion social organization in the Idaho Primitive Area.* Wildlife Monographs 35.

Shaw, H. G. 1987. *Mountain lion field guide.* Third edition. Arizona Fish and Game Department, Special Report No. 9, Phoenix, USA.

Shermer, M. 1997. *Why people believe weird things: pseudoscience, superstition, and other confusions of our time.* W. H. Freeman, New York, New York, USA.

Shoemaker, H. W. 1917. *Extinct Pennsylvania animals. Part I. The panther and the wolf.* Altoona Tribune Publishing Company, Altoona, Pennsylvania, USA.

Sinclair, A. R. E. 1991. Science and the practice of wildlife management. *Journal of Wildlife Management* 55:767–773.

Stocek, R. F. 1995. The cougar, *Felis concolor*, in the Maritime Provinces. *Canadian Field-Naturalist* 109:19–22.

Stoner, D. 1950. *Extant New York State specimens of the Adirondack cougar.* New York State Museum, Circular 25, Albany, USA.

Sweanor, L. L., K. A. Logan, and M. G. Hornocker. 2000. Cougar dispersal patterns, metapopulation dynamics, and conservation. *Conservation Biology* 14:798–808.

Tischendorf, J. W. 1996. Bruce S. Wright, the ghost cat, and other players. Pages 39–45 in J. W. Tischendorf and S. J. Ropski, editors. *Proceedings of the eastern cougar conference, 3–5 June 1994,* Erie, Pennsylvania, USA. American Ecological Research Institute, Fort Collins, Colorado, USA.

Torres, S. G., T. M. Mansfield, J. E. Foley, T. Lupo, and A. Brinkhaus. 1996. Mountain lion and human activity in California: testing speculations. *Wildlife Society Bulletin* 24:451–460.

True, E. W. 1891. The puma, or American lion: *Felis concolor* of Linnaeus. *Annual Report of the Board of Regents of the Smithsonian Institution for the year ending June 30, 1889:* 591–608.

United States Fish and Wildlife Service. 1982. *Eastern cougar recovery plan.* United States Fish and Wildlife Service, Atlanta, Georgia, USA.

Uttal, W. R. 1981. *A taxonomy of visual processes.* Lawrence Erlbaum, Hillsdale, New Jersey, USA.

Van Dyke, F. G., R. H. Brocke, H. G. Shaw, B. B. Ackerman, T. P. Hemker, and F. G. Lindzey. 1986a. Reactions of mountain lions to logging and human activity. *Journal of Wildlife Management* 50:95–102.

Van Dyke, F. G., R. H. Brocke, and H. G. Shaw. 1986b. Use of road track counts as indices of mountain lion presence. *Journal of Wildlife Management* 50:102–109.

Van Dyke, F. G. and R. H. Brocke. 1987a. Searching technique for mountain lion sign at specific locations. *Wildlife Society Bulletin* 15:256–259.

Van Dyke, F. G. and R. H. Brocke. 1987b. Sighting and track reports as indices of mountain lion presence. *Wildlife Society Bulletin* 15:251–256.

Warren, R. J. 1997. The challenge of deer overabundance in the 21st century. *Wildlife Society Bulletin* 25:213–214.

Wobeser, G. 1996. Forensic (medico-legal) necropsy of wildlife. *Journal of Wildlife Diseases* 32:240–249.

Wright, B. S. 1948. Survival of the northeastern panther *(Felis concolor)* in New Brunswick. *Journal of Mammalogy* 29:235–246.

Wright, B. S. 1953. Further notes on the panther in the northeast. *Canadian Field-Naturalist* 67:12–28.

Wright, B. S. 1959. *The ghost of North America: the story of the eastern panther.* Vantage, New York, New York, USA.

Wright, B. S. 1972. *The eastern panther: a question of survival.* Clarke and Irwin, Toronto, Ontario, Canada.

Young, S. P. and E. A. Goldman. 1946. *The puma: mysterious American cat.* American Wildlife Institute, Washington, D.C., USA.

Five officers and members of the Board of Directors of the Eastern Cougar Foundation responded to the article above (David S. Maehr, Marcella J. Kelly, Chris Bolgiano, Todd Lester, Helen McGinnis. "Eastern Cougar Recovery Is Linked to the Florida Panther: Cardoza and Langlois Revisited." Wildlife Society Bulletin *31(3): 849–85, 2003). The authors commended Cardoza and Langlois on their recommendations for a science-based approach to eastern cougar investigations, and linked the Florida Panther Recovery Project to potential recovery of cougars elsewhere in the East. That theme is pursued in the next section.*

HABITAT AND ECOSYSTEM ROLE

In the original essay below, Dr. David S. Maehr, former field leader for the Florida Panther Recovery Project, elaborates on the comparison between the Florida panther and eastern cougars.

Can the Florida Panther Provide Insight into Restoring the Eastern Cougar?

by David S. Maehr
University of Kentucky

A mere decade ago the idea of cougars outside of well-known populations in the West or Florida panthers outside the remnant population in Florida would have been viewed with great skepticism. Today, appearances of individuals outside of known breeding range, even in the East, are almost commonplace. This is in keeping with the repair of other components of the eastern biota. With little purposeful help from humans, eastern forests and bears have returned to landscapes that are now inhabited by people who value their aesthetic and ecological attributes. Will the cougar/panther become part of this eastern rewilding? I believe that the adaptability and stealth of *Puma concolor* are in its favor, but that its return is not as simple as welcoming it home.

I am naturally a skeptic. I doubted the Florida panther's potential for recovery when I reluctantly accepted the job of studying it in 1985. Before I moved to steamy south Florida, the project had produced only a handful of study animals (reputed to be parasite-infested and decrepit), and the two previous chief researchers had been run off by unsavory internal politics. I've never claimed a particularly sane approach to running my life, but I figured that if I was going to preside over an extinction event, it might as well be in an interesting place. As it turned out, the panther was a very interesting story (still is), and I became a believer in its revival after a few short years of documenting a distribution and reproductive capacity that were at odds with the accepted vision of a declining population.

But there remains plenty to be skeptical about. I remain unconvinced that recovery agencies are capable of or willing to assist panthers and cougars in their own efforts to recolonize vast areas of former range. However, I believe that the species is sufficiently flexible in its resistance to human activities that it can live almost anywhere with enough food and cover. And, I am exceedingly skeptical of arguments that downplay the uniqueness of the *Puma concolor coryi* genome. In this age of biotic homogenization (e.g., European starlings in North America, Canada geese in Sweden, hatchery-raised salmon in the Atlantic), it might be instructive to remember that the great variety of recognized races of the cougar (and other vertebrates) was the result of recognized anatomical differences between populations. Certainly, such descriptions were based on small samples of scattered individuals, and the early taxonomists may have been overly generous in the naming and subdividing, but as a conservation biologist, I am reluctant to embrace the view of the cougar in North America as a single, intermixing population that is not influenced by isolating mechanisms. Such isolation, even if it is not complete, is a pathway to speciation. While the cougar's most recent invasion of the continent may be measurable in mere millennia, the evolutionary forces that act on *P. c. stanlyana* (or what passes for that regional population in Texas) are clearly different than those that act on *P. c. coryi* in Florida. Whereas recent genetic analyses might suggest more similarities than differences among populations of the species in North America, this should not diminish the importance of the unique characters that make a mountain lion at White Sands Missile Base a New Mexico puma and another in the Big Cypress Swamp a Florida panther. Such differences, I believe, are related to more than just geography.

My skeptic's antennae turn on around the subject of the eastern cougar. I would bet the farm that there are no self-sustaining populations anywhere between Lake Arbuckle, Florida, and Toronto, Canada. After entertaining hundreds of phone calls, letters with photographs, and countless emails since the mid-1980s, I am convinced that most claims of cougar sightings are, at best, cases of mistaken identity. Sure, the odd specimens have turned up from time to time in a variety of unexpected places, but their distribution in time and space provide no evidence of ongoing reproduction and permanent residence outside of the Big Cypress region. Thus, I do not believe that a road-killed cougar kitten in

Kentucky, for example, proves anything beyond the fact that it was there. On the other hand, do apparently wild specimens recovered in Iowa, Missouri, and Illinois mean any more than Kentucky's roadkill? I suspect so, and will get back to this point in a bit.

I admire and embrace the vision of large carnivores in the Appalachians. My mind's eye sees them in much of eastern Kentucky. I'm an advocate. Populations of white-tailed deer, raccoons, and humans (the former two overabundant, the latter superabundant) could sure use them for a number of biological and psychological reasons. However, with the exception of the plant-loving black bear, it seems that there are no viable populations of carnivores in the East to limit densities of big herbivores and smaller carnivores. If they were here, it would not be difficult to tell. One of the simple facts of cougar populations anywhere in the Western Hemisphere is that they provide physical evidence of their day-to-day existence. A resident individual, and certainly a population, cannot help but leave pugmarks, scats, scrapes, and kills scattered about a large area. Such artifacts can be found if a cougar lives there. If a population is bordered or bisected by highways, sooner or later a traveling cougar will throw itself in front of a hurtling vehicle (this happened regularly in south Florida even when it appeared the population was nearly extinct).

Such events are sad but often sure signs that cougars live nearby. While I will be the first to acknowledge that the inability to document sign does not disprove a cougar's presence, without it one is increasingly challenged to argue the existence of a population. Although a variety of "expert" opinion surveys over the years have repeatedly tantalized us about their likely existence in places such as Arkansas, when actual searches for these cougars are made, whether by well-experienced biologists, technicians with hounds, or strategically placed cameras, the results have always been the same—no big cats at home. Although there may be some population-wide changes occurring in the easternmost reaches of western cougar range, the recovery of an eastern cougar population any time soon will require significant human intervention and probably a bit of luck.

How might the cougar return to the East? Natural colonization of vacant range is preferable to moving cougars from place to place. Quite simply, as soon as a public agency jumpstarts a population by transporting cougars, liability issues will surface. Suddenly, in some folks' minds human life and property will be less secure, and a lawsuit will be around the corner. The last thing that Florida panther or eastern cougar recovery efforts need is for a young high school athlete to be eaten at the edge of town—as happened in Boulder, Colorado, just a few years ago—especially if the presence of the marauding cat was even remotely linked to an agency translocation. Such tragedies create sufficiently bad karma to give agencies icy feet. Elsewhere I have suggested that "the existing population in extreme south Florida is so profoundly isolated, and its social fabric so challenged by male-biased dispersal, that human-assisted colonization may be the only practical way to help it overcome nearly 5 centuries of anthropogenic landscape change and range reduction."[1] How can we expect natural colonization to occur—say in the central Appalachians—when a nearby source population is not available, and when wildlife agencies are generally resistant to the challenges of managing large carnivores? Might the Florida situation offer some hope in this regard? Perhaps.

One of the unexpected outcomes of introducing Texas cougars into south Florida to stem genetic deterioration in the Florida panther was an increase in density that promoted unprecedented long-distance dispersal across landscape features that were previously thought of as barriers. In most places, cougars disperse among nearby populations or within large areas of occupied range. Such behavior helps to reduce inbreeding in a species where females usually establish home ranges that are near their birth places. In other words, only males regularly attempt to move long distances. In 1998, male panther #62 made it to the outskirts of Orlando (about one hundred miles as the crow flies) before retreating to south Florida after failing to find a mate. No one would have predicted this long movement, but it helped to illustrate the capacity for the species to colonize new range. Since this time at least three other males have repeated this feat.

Even before Texas cougars were introduced, the panther surprised us. For example, after the early years of monitoring a handful of mostly old, decrepit panthers, documentation of a younger, more widespread population emerged from annual capture efforts. Whether these young animals were always there, or were the vanguard of a natural recovery following decades of overexploitation, is not known. But we were surprised that

[1]Maehr, D. S., M. J. Kelly, C. Bolgiano, T. Lester, and H. McGinnis. 2003. Eastern cougar recovery is linked to the Florida panther: Cardoza and Langlois revisited. *Wildlife Society Bulletin* 31:849–853.

Florida panther females began breeding at less than two years of age versus the more common three years in western populations (as with humans, age of first reproduction is an important factor influencing potential growth in populations—the earlier reproduction begins, the faster the population can grow). Perhaps the biggest surprise in panther research was the successful reproduction of experimental Texas female cougars in north Florida that had been impregnated by vasectomized experimental males. All that is needed for an expansion of panther range to occur is for a female or two to disperse at the same time that a male does. This could be exactly what is driving the increase in cougar records in the Midwest. A lesson to be learned from long-term studies of wildlife is to expect the unexpected. Thus, wildlife agencies in states with apparently expanding populations of cougars/panthers should be prepared to have another large mammal to manage, even if it is not a welcome addition to their list of charges.

What can we expect in the next few years? If a female Florida panther does not successfully cross the Caloosahatchee River (one of the former dispersal "barriers"), will managers embrace the idea of moving one across it? If a female does successfully disperse and establish a breeding territory, will managers safeguard the expanding population? Given what appears to be fairly regular occupation of Glades and Highlands counties by young male panthers that have dispersed from south Florida, and because regional conservation lands are on the increase in south central Florida (e.g., Fisheating Creek), the translocation of a female should be considered a reasonable recovery strategy in this area. Certainly, it would be helpful to have the full support of local citizens, but such an action should not rise to the level of a reintroduction because south central Florida appears to have been occupied (at least by males) since the 1980s. For such a strategy to work in the East, cougars must be proven to be regular residents. Perhaps consistent documentation of dispersing animals from the West (likely to be males) might be sufficient for agencies to consider the potential for some eastern regions to support a big cat population once again, and to investigate the feasibility of relocating females to suitable locations. Planning for female translocation now could avoid the consequences of a rapid decline and extinction in the only known breeding population of cougar in eastern North America, and could facilitate the return of breeding populations outside of Florida. Despite the Florida panther's recent positive population growth, its numbers are still sufficiently small that any number of factors could quickly reverse its growth.

Growing populations in the West are most certainly the sources for the recent phenomenon of cougars in Iowa and Illinois. I suspect the young males that have been throwing themselves in front of midwestern cars and trains may be compelled to disperse for the same reasons that young Florida panthers have recently moved north into vacant range. They are like steam venting from a pressure-cooker—escaping the centers of populations where intolerant resident males frequently kill loitering and all-too-common subadult males that may represent half of the males in a given area. In Florida, the surplus of motivated male dispersers was enhanced by the introduction of Texas cougars. In the West, naturally growing populations in many areas have probably driven the move of dispersing males eastward. In south Florida,

> the additive productivity of Texas females may have had no measurable impact on most aspects of panther demography [litter size, mortality patterns, etc.]. The occurrence of unprecedented, semi-directional and long-distance dispersal attempts by males is best explained by a recent and rapid increase in panther population density [more panthers producing kittens]. This phenomenon is in keeping with a population that is attempting to relieve the stresses of high density—including food limitations, competition for finite resources, and inbreeding avoidance. . . . We suspect that before the introduction of Texas cougars, south Florida supported a population that was at carrying capacity or at pre-saturation density [that is, there was no room left]. Dispersal attempts by males were routinely made, but remained south of the Caloosahatchee River. In the 3 years since the introduction of eight Texas cougar females, more than 36 hybrid kittens have been produced. This number represents 75% of all known reproduction from 1985 through 1993 and was likely additive to reproduction that was already occurring at a rate that was sufficient to facilitate population growth. Thus, we suggest that the rapid increase in density created the motivation for adult males to cross this landscape filter. We did not document any river crossings during the 15 years prior to these events.[2]

---

[2]Maehr, D. S., E. D. Land, D. B. Shindle, O. L. Bass, and T. S. Hoctor. 2002. Florida panther dispersal and conservation. *Biological Conservation* 106:187–197.

Basically, lots of panthers in a confined space translate into a higher likelihood of colonization attempts. Recent surges in western cougar population densities may well explain the occurrence of pioneers that have appeared as far east as southern Illinois. Young male cougars born in the expanding populations of Oklahoma and the Dakotas may be experiencing the same frustrations that face young male panthers in south Florida: danger at home, but an absence of females beyond. Perhaps east-west oriented rivers and streams such as the Missouri, Niobara, and Platte act as conduits to eastern locales. What these east-traveling dispersers anticipate as their destination is anyone's guess, but an unknown outcome must be better than the likelihood for conflict and death back home. And, sooner or later, a female will join in the colonization pulse and another former chunk of cougar range will be filled. I suspect it is just a matter of time before the cougar reclaims more of its eastern range. The distance and speed of such colonization, however, will depend on continued pressure from source populations and the willingness of wildlife agencies and the public to have them back. At the moment, the sociological hurdles seem more resistant to the cougar than do landscape barriers.

How badly do we really want them back in the East? Would we do more for the maintenance and conservation of biodiversity by physically restoring a population, or by letting individuals do the job naturally, without assistance? For me, the ecological and evolutionary benefits of returning large carnivores to a landscape that has been dominated by raccoons and white-tailed deer for two centuries outweigh the negative consequences that will be borne by local human residents. Translocation might provide a quick result, but how lasting would it be if the outcome was viewed as a heavy-handed government plot? Natural colonization may be hampered by other challenges. Part of the problem is that the North American landscape has changed drastically in the two centuries since cougars were mostly eliminated. Highways, cities, reservoirs, vast expanses of agriculture, backyard dogs throughout suburbia and farmland, fearful residents with guns, and agencies trying to balance the demands of a diverse public, have all combined to create formidable barriers to colonizing big cats. Even if wonderful habitats exist—complete with productive deer herds, plenty of space, and lots of cover in, say, West Virginia—how will a population become established, especially because females are much less likely to disperse long distances? Ignoring a galaxy of societal issues, I could argue that natural recolonization is a perfectly acceptable approach so long as the landscape has been repaired to the extent that dispersal into suitable range by male and female cougars becomes more likely than it is today.

Of course, the toughest issue to deal with is the eventuality of a human death by cougar. We can celebrate the ecological, evolutionary, and aesthetic benefits, but the thought of a grotesque mauling or act of predation is a virtual deal-breaker. How could any responsible agency advocate the return of a species that occasionally produces an individual brazen enough to consider a jogger as food? The dilemma is certainly clear to me. Still, it is interesting that we do not hear more about the dangers posed by the cougar's primary prey. For example, in Michigan alone, vehicle collisions with deer approach 70,000 per year, injuring 2,100 people and killing more than 10. Hundreds of people are killed annually this way in the U.S. The nationwide cost of human injury, death, and vehicle damage approaches one billion dollars each year. How many of us do not know someone who has had a vehicular encounter with a deer?

Some have suggested that signs, fences, walls, underpasses, strategically located feeding areas, liberalized hunting seasons, contraception campaigns, highway reflectors, noise-making devices, and bumper-mounted whistles will solve the overabundant deer problem. But these devices can be costly, none are proven effective against crop-subsidized fecundity in local deer populations, and they do little to address the problem of overabundant suburban herds. While large carnivores may not be the single solution to deer population growth, there is no doubt that they dramatically affect deer behavior and distribution. The presence of the cougar in eastern North America will change patterns of deer movements, make them more wary, and may ultimately reduce the frequency of deer highway crossings and collisions. The potential for an occasional attack on a person will be offset by protecting property, promoting animal and human health, and saving human lives that would otherwise be lost due to collisions with deer from herds unencumbered by predatory tension. It may be easy to doubt the prospects for premeditated introductions of cougars in the East. But it is difficult to be skeptical about the benefits to the environment and the human landscape that would occur if the species could be reestablished, especially where deer are like a plague.

As I have observed elsewhere with colleagues in the Eastern Cougar Foundation, "Florida has been aggressive in protecting its sensitive ecological heritage and landscapes, but it must redouble efforts to generate support for panther reintroduction. If success can be demonstrated in Florida—where a population already exists and is making spectacular efforts to escape the boundaries of constrained space—it will be the precedent needed to drive the human-assisted return of the eastern cougar. Without this step, it will be too easy for unmotivated agencies and a misinformed public to deny the ecological and sociological benefits of restoring populations of large carnivores by correctly observing that if it can't be done in Florida, it can't happen anywhere in the East." Florida currently supports a panther population that is on the verge of expanding a range that has been constrained for more than a century. Yet, despite a mandate to increase numbers and distribution, recovery agencies have been slow to take advantage of what the panther has been telling them. Without proactive management that moves individuals or restores key landscapes, both the eastern cougar and the Florida panther are unlikely to reclaim their former range in the near future. Yes, I'm skeptical—but more in society's capacity to live with large carnivores than in their ability to restore themselves and live with us.

Maehr's essay touches on the cover and prey abundance necessary to support cougars, which many experts agree are sufficient in wilder parts of the East, especially the extensive public lands of the Adirondacks and the Southern Appalachians. In 1999, the environmental group Heartwood (based in Bloomington, Indiana) funded an effort to use geographic information systems (GIS) to identify suitable cougar habitat in the central Appalachians based on four critical parameters. The composite map is reproduced in this chapter. Authors Kristin Taverna, Jason E. Halbert, and David M. Hines concluded that "Large areas of suitable habitat were identified within central West Virginia and along the Appalachian mountains from western Virginia to the northern Allegheny plateau."

However, back in 1981, Dr. Ranier H. Brocke of the State University of New York at Syracuse completed an extensive study on the possibility of reintroducing cougars into the Adirondack State Forest Preserve for the New York State Department of Environmental Conservation. His conclusion: "For reasons of high human density and road penetration in the [study area], I believe that potential man-induced cougar mortality would exceed the level that a potentially reintroduced

Central Appalachian Study Area
COUGAR HABITAT SUITABILITY COMPOSITE MAP
Incorporating Deer Density, Human Population Density, Land Use, and Road Density

CAA Boundary
State Boundary
Composite Score

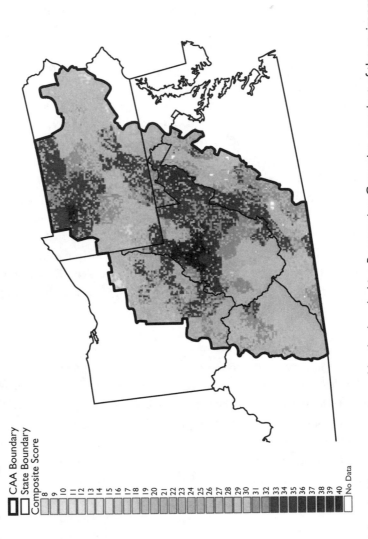

This central Appalachian map was created by the Appalachian Restoration Campaign, a project of the environmental group Heartwood. The darkest areas indicate suitable cougar habitat.

cougar population could sustain and still survive." The fragmentation of habitat by roads and the intrusion of humans that roads allow have increased dramatically in the decades since Brocke's study, raising a serious question about the long-term viability of cougar habitat if these destructive land use patterns continue.

TOLERANCE

Three broad groups are most likely to object to cougar recovery in the East: deer hunters, livestock farmers, and that segment of the general public that fears for human safety. Nationally known carnivore expert Susan C. Morse chided deer hunters for their narrow-mindedness toward predators in a March 2002 interview with James Ehlers in Vermont's Outdoors Magazine.

The esteemed conservationist hunter Aldo Leopold taught us the extraordinary ways in which predators influence the health of ungulates. . . . Today, some hunters still don't get it. Some openly detest large and small carnivores alike, and resent the competition. Excuse me, but how can we pass judgment on predators and call ourselves hunters? For thousands of years, pumas throughout the North American continent have coexisted handsomely with their principal prey: deer species. As an avid elk and deer hunter I feel I'm in good company with cougars.

Although cougar depredations on livestock have traditionally been a source of conflict, it is undoubtedly the ability of cougars to attack and kill humans that poses the most difficult obstacle to the reestablishment of cougars in the East. Young and Goldman, in their classic 1946 book The Puma, Mysterious American Cat, *record three human deaths by cougars in the East since European settlement began, although the documentation is sparse. The only confirmed modern account of a cougar attacking a person in the East was given in an August 15, 2001, article by Matthew Sekeres in the* Ottawa Citizen. *A man near Monkland, Ontario, was bitten on the arm (not fatally) by an animal that jumped at him as he approached a goat pen shortly after midnight. The tooth marks were analyzed by Dr. Lee Fitzhugh of the University of California–Davis and independent researcher Michael Sanders of Livingston, Montana, who agreed that the bite was most likely inflicted by a cougar.*

In the West, where documentation is extensive, nineteen people have been killed by cougars since 1890 (a comparison is often made to the fact that dogs kill approximately that many people every year, but with far less public outcry). Most attacks have occurred since 1970, as human development has rapidly moved into western cougar habitat. The risk of attack by cougar is very, very low; nonetheless, that risk must be acknowledged. Research in the West has identified techniques to avoid or mitigate both livestock and human encounters with cougars, so considerable knowledge is available to assist easterners in living with the cats—if easterners decide they are willing to take the risk. Willingness will arise only from the kind of emotion expressed in these two following pieces.

Ghost of Supposedly Extinct Cat Leaves a Real Devil of a Void

by Pete Bodo
The New York Times, September 12, 1993
Copyright 1993 by *The New York Times,* reprinted with permission

The creature appeared at twilight, crossing the pasture above the old sap house on Little View Farm, not far from the dense woods where Bob and Dick Little had put the carcass of a pregnant cow that died in March.

At first, I thought the animal was my dog. But it slipped like smoke over the rough stones and between the pale green burdocks, moving with a fabulous and silent grace that no canine possesses. The creature was dark, almost black. It stood about two-and-a-half feet tall, and the end of its long tail curled up. Then it was gone, just like that. And the hiss of the cicadas rose like a fever, until it was almost deafening and I couldn't stare at the empty pasture any longer.

That was how I became one of hundreds of people who believe, with varying degrees of conviction, that they might have seen an Eastern cougar, or even a black panther. And the only thing wrong with this picture is that the Eastern cougar, one of some 30 different subspecies of the North American cougar, is considered extinct. The last confirmed cougar in New York State was killed in the Adirondacks by a bounty hunter in the 1920s.

As the popular saying goes, "Extinct is forever." Nevertheless, the Eastern cougar lives on, and whether it does so in the deep woods or on the fields of the imagination is a matter of nagging debate. This I know for sure: If you believe you have seen the big cat, you may find yourself stricken now and then by a deep, abiding ache, in a place too remote to reach and relieve. I believe this is called grief.

Most biologists, state officials and even visiting experts who study the relatively abundant Western cougar, or mountain lion, have traditionally pointed to the paucity of "sign," including positively identified tracks and scat, as proof that the cat is indeed extinct. Unlike the endangered lynx, no cougar has been killed on the road, inadvertently trapped or shot by hunters. Thus, most biologists have put down the frequent sightings to "cougar hysteria."

But a curious thing happened near McKell Lake, in New Brunswick, Canada, last November. Responding to a call from a baffled logger, provincial officials examined a two-mile trail of mysterious tracks. They also found some scat. Lab tests and track analysis positively identified the sign as that of a cougar.

"We made some 30 measurements, covering stride, size and pattern," Rod Cumberland, the provincial fur biologist for New Brunswick, told me. "They checked out in every way, including the cougar's habit of walking across logs instead of avoiding them. The scat contained hair that was unquestionably from a cougar."

Skeptics will suggest that the cougar was an "escapee" from a zoo or a runaway/pet whose lineage traces to the colony of one species of Eastern cougar that still exists in Florida. But the wilds of New Brunswick is an unlikely place for such a creature to turn up. The province has declined to speculate on the origin of the cat, nor has anyone seen sign of the animal since.

But if a domestic cat called Mittens can disappear in a Manhattan studio apartment, a wild cougar can surely avoid man in Woodland Gates, the uninhabited, million-acre timber lot in New Brunswick. Perhaps even on the great tracts of undeveloped New York City watershed property near my farm.

The field above the old sap house is a tamer place than Woodland Gates. Much of the time, cows graze in it, switching their tails as they forage amid the lichen-covered boulders. In the green fog of twilight, I sit and watch, until the shrieking of the crickets reaches a crescendo, and the emptiness becomes unbearable again.

Todd Lester, founder and president of the Eastern Cougar Foundation, is a third-generation Appalachian coal miner who has taught himself to become one of the leading cougar experts in the East.

My Search for Cougars

by Todd Lester
President of the Eastern Cougar Foundation

Growing up in the mountains of southern West Virginia, I spent an enormous amount of time in the woods and hollows coon-hunting and learning about the animals native to this area. I had always heard people telling stories about seeing cougars, mountain lions, and panthers. Even though I had never seen one myself, in the back of my mind I thought there must be a few around in our forests.

On several coon-hunts, I came across a few deer kills, tracks and scats that I credited to a cougar, but at the time I didn't know their true status in the eastern U.S. or the need to collect potential evidence of their existence. Then on one fateful coon-hunt in 1983 all that changed.

I was hunting in a remote area in Wyoming County, West Virginia, and lost a redbone hound during a rainstorm. I headed to the truck to seek shelter from the rain, and at dawn the rains had stopped and my hound still hadn't come back, so I decided to walk back into that remote area to look for him. The only thing on my mind was finding my dog and heading back home. I headed up the game trail and all the leaves were wet and I wasn't making any noise with my footsteps. Approximately one mile from the truck, I came around a bend in the trail when something caught my attention on the mountainside across from me. At first glance, the animal appeared brown in color and the first thing that entered my mind was it's my dog and a feeling of relief came over me.

But as my eyes focused on the animal, it saw me and immediately crouched down and stared at me. I'm sure my mouth dropped open in amazement when I realized just exactly what the animal was that I was looking at. It wasn't my dog at all but a beautiful adult cougar. We stared at each other for what seemed like an eternity at the time, but actually only a few seconds passed. Then suddenly, without warning, it rose up and spun around and bounded up the mountainside out of sight. I remember the big, long, thick tail trailing behind the cat as it disappeared into the forest.

When the cougar ran away, it took part of me with it, and I just haven't been the same since. It's hard to describe this encounter with words, or to imagine just what impact this event would have on my life. A short time later, a couple of conservation officers stopped me to check my hunting license, and I mentioned my cougar sighting to them. Those officers immediately gave me my first lesson on cougars and their status in the East. "No, what you saw wasn't a cougar, it must have been a big brown dog, because there haven't been any cougars in these parts for over a hundred years." I replied that I had been looking for a dog when I saw this cat, and that I knew the difference between a dog and a cougar. What I saw was a cougar!

My interest in cougars began to grow and I gradually gave up coon-hunting to pursue it. In 1986 I joined the U.S. Air Force and was stationed at Homestead Air Force Base in Florida. As fate would have it, this base was on the outskirts of the Florida panther's home range. Florida panthers are the only recognized breeding population of cougars in the eastern U.S. I spent most of my spare time in the Everglades or Big Cypress areas looking for Florida panthers or their sign. I began reading all I could about the animals. Then I met Frank Weed, who lived in Immokalee. Frank owned an animal compound that housed twenty-six cougars, and he was a walking, talking encyclopedia on them. He taught me a wealth of knowledge.

In 1990, I got out of the Air Force and headed back to West Virginia. I continued to read and learn all I could about cougars. In 1995, I decided to prove that cougars existed in the eastern U.S. I ran a few ads in local papers asking for information on cougar sightings. I wanted to know what areas they were being seen in so I could search for evidence. The reports began to come in, but most were months or years old. When I did get a good, hot report, it was still hard to collect good evidence. Finding cougar tracks in this mountainous terrain is not an easy chore. Frequent rains wash out tracks quickly, or the hot sun bakes the ground so hard that a cougar won't leave a track. And the snowfalls we get last only for a couple of days and then melt off.

But in 1996, I managed to find a track near the location of my 1983 sighting. I took photos of the track and made a plaster cast of it. Then I contacted Dr. Lee Fitzhugh in California, who is a renowned cougar expert. Dr. Fitzhugh confirmed that the track was the right front foot of an adult male cougar. Since the cougar I saw in 1983 appeared to be an adult, I seriously doubted that this 1996 track (thirteen years later) could be the same cougar. This enforced my belief that these cougars may be reproducing.

Over the next few years, I began to meet other people who shared my interest in cougars, and I felt that an organization would accomplish more than a single person ever could. So with their help we founded the Eastern Cougar Foundation (ECF) in 1998. The ECF would go on to become a nonprofit organization that conducts field investigations to document reproducing cougar populations, promotes full legal protection of all cougars living wild in the East regardless of origins, and builds tolerance through education.

There were other cougar research groups around during this time, but they seemed to be building walls between themselves and the various state and federal wildlife agencies. And they weren't willing to have potential cougar evidence confirmed by cougar experts and presented in a scientific manner. This approach had been going on for half a century and wasn't going anywhere.

I wanted to do it differently—engage and work with the various wildlife agencies and not build these walls of isolation. I wanted to have any potential evidence examined by cougar experts and confirmed and then present it to the scientific community and the public. The ECF would search for the "true" status of cougars in the eastern U.S. and make its findings known.

The Internet has proven to be an invaluable tool in our efforts. We established a website, www.easterncougar.org, which receives thousands of visitors every year and helps educate the public about cougars in the East. We also started two very popular listservs, "ecougar" and "eastern-cougar," which continue to prosper. Email plays a tremendous role in keeping everyone up to date and informed. I don't know if the ECF would have ever been formed without the help of cyberspace.

Taking an active role in searching for cougars led the ECF to pursue grants to purchase some automatic remote cameras. In 2003, we purchased twenty such cameras. A field advisory committee was formed consisting of cougar experts and state and federal wildlife agencies. These cameras were deployed for six months in a remote area of West Virginia, but unfortunately, no confirmable cougars were photographed. The camera project will continue as long as funds are available. Also, a number of scats have been collected and sent off to a lab for DNA testing. Results are still pending.

What I hope to accomplish is to someday take away the shroud of mystery that has clouded the controversy of cougars in the East for over a century and determine once and for all the status of cougars in the East. So many questions remain unanswered, and with the technology we have today it would be a shame not to seek out the truth. The evidence is out there, if we will only look for it.

The confirmed evidence that has been gathered so far indicates that we do indeed have some cougars roaming our woods. But are these released or escaped pets, transients from western populations, or remnant natives? Do we have any breeding populations, and if so, where are they? Questions like these continue to drive me, and I can't rest until I find the answers.

Twenty years ago, I looked into the eyes of a cougar in a forest of the eastern U.S. It's a memory that will always stay with me. Such a beautiful and magnificent creature changed my life at that moment and I wouldn't trade that experience for the world. And I want to do everything I can to help its kind survive.

Bibliography

BOOKS

Ackerman, B. B., F. G. Lindzey and T. P. Hemker. "Predictive Energetics Model for Cougars." In *Cats of the World: Biology Conservation, and Management,* edited by S. D. Miller and D. D. Everett. Washington, D.C.: National Wildlife Federation, 1986: 333–352.

Adams, A. Leith. *Field and Forest Rambles with Notes and Observations on the Natural History of Eastern Canada.* London: Henry S. King and Co., 1873.

Allen, G. M. *Extinct and Vanishing Mammals of the Western Hemisphere.* Washington, D.C.: American Committee for International Wildlife Protection, Special Publication 11, 1942.

Alvarez, Ken. *Twilight of the Panther: Biology, Bureaucracy and Failure in an Endangered Species Program.* Sarasota, Fla.: Myakka River Publishing, 1993.

Alvord, C. W., and L. Bidgood. *First Exploration of the Trans-Allegheny Region by the Virginians, 1650–1675.* Cleveland: Arthur Clarke, 1912.

Anderson, Allen E. *A Critical Review of Literature on Puma* (Felis concolor). Denver: Colorado Division of Wildlife, 1983.

Arant, Frank Selman. *The Status of Game Birds and Mammals in Alabama.* Birmingham: Alabama Cooperative Wildlife Research Institute, 1939.

Ash, Thomas. *Carolina, or a Description of the Present State of That Country.* London: 1682.

Audubon, John James, and John Bachman. *The Viviparous Quadrupeds of North America.* New York: J. J. Audubon, 1845–48.

Aughey, Samuel. *Sketches of the Physical Geography and Geology of Nebraska.* Omaha: 1880: 119.

Baird, Spencer Fullerton. *General Report of the North American Collection, Including Descriptions of All Known Species Chiefly Contained in the Museum* [Smithsonian Institute]. Philadelphia: J. B. Lippincott & Co., 1857: 85–86.

Baird, Spencer Fullerton. *Mammals of North America.* Philadelphia: J. B. Lippincott & Co., 1859: 83–86.

Baker, Rollin H. *Michigan Mammals.* East Lansing: Michigan State University Press, 1983.

Banfield, W. F. *The Mammals of Canada.* Toronto and Buffalo: University of Toronto Press, 1974.

Barbour, Philip. *Jamestown Voyages Under the First Charter 1606–1609.* London: Hakluyt Society, 1969.

Barbour, Roger W., and Wayne H. Davis. *Mammals of Kentucky.* Lexington: University of Kentucky Press, 1974.

Barnes, Claude. *The Cougar or Mountain Lion.* Salt Lake City: Ralton Co., 1960.

Baron, David. *The Beast in the Garden: A Modern Parable of Man and Nature.* New York: W. W. Norton & Co., 2004.

Bartlett, Charles A. *Tales of Kankakee Land.* New York: Charles Scribner's Sons, 1904: 95–97.

Bartram, William. *The Travels of William Bartram.* Edited by Mark Van Doren. Macy-Masius, 1928: 34, 63.

Bartram, William, and John Bartram. *Travels Through North and South Carolina, Georgia and Eastern and Western Florida* [1792]. Savannah, Ga.: Beehive Press, 1973.

Bayard, Ferdinand M. *Travels of a Frenchman in Maryland and Virginia— Valley of the Shenandoah* [1791]. Ann Arbor: Edward, 1950.

Beard, D. B. *Fading Trails: The Story of Endangered American Wildlife.* New York: Macmillan, 1942: 109–117.

Beebe, B. F. *American Lions and Cats.* New York: D. McKay Inc., 1963.

Beverley, Robert. *A History of the Present State of Virginia* [1705]. Chapel Hill: University of North Carolina Press, 1947.

Bewick, Thomas. *A General History of Quadrupeds.* Newcastle upon Tyne, England: 1824.

Boardman, G. A. *The Naturalist of the St. Croix.* Bangor, Maine: 1903: 319–321.

Boatwright, Mody, and Donald Day, editors. *From Hell to Breakfast.* Austin: Texas Folklore Society, 1944.

Bolgiano, Chris. *The Appalachian Forest.* Mechanicsburg, Pa.: Stackpole Books, 1998.

Bolgiano, Chris. *Living in the Appalachian Forest: True Tales of Sustainable Forestry.* Mechanicsburg, Pa.: Stackpole Books, 2002.

Bolgiano, Chris. *Mountain Lion: An Unnatural History of Pumas and People.* Mechanicsburg, Pa.: Stackpole, 1995.

Bombonnel. *Bombonnel le Tueur de Pantheres: Ses Chasses Ecrites par Lui-meme.* Paris: L. Hachette, 1863.

Boone & Crockett Club. *North American Big Game.* New York: Charles Scribner's Sons, 1939.

Bossu, M. *Travels in the Interior of North America 1751–62* [1765]. Translated by Seymour Feiles. Norman: University of Oklahoma Press, 1962.

Bradbury, John. *Travels in the Interior of North America in the Years 1809, 1810, & 1811.* London: 1819 [Lincoln: University of Nebraska Press, 1986].

Brickell, John. *Natural History of North Carolina* [1737]. New York: Johnson Reprints, 1969.

Brimley, C. S. *Mammals of North Carolina.* Burlington, N.C.: North Carolina Department of Agriculture, Division of Entomology 2, 1939; and Carolina Biological Supply Co., 1946.

Brock, Stanley E. *Leemo: A True Story of a Man's Friendship with a Mountain Lion.* New York: Taplinger Publishing Co., 1967.

Brock. Stanley E. *More About Leemo: The Adventures of a Puma.* New York: Taplinger Publishing Co., 1968.

Brocke, Rainer, et al. "Restoration of Large Predators: Potentials and Problems." In *Challenges in the Conservation of Biological Resources: A Practitioner's Guide,* edited by D. J. Decker, et al. Boulder, Colo.: Westview Press, 1991.

Bronner, Simon J. *Popularizing Pennsylvania: Henry W. Shoemaker and the Progressive Uses of Folklore and History.* University Park: The Pennsylvania State University Press, 1996.

Brooks, Maurice. *The Appalachians.* Boston: Houghton Mifflin, 1965.

Browning, Meshach. *Forty-four Years of the Life of a Hunter* [1859]. Baltimore: Gateway, 1994.

Bryan, Daniel. *The Mountain Muse, Comprising the Adventures of Daniel Boone; and the Power of Virtuous and Refined Beauty.* Harrisonburg, Va.: Davidson & Bourne, 1813.

Buffon, Georges Louis Leclerc Comte de. *Natural History, General and Particular* [1776]. Translated with Notes and Observations by William Smellie. London: T. Caddell & W. Davies, 1812.

Burnaby, Andrew. *Travel Through the Middle Settlement in North America in the Years 1759 & 1760.* London: 1775.

Burrage, Henry S. *Early English and French Voyages, Chiefly from Hackluyt, 1534–1608.* London: 1906 [New York: Barnes & Noble, 1967].

Burt, William Henry. *The Mammals of Michigan.* Ann Arbor: University of Michigan Press, 1946.

Burt, William Henry, and R. P. Grossenheider. *A Field Guide to the Mammals.* Boston: Houghton Mifflin Co., 1976.

Busch, Robert. *The Cougar Almanac: A Complete Natural History of the Mountain Lion.* New York: Lyons & Burford, 1996.

Butz, Bob. *Beast of Never, Cat of God.* Guilford, Conn.: Lyons Press, 2005.

Byrd, William. *William Byrd's Histories of the Dividing Line* [1728–29]. Raleigh: North Carolina Historical Commission, 1929.

Byrd, William, et al., and Marion Tinling, editor. *Correspondence of the Three William Byrds of Westover, Virginia, 1684–1776.* Charlottesville: Charlottesville Historical Society, 1977.

Cahalane, Victor H. *Mammals of North America.* New York: Macmillan, 1958.

Cahalane, Victor H. "The American Cats." In *Wild Animals of North America,* edited by M. B. Grosvenor. Washington, D.C.: National Geographic Society, 1963.

Cameron, A. W. *A Guide to Eastern Canadian Mammals.* Ottawa: Natural Museum of Canada, 1956.

Campbell, John Wilson. *History of Virginia from Its Discovery Till the Year 1781.* Philadelphia: Campbell & Carey, 1813.

Carter, M. H., editor. *Panther Stories Retold from St. Nicholas.* New York: Century, 1904.

Carver, Jonathan. *Travels Through the Interior Parts of North America in the Years 1766, 1767, 1768.* London: 1781 [Reprinted as *Carver's Travels in Wisconsin,* 1838, and under original title, Minneapolis: Ross & Haines, 1956].

Catesby, Mark. *The Natural History of Carolina, Florida and the Bahama Islands* [1743]. Chapel Hill: University of North Carolina Press, 1985.

Charlevoix, P. de. *Journal of a Voyage to North America* [1720]. Translated from the French. London: Dodsley, 1761.

Chase, Stuart. *Rich Land; Poor Land: A Study of Waste in the Natural Resources of America.* New York: Whittlesey House, 1936: 178–191.

Chateaubriand. *Chateaubriand's Travels in America.* Translated by Richard Switzer. Lexington: University of Kentucky Press, 1969.

Clark, Thomas D. *Travels in the Old South.* Norman: University of Oklahoma Press, 1956.

Clark, Walter van Tilburg. *Schwarze Panther* [Track of the Cat]. Vienna, Austria: Humboldt, 1951.

Clarke, Samuel. *True & Faithful Account of the Four Chieftest Plantations of the English in America.* London: 1670.

Collinson, Peter. *Selected Letters of Peter Collinson 1725–1768.* Philadelphia: American Philosophical Society, 2002.

Columbus, Christopher, and R. H. Major, editor and translator. *Four Voyages to the New World: Letters and Selected Documents.* London Hakluyt Society, 1961 [as *Selected Letters of Christopher Colmbus, With Other Original Documents.* New York: Corinth, 1961].

Conrad, Margaret, editor. *They Planted Well: New England Planters in Maritime Canada.* Fredericton, New Brunswick: Acadiensis Press, 1988.

Cooney, R. *A Compendious History of the Northern Part of the Province of New Brunswick and the District of Gaspe in Lower Canada.* Halifax, Nova Scotia: Joseph Howe, 1832.

Corelli, Marie. *Love of Long Ago, and Other Stories.* London: Methuen & Co., 1920.

Cory, Charles B. *Hunting and Fishing in Florida.* Boston: Estes and Lauriat, 1896: 41–49 and 109–110.

Cory, Charles B. *The Mammals of Illinois and Wisconsin.* Chicago: Field Museum of Natural History 11, 1912: 153 and 180.

Cresswell, Nicholas. *The Journal of Nicholas Cresswell 1774–1777.* New York: The Dial Press, 1924.

Cruickshank, Helen G., editor., *Selected Writings of Philadelphia Naturalists.* New York: Devin-Adair, 1957.

Cutler, B. L., and S. D. Penrod. *Mistaken Identification: The Eyewitness, Psychology, and the Law.* New York: Cambridge University, 1995.

Cuvier, Baron Georges, and E. Griffith. *The Animal Kingdom Arranged by Conformity.* London: Whitaker, 1827: 438–439.

Danz, Harold P. *Cougar!* Athens: Swallow Press/Ohio University Press, 1999.

Dashwood, R. L. *Chiploquorgan, or Life by the Campfire in the Dominion of Canada and Newfoundland.* Dublin: Robert T. White, 1871.

DeGraaf, R. M., G. W. Witman, and D. D. Rudis. *Forest Habitat for Mammals of the Northeast.* Washington, D.C.: U.S. Dept. Agriculture, Forest Service, 1981.

DeKay, James. *Anniversary Address of the Progress of the Natural Sciences in the U.S.* New York: G&C Carvill, 1826 [New York: Arno Press, 1970].

DeKay, James. *Natural History of New-York: Zoology.* New York: Appleton, 1842.

DeKay, James. *The Zoology of New York and the New-York Fauna.* Albany: 1842.

Deurbrouck, Jo, and Dean Miller. *Cat Attacks: True Stories and Hard Lessons from Cougar Country.* Seattle: Sasquatch Books, 2001.

Dionne, C. E. *Les Mammiferes de la Province de Quebec.* Quebec: Dussault & Proulx, 1902.

Dixon, K. R. "Mountain Lion." In *Wild Mammals of North America,* edited by J. A. Chapman and G. A. Feldhammer. Baltimore: Johns Hopkins University Press, 1982.

Doddridge, Joseph. *Notes on the Settlements and Indian Wars of the Western Parts of Virginia and Pennsylvania from 1763 to 1783* [1824]. [Pittsburgh: John S. Ritenour & Wm. T. Lindsey, 1912; and Parsons, W. Va.: McClain Printing Co., 1960].

Doutt, J. Kenneth, Caroline A. Heppenstall, John E. Guilday, and Roger M. Latham, editors. *Mammals of Pennsylvania.* Harrisburg and Pittsburgh: The Pennsylvania Game Commission and Carnegie Museum, Carnegie Institute, 1966.

Dryden, John. *Hind and the Panther, and Other Works.* New York: Garland, 1974.

Du Pratz, M. Le Page. *The History of Louisiana.* Paris: 1758 [English translation of the French edition, London: 1774].

Eastman, Charles A. *Red Hunters and the Animal People.* New York: Harper & Brothers, 1904.

Ely, A., and R. R. M. Carpenter. *North American Big Game*. New York: Scribner's, 1939.

Emmons, Ebenezer. *Report on the Quadrupeds of Massachusetts*. Cambridge, Mass.: 1840: 36.

Esposito, Jackie R., and Steven L. Herb. *The Nittany Lion*. University Park, Pa.: Pennsylvania State University Press, 1997.

Etling, Kathy. *Cougar Attacks: Encounters of the Worst Kind*. Guilford, Conn.: Lyons Press, 2001.

Evers, David C., editor. *Endangered and Threatened Wildlife of Michigan*. Ann Arbor: University of Michigan Press, 1994.

Ewan, Joseph, and Nesta Ewan. *John Banister and His Natural History of Virginia, 1678–1692*. Urbana, Ill.: University of Chicago Press, 1970.

Ewer, R. E. *The Carnivores*. Ithaca: Cornell University Press, 1973.

Ewing, Susan, and Elizabeth Grossman, editors. *Shadow Cat: Encountering the American Mountain Lion*. Seattle: Sasquatch Books, 1999.

Eyes in the Night. New York: Thomas Y. Crowell, 1939: 157–185.

Faull, J. H. *The Natural History of the Toronto Region, Ontario, Canada*. Toronto: Canadian Institute of Toronto, 1913.

Ferrell, Dorothy M. *Bear Tales and Panther Tracks*, Books 1, 2, 3. Atlanta: Appalachian Publisher, 1965, 1968, 1969.

Flint, Timothy. *The First White-Man of the West, or the Life and Exploits of Colonel Daniel Boone*. Cincinnati: 1856: 74.

Force, Peter. *Tracts and Other Papers . . .* [1836]. Gloucester, Mass.: P. Smith, 1963.

Founatain, Paul. *The Great Mountains and Forests of South America*. London: Longmans Green & Co., 1902.

Francis, Di. *Cat Country: The Quest for the British Big Cat*. Newton Abbot, UK: David & Charles, 1983.

Funkhouser, William Delbert. *Wild Life in Kentucky*. Frankfort: Kentucky Geological Survey, 1925: 38–40.

Geological Survey of Ohio. Vol. IV. "Zoology and Botany, Part 1: Zoology." Columbus: Nevin and Myers, State Printers, 1882.

Gesner, A. *New Brunswick, with Notes for Immigrants (Including a Catalogue of Mammals)*. London: Simmonds & Ward, 1847.

Godman. John. *American Natural History*. Philadelphia: Carey & Lea, 1826.

Godman, John. *Rambles of a Naturalist.* Philadelphia: Hogan & Thompson, 1836.

Goldman, Edward A. "Classification of the Races of Puma, Part 2." In *The Puma: Mysterious American Cat,* by Stanley P. Young and Edward A. Goldman. Washington, D.C.: American Wildlife Institute, 1946.

Golley, Frank B. *Mammals of Georgia.* Athens: University of Georgia, 1962.

Goodwin, G. G. *The Mammals of Connecticut.* Hartford: *Bulletin of the State Geological and Natural History Service* 53, 1935: 84–86.

Gordon, Hon. Arthur Hamilton. *Wilderness Journeys in New Brunswick in 1862–63.* St. John: J. and A. McMillan, 1864.

Gosse, P. H. *The Canadian Naturalist.* London: John Van Noost, 1840.

Graham, Gid. *Animal Outlaws.* Collinsville, Okla.: Graham, 1938.

Gray, Lewis Cecil. *History of Agriculture in the Southern United States.* Washington, D.C.: Carnegie Institute, 1933.

Gray, Robert. *Cougar: The Natural Life of a North American Mountain Lion.* New York: Grosset & Dunlap, 1972.

Greenbie, Sydney. "Frontiers in the Fur Trade." In *The Puma: Mysterious American Cat,* by Stanley P. Young and Edward A. Goldman. Washington, D.C.: American Wildlife Institute, 1946.

Greene, Jack. "Recent Developments in the Historiography of Colonial New England." In *They Planted Well: New England Planters in Maritime Canada,* edited by Margaret Conrad. Fredericton, New Brunswick: Acadiensis Press, 1988.

Gregory, T. *Mammals of the Chicago Region.* Chicago: Chicago Academy of Science, 1936.

Griffith, Edward. *General and Particular Descriptions of the Vertebrate Animals—Order Carnivora.* London: 1821: 74–79.

Guggisberg, G. A. W. *Wild Cats of the World.* New York: Taplinger Publishing Co., 1975.

Haig-Brown, Roderick. *Panther.* United Kingdom: Collins, 1946.

Hakluyt, Richard. *Collection of the Early Travels and Discoveries of the English Nation.* Vol. 3, 1810: 333, 373, and 616.

Hakluyt, Richard. *Principal Navigations, Voyages, Traffiques & Discoveries of the English Nation.* Glasgow: 1565.

Hall, Basil. *Travels in North America in the Years 1827 & '28.* Philadelphia: Lea & Carey, 1829.

Hall, E. R., and K. R. Kelson. *The Mammals of North America,* 2nd Edition. New York: John Wiley and Sons, 1981.

Hallock, C. *The Sportsman's Gazetteer and General Guide. . . .* New York: Forest & Stream Publishing Co., 1880.

Hamilton, William J. *American Mammals.* New York: McGraw-Hill, 1939.

Hamilton, William J. *The Mammals of the Eastern United States.* Comstock, N.Y.: Comstock Publishing, 1943.

Hamor, Ralphe. *A True Discourse on the Present State of Virginia* [1615]. Richmond: Virginia State Library, 1957.

Hansen, Kevin. *Cougar, the American Lion.* Flagstaff, Ariz.: Northland Publishing Co., 1992.

Hariot, Thomas. *A Brief and True Report on the Present State of Virginia* [1584]. Raleigh: North Carolina State Department of Archives and History, 1953: 84–85.

Harlan, Richard. *Fauna Americana: Being a Description of the Mammiferous Animals Inhabiting North America.* Philadelphia: Anthony Finley, 1825.

Hayes, Edward. "The Voyages of Sir Humfrey Gilbert, Knight, 1583." In *Early English and French Voyages, Chiefly from Hakluyt, 1534–1608,* edited by Henry S. Burrage. New York: Charles Scribner's Sons, 1906: 177–222.

Haynes, Nelma. *Panther Lick Creek.* Nashville: Abingdon Press, 1970.

Haywood, Charles. *Bibliography of North American Folklore & Folksongs.* New York: Dover, 1961.

Henderson, A. *The Conquest of the Old Southwest: The Romantic Story of the Early Pioneers into Virginia, the Carolinas, Tennessee and Kentucky 1740–1790.* 1920.

Hening, William Waller, compiler. *The Statutes at Large of Virginia, 1619–1792* ["Hening's Statutes"], 13 Vols. New York: AMS Press.

Hewitt, C. Gordon. *The Conservation of Wildlife of Canada.* New York: Charles Scribner's Sons, 1921.

Hibben, Frank C. *Hunting American Lions.* New York: Thomas Crowell Co., 1948.

Hoagland, Edward. *Walking the Dead Diamond River.* New York: Random House, 1973: 46–68.

Hoffmeister, Donald F. *Mammals of Illinois.* Urbana and Chicago: University of Illinois Press, 1989.

Hollingsworth, S. *The Present State of Nova Scotia*. Edinburgh: William Creach, 1787.

Hornaday, W. T. *Our Vanishing Wildlife*. New York: New York Zoological Society, 1913.

Hoyt, William Dana. *Colonel William Fleming's Scientific Observations in Western Virginia*. Ann Arbor: Edwards Brothers, 1941.

Hudson, Charles. *Southeastern Indians*. Knoxville: University of Tennessee Press, 1976.

Hummel, Monte, and Sherry Pettigrew. *Wild Hunters: Predators in Peril*. Toronto: Key Porter, 1991.

Humphreys, Charles R. *Panthers of the Coastal Plain*. Wilmington, N.C.: The Fig Leaf Press, 1994.

Hunt, Leigh. *Hero and Leander, and Bacchus and Adriadne*. London: C & J Ollier, 1819.

Ingersoll, E. *The Life of Animals: The Mammals*. New York: 1906.

Jackson, H. H. T. *Mammals of Wisconsin*. Madison: University of Wisconsin Press, 1961.

James, Edwin, editor, and Stephen H. Long, T. Say, et al. *Account of an Expedition from Pittsburgh to the Rocky Mountains, Performed in the Years 1819 and 1820*. 1823: Vol. 2, 369.

Jardine, Sir William. *Sir William Jardine's Naturalists' Library, The Felidae*. Edinburgh: 1843.

Jefferson, Thomas. *Notes on the State of Virginia* [1784]. Chapel Hill: University of North Carolina Press, 1955.

Jenkins, J. H. *The Game Resources of Georgia*. Atlanta: Georgia Game and Fish Commission, 1953.

Johnson, Samuel, and E. L. McAdam, editors. *Johnson's Dictionary, a Modern Selection*. London: [1755].

Josselyn, John. *New England's Rarities Discovered in Birds, Beasts, Fishes*. London: Printed for G. Widdowes, 1672.

Kalm, Peter. *Travels into North America*. London: Printed for T. Lowndes, 1773.

Keller, W. B. *Under Wilderness Skies*. Toronto: McLelland & Stewart, 1966.

Kerr, R. *The Animal Kingdom, or Zoological System of the Celebrated Linnaeus*. London: 1792.

Kerscheval, Samuel. *History of the Valley of Virginia*. Strasburg, Va.: Shenandoah Publishing House, 1925: 379–380.

King, Major W. R. *The Sportsman and Naturalist in Canada*. London: Hurst & Blacket, 1886.

Kingsbury, Susan Myra, editor. *The Records of the Virginia Company of London,* 4 Vols. Washington, D.C.: Government Printing Office, 1906, 1933, and 1935.

Kirkland, Caroline. *Forest Life*. New York: C. Francis & Co., 1842.

Kirkland, Caroline. *Western World* [1845]. New York: Garrett, 1969.

Knox-Jones, J., and E. C. Birney. *Handbook of Mammals of the North-Central States*. Minneapolis: University of Minnesota Press, 1988.

Kosack, Joe. *The Pennsylvania Game Commission 1895–1995: 100 Years of Wildlife Conservation*. Harrisburg: The Pennsylvania Game Commission, 1995.

Kurten, B., and E. Anderson. *Pleistocene Mammals of North America*. New York: Columbia University Press, 1980.

Lamb, Harold. *The Crusades*. Garden City, N.Y.: Garden City Publishers, 1930.

Lanman, Charles. *Adventures in the Wilds of the United States and British American Provinces*. Philadelphia: 1856: Vol. 1, 352.

Latrobe, Benjamin Henry. *Journal of Latrobe—1796–1820*. New York: Franklin, 1971.

Laudonniere, Rene Goulaine de. *Notable History Containing Four Voyages Made by Certain French Captains unto Florida* [1564–65]. London: 1587.

Lawrence, R. D. *The Ghost Walker*. New York: Holt, Rinehart and Winston, 1983.

Lawson, John. *The History of North Carolina*. London: T. Warner, 1718.

Lawson, John, and F. L. Harris, editors. *Lawson's History of North Carolina* [1709]. Richmond: Garrett & Massie, 1937.

Laycock, George. *The Hunters and the Hunted*. New York: Outdoor Life Books/Meredith Press, 1991.

Lederer, John. *Discoveries of John Lederer, in Three Several Marches from Virginia to the West of Carolina*. London: Printed by J.C. for Samuel Heyrick at Grays-Inne-Gate in Holborn, 1672.

Lee, William. *True and Interesting Travels of William Lee* [1768]. London: T & R Hughes, 1808.

Leopold, Aldo. *Game Management*. New York: Charles Scribner's Sons, 1936.

Le Page du Pratz, Antoine Simon. *History of Louisiana, or of the Western Parts of Virginia and Carolina.* London: 1763.

Lester, C. Edwards. *The Life and Voyages of Amerigo Vespucci.* New York: New Amsterdam Book Company Publishers, 1903.

Linderman, Frank B. *Why the Mountain Lion Is Long and Lean.* New York: Charles Scribner's Sons, 1915.

Lindholdt, Paul J., editor. *John Josselyn, Colonial Traveler: A Critical Edition of Two Voyages to New England.* Hanover: University Press of New England, 1988.

Lindzey, F. G. "Mountain Lion." In *Wild Furbearer Conservation and Management in North America,* edited by M. Novak, J. A. Baker, M. E. Obbard, and B. Malloch. Toronto: Ontario Ministry of Natural Resources, 1987: 657–668.

Linne, Carl von [Carolus Linnaeus]. *Regni Animalis.* Stockholm: 1771.

Linzey, D. W. *The Mammals of Virginia.* Blacksburg, Va.: McDonald and Woodward, 1998.

Lloyd, Owen. *The Panther Prophesy, or A Premonition to All People of Sad Calamities and Miseries Like to Befal These Islands.* London: 1662.

Logan, Kenneth A., and Linda L. Sweanor. *Desert Puma: Evolutionary Ecology and Conservation of an Enduring Carnivore.* Washington, D.C.: Island Press, 2001.

Long, J. *Voyages and Travels of an Indian Interpreter and Trader.* London: 1791. In *Early Western Travels,* by R. H. Thwaites. Cleveland: A. H. Clark, 1904.

Lowery, George H. Jr. *The Mammals of Louisiana and Its Adjacent Waters.* Baton Rouge: Louisiana State University Press, 1974.

Maehr, David S. *The Florida Panther: Life and Death of a Vanishing Carnivore.* Washington, D.C.: Island Press, 1997.

Maehr, David S., R. F. Noss, and J. L. Larkin, editors. *Large Mammal Restoration: Ecological and Sociological Challenges in the 21st Century.* Washington, D.C.: Island Press, 2001.

Maehr, David S., T. S. Hoctor, and L. D. Harris. "The Florida Panther: A Flagship for Regional Restoration." In *Large Mammal Restoration: Ecological and Sociological Challenges in the 21st Century,* edited by David S. Maehr, R. F. Noss, and J. L. Larkin. Washington, D.C.: Island Press, 2001.

Major, R. H., editor. *Select Letters of Christopher Columbus, with Other Original Documents Relating to His Four Voyages to the New World.* London: The Hakluyt Society, 1847.

Marcy, Randolph B. *Exploration of the Red River in Louisiana in Year 1852.* Washington, D.C.: Doc. 54, 1853: 11, 50–55, and 59.

Marcy, Randolph B. *The Prairie Traveler: A Handbook for Overland Expedition with Maps.* New York: Harper & Brothers, 1859: 242.

Marshall, Marilyn. *Cougar or the First Mosquitoes: Tales from the Longhouse.* Sidney, B. C.: Gray's Publishing, Ltd., 1973.

Marshall, Robert E. *The Onza: The Search for the Mysterious Cat of the Mexican Highlands.* New York: Exposition Press, 1961.

Martin, Calvin. *Keepers of the Game.* Berkeley: University of California Press, 1978.

Maxwell, Hu. *The History of Randolph County, West Virginia.* Morgantown: 1898.

McQueen, A. S., and Hamp Mizell. *History of Okefenokee Swamp.* Clinton, S.C.: 1926.

McShea, W. J., H. B. Underwood, and J. H. Rappole, editors. *The Science of Overabundance: Deer Ecology and Population Management.* Washington, D.C.: Smithsonian Institution, 1997.

McWhorter, Lucullus Virgil. *The Border Settlers of Northwestern Virginia, from 1768 to 1795, Embracing the Life of James Hughes and Other Noted Scouts of the Great Woods of the Trans-Allegheny.* Hamilton, Ohio: 1915.

Meisel, Max. *Bibliography of American Natural History.* New York: Hafner Publishing Co., 1967.

Mereness, Newton Dennison. *Travels in the American Colonies.* New York: Macmillan, 1917.

Mighetto, Lisa. *Wild Animals and Environmental Ethics.* Tucson: University of Arizona Press, 1991.

Miller, S. D., and D. D. Everett, editors. *Cats of the World: Biology Conservation, and Management.* Washington, D.C.: National Wildlife Federation, 1986.

Mills, Enos A. *Watched by Wild Animals.* Boston: Houghton Mifflin Co., 1932.

Monroe, A. *New Brunswick, Nova Scotia and Prince Edward Island.* Halifax, Nova Scotia: Nugent, 1855.

Moorehead, Warren K. *A Report on the Archaeology of Maine*. Andover, Mass.: Andover Press, 1922.

Morton, Thomas. *New English Caanan*. London: Charles Green, 1632 [In *Tracts and Other Papers . . .* , by Peter Force. Gloucester, Mass.: Peter Smith, 1693].

Murie, O. J. *A Field Guide to Animal Tracks*. Boston: Houghton Mifflin (Peterson's Field Guide Series, Second Edition), 1974.

Murphy, Robert. *Mountain Lion*. New York: Dutton, 1969.

Murray, Sir Charles Augustus. *Travels in North America During the Years 1834, '35 & '36*. New York: Da Capo Press, 1974.

Nash, C. W. *Manual of Vertebrates of Ontario*. Toronto: Ontario Department of Education, 1908.

Nelson, Edward W. *Wild Animals of North America*. Washington, D.C.: National Geographic Society, 1918.

Nesbit, William H., and Jack Reneau, editors. *Records of North American Big Game,* 9th Edition. Dumfries, Va.: Boone & Crockett Club, 1988.

Newhouse, Sewell. *The Trapper's Guide*. New York: Oakley, Mason & Co., 1869: 58–59.

Novak, M., J. A. Baker, M. E. Obbard, and B. Malloch. *Wild Furbearer Conservation and Management in North America*. Toronto: Ontario Ministry of Natural Resources, 1987: 657–668.

Nuttall, Thomas. *A Journal of Travels into the Arkansas Territory During the Year 1819*. Philadelphia: 1821: 118 and 149.

Ord, George. *A Reprint of the North American Zoology by George Ord, Being an Exact Reproduction* [1815]. Hoddonfield, N.J.: Samuel N. Rhoads, 1894.

Paquet, E., and D. A. Hackman. *Large Carnivore Conservation in the Rocky Mountains: A Long-Term Strategy for Maintaining Free-Ranging and Self-Sustaining Populations of Carnivores*. Toronto and Washington: World Wildlife Fund of Canada and World Wildlife Fund, U.S., 1995.

Parker, Gerry. *The Eastern Coyote: The Story of Its Success*. Halifax, Nova Scotia: Nimbus Publishing, Ltd., 1995.

Parker, Gerry. *The Eastern Panther: Mystery Cat of the Appalachians*. Halifax, Nova Scotia: Nimbus Publishing, Ltd., 1998.

Peattie, D. C., editor. *Audubon's America: The Narratives and Experiences of John James Audubon*. Boston: Houghton Mifflin, 1940.

Pennant, Thomas. *History of Quadrupeds.* London: B. White, 1781: Vol. 1, 289–290.

Perry, W. A. "The Cougar." In *The Big Game of North America,* edited by G. O. Shields. Chicago: 1890: 405–427.

Peterson, R. L. *The Mammals of Eastern Canada.* Toronto: Oxford Press, 1966.

Philp, James, and William D. Haley, editors. *Philp's Washington Described.* New York: Rudd & Carleton, 1861: 22.

Pliny the Elder. *The Natural History of Pliny.* Translated by John Bostock and H. T. Riley. London: H. G. Bohn, 1855.

Priest, Josiah. *Stories of the Revolution.* Albany: Hoffman & White, 1838.

Quinn, David Beers. *Roanoke Voyages, 1584–1590; Documents to Illustrate the English Voyages.* London: Hakluyt Society, 1955.

Ramsey, J. G. M. *The Annuals of Tennessee to the End of the 18th Century.* Philadelphia: 1853.

Ratti, J. T., and E. O. Garten. "Research and Experimental Design." In *Research and Management Techniques for Wildlife and Habitat,* edited by T. A. Bookhout. Bethesda, Md.: The Wildlife Society, 1994: 1–23.

Ray, John. *Synopsis Methodica Animalium Quadrupedum.* London: Robert Southwell, 1693 [New York: Arno Press, 1978].

Ray, John, and Edwin Lankester, editors. *The Correspondence of John Ray.* London: The Ray Society, 1848.

Read, J. D. "Understanding Bystander Misidentifications: The Role of Familiarity and Contextual Knowledge." In *Adult Eyewitness Testimony: Current Trends and Developments,* edited by D. F. Ross, J. D. Read, and M. P. Toglia. New York: Cambridge University Press, 1994: 56–79.

Rhoades, Samuel Nicholson. *The Mammals of Pennsylvania and New Jersey.* Philadelphia: 1903.

Richter, Conrad. *Trees* (The Awakening Land series). New York: Knopf, 1940.

Roberts, Sir Charles G. D. *Around the Camp-Fire.* Boston: Thomas W. Crowell & Co., 1896.

Roberts, Sir Charles G. D. *Kindred of the Wild.* New York: Stitt, 1905.

Roberts, Sir Charles G. D. *The Watchers of the Camp-Fire.* Boston: The Page Co., 1902.

Roberts, Jerry. *Rain Forest Bibliography: An Annotated Guide to Over 1,600 Nonfiction Books About Central and South American Jungles.* Jefferson, N.C.: McFarland & Company, Inc., 1999.

Robertson, William. *History of America.* London: Strahan, 1778.

Rogers, Robert. *Concise Account of North America.* London: 1765.

Rogers, Robert. *Journals* [1765]. New York: Corinth, 1961.

Roosevelt, Theodore. *The Wilderness Hunter.* New York: G. P. Putnam's Sons, 1893.

Ross, D. F., J. D. Read, and M. P. Toglia, editors. *Adult Eyewitness Testimony: Current Trends and Developments.* New York: Cambridge University Press, 1994.

Rowland, Beryl. *Animals with Human Faces: A Guide to Animal Symbolism.* Knoxville: University of Tennessee Press, 1973.

Ruggiero, Leonard F., Keith B. Aubry, Stephen W. Buskirk, Gary M. Koehler, Charles R. Krebs, Kevin S. McKelvey, and John R. Squires. *Ecology and Conservation of Lynx in the United States.* Boulder: University Press of Colorado and the U.S. Department of Agriculture Rocky Mountain Research Station, 1999.

Russell, K. R. "Mountain Lion." In *Big Game of North America: Ecology and Management,* by J. L. Schmidt and D. L. Gilbert. Harrisburg: Stackpole Books, 1978.

Sally, Alexander S. *Narratives of Early Carolina.* New York: Charles Scribner's Sons, 1911.

Savage, D. E., and D. E. Russell. *Mammalian Paleofaunas of the World.* Reading, Mass.: Addison-Wesley Publishing Co., 1983.

Schlebecher, John T. *Bibliography of Books and Pamphlets of the History of Agriculture in the United States 1607–1967.* Santa Barbara, Calif.: Smithsonian, 1969.

Schoepf, David Johann. *Travels in the Confederation, 1783–1784.* Philadelphia: 1911: 107–108.

Schultz, Christian. *Travels on an Inland Voyage Through New York, Pennsylvania, Virginia, Ohio, Kentucky & Tennessee 1807 & 8.* New York: Riley, 1810.

Schwaab, Eugene Lincoln. *Travels in the Old South, Selected from Periodicals of the Times.* Lexington: University of Kentucky Press, 1973.

Schwartz, C. W., and E. R. Schwartz. *The Wild Animals of Missouri.* Jefferson City, Mo.: University of Missouri Press, 1959.

Scott, Joseph A. *A Geographical Description of the States of Maryland and Delaware.* 1807.

Scott, William Berryman. *A History of Land Mammals in the Western Hemisphere.* New York: Macmillan Co., 1929.

Sealander, J. A. *A Guide to Arkansas Mammals.* Conway, Ark.: River Road Press, 1979.

Seton, Ernest Thompson. *The Lives of Game Animals.* Boston: Charles T. Branford Co., 1925 [also Garden City, N.Y.: Doubleday Doran & Co., 1929].

Shaw, Harley G. *Soul Among Lions: The Cougar as Peaceful Adversary.* Boulder, Colo.: Johnson Books, 1989.

Sheilds, G. O., editor. *The Big Game of North America.* Chicago: Rand McNally & Co., 1890: 405–427.

Shermer, M. *Why People Believe Weird Things: Pseudoscience, Superstition, and Other Confusions of Our Time.* New York: W.H. Freeman, 1997.

Shoemaker, Henry W. *Extinct Pennsylvania Animals, Part I: The Panther and the Wolf.* Altoona, Pa.: Altoona Tribune Publishing Co., 1917 [reprinted, Baltimore: Gateway, 1993].

Shoemaker, Henry W. *In the Seven Mountains.* Reading, Pa.: Bright Printing, 1913.

Shoemaker, Henry W. *The Pennsylvania Lion or Panther.* Altoona, Pa.: Altoona Tribune Publishing Co., 1914.

Shoemaker, Henry W. *Stories of Pennsylvania Animals.* Altoona, Pa.: Altoona Tribune Publishing Co., 1913.

Shrigley, Nathaniel. *A True Relation of Virginia and Maryland.* London: Printed by Tho. Milbourn for Thomas Hudson, Book-binder, 1669.

Shuker, Karl P. N. *Mystery Cats of the World: From Blue Tigers to Exmoor Beasts.* London: Robert Hale, 1989.

Silver, Helenette. *History of New Hampshire Game and Furbearers.* Concord: Survey No. 6, New Hampshire Fish and Game Department, 1957.

Small, H. Beaumont. *The Animals of North America.* Montreal: John Lovell, 1864: 48–50.

Smith, James. *Account of the Remarkable Occurrences in the Life & Travels of Col. James Smith.* Philadelphia: J. Grigg, 1831.

Smith, Captain John, and Edward Arbor, editors. *Captain John Smith's Works (1608–1631).* In *The Puma: Mysterious American Cat,* by Stanley P. Young and Edward A. Goldman. Washington, D.C.: American Wildlife Institute, 1946.

Smith, Samuel. *The History of the Colony of Nova-Caesaria or New Jersey.* Burlington, N.J.: James Parker, 1765 [and Philadelphia: David Hall, 1765].

Smucker, Isaac. *Centennial History of Licking County, Ohio.* Newark, Ohio: Clark & Underwood, 1876.

Smyth, John Ferdinand Dalziel. *Tour in the United States of America.* London: G. Robinson, 1784.

Spargo, John. *The Catamount in Vermont.* Montpelier: State of Vermont Free Public Library Commission, 1950.

Sparke, John. "The Voyages Made by M. John Hawkins Esquire, 1565." In *Early English and French Voyages, Chiefly from Hakluyt, 1534–1608,* edited by Henry S. Burrage. New York: Charles Scribner's Sons, 1906: 113–132.

Spelman, Henry. *Relation of Virginia* [1609]. London: Chiswick Press, 1872.

Springer, John. *Forest Life and Forest Trees.* New York: Harper & Bros., 1851.

Stearns, William P. *Science in the British Colonies of America.* Urbana, Ill.: University of Illinois Press, 1970.

Stone, Witmer, and William Everett Cram. *American Mammals.* New York: Doubleday, Page & Co., 1903: 290–291.

Strachey, William. *Historie of Travell into Virginia Britannia* [1612]. London: Hakluyt Society, 1953.

Swanton, John Reed. *Indians of the Southeastern United States.* Washington, D.C.: Government Printing Office, 1946.

Swem, E. G., editor. *Brothers of the Spade; Correspondence of Peter Collinson of London and John Custis of Williamsburg, Virginia.* Barre, Mass.: Proceedings of the American Antiquarian Society, 1957.

Thomas, Roy Edwin, editor and compiler. *Authentic Ozarks Stories, Big Varmints: Bears, Wolves, Panthers.* Little Rock: Dox Books, 1972.

Thompson, Ernest Seton [original name]. *The Lives of Game Animals.* Garden City, N.Y.: Doubleday Doran & Co., 1929.

Thompson, Stith. *Motif-Index of Folk Literature.* Bloomington: Indiana University Press, 1966.

Thompson, Zadock. *The Natural History of Vermont* [1853]. Rutland, Vt.: reprint 1972: 37.

Thomson, William. *Great Cats I Have Met; Adventures in Two Hemispheres.* Boston: Alpha Publishing Co., 1896.

Thwaites, Reuben G., editor. *Early Western Travels 1748–1846,* 32 Vols. Cleveland: 1904–07.

Timberlake, Henry, and Samuel Cole Williams, editors. *Lieutenant Henry Timberlake's Memoirs, 1756.* Johnson City, Tenn.: Watauga, 1927.

Tinling, Marion, editor. *The Correspondence of the Three William Byrds of Westover, Virginia, 1684–1776.* Charlottesville: University of Virginia Press for Virginia Historical Society, 1977.

Tinsley, Jim Bob. *The Puma, Legendary Lion of the Americas.* El Paso: Texas Western Press/University of Texas at El Paso, 1987.

Tome, Philip. *Pioneer Life: or, Thirty Years a Hunter* [1854]. Baltimore: Gateway Press, 1992.

Torres, Steve. *Mountain Lion Alert: Safety Tips for Yourself, Your Children, Your Pets and Your Livestock in Lion Country.* Helena, Mont.: Falcon, 1997.

Turnbo, Silas Claborn, and Desmond Walls Allen, editors. *Turnbo's Tales of the Ozarks: Panther Stories.* Conway, Ark.: Arkansas Research, 1989.

Uttal, W. R. *A Taxonomy of Visual Processes.* Hillsdale, N.J.: Lawrence Erlbaum, 1981.

Van der Donck, Adriean. *A Description of the New Netherlands.* Amsterdam: 1656.

Vespucci, Amerigo. *First Four Voyages of Amerigo Vespucci* [Florence: 1505–6]. London: B. Quaritch, 1893.

Vosburgh, John R. *Texas Lion Hunter.* San Antonio: Naylor Co., 1949.

Walker, E. P. *Mammals of the World.* Baltimore: Johns Hopkins University Press, 1964.

Warden, D. B. *Statistical, Political and Historical Account of the United States of North America, From the Period of Their First Colonization to the Present Day.* Edinburgh: 1819.

Warren, Louis S. *The Hunter's Game: Poachers and Conservationists in Twentieth-Century America.* New Haven: Yale University Press, 1997.

Webber, C. W. *Hunter-Naturalist: Romance of Sporting, or Wild Scenes and Wild Hunters.* Philadelphia: J. W. Bradley, 1851.

Webster, David, James F. Parnell, and Walter C. Biggs Jr. *Mammals of the Carolinas, Virginia, and Maryland.* Chapel Hill: University of North Carolina Press, 2004.

Whitaker, Alexander. *Good News from Virginia.* London: William Welby, 1613.

Wied-Neuwied, Maximillian. *Travels in the Interior of North America.* Cleveland: A. H. Clark, 1906.

Wilcox, Alvin H. *A Pioneer History of Becker County, Minnesota.* St. Paul: Pioneer Press, 1907: 73–76.

Wildman, Edward Embree. *Penn's Woods, 1682–1932.* Philadelphia: Privately published, 1944: 14.

Williams, Samuel Cole. *Beginnings of West Tennessee: In the Land of the Chickasaws, 1541–1841.* Johnson City, Tenn.: Watange Press, 1930.

Wood, J. G. *Illustrated Natural History.* London: Routledge, 1871.

Wood, William. *New England's Prospect.* London: 1639 [Amsterdam: Da Capo Press, 1968].

Wright, Bruce S. *The Eastern Panther: A Question of Survival.* Toronto: Clarke, Irwin & Co., Ltd., 1972.

Wright, Bruce S. *The Ghost of North America: The Story of the Eastern Panther.* New York: Vantage Press, 1959.

Wrigley, Robert E., and Robert W. Nero. *Manitoba's Big Cat: The Story of the Cougar in Manitoba.* Winnipeg: Manitoba Museum of Man and Nature, 1982.

Young, Stanley P. *Sketches of American Wildlife.* Baltimore: The Monumental Press, 1946.

Young, Stanley P., and Edward A. Goldman. *The Puma: Mysterious American Cat.* Washington, D.C.: American Wildlife Institute, 1946 [New York: Dover, 1964].

Zeigler, Wilbur Gleason, and Ben S. Grosscup. *The Heart of the Alleghenies; or Western North Carolina.* Raleigh: A. Williams & Co., 1883.

PERIODICALS

Allen, J. A. "The Former Range of Some New England Carnivorous Mammals." *American Naturalist* 10, 1876: 708–715.

Allen, Thomas B. "Vanishing Wildlife of North America." Washington, D.C.: National Geographic Society, 1974.

Ames, C. H. "Maine Panthers Again." *Forest & Stream* 56(20), May 18, 1901: 385.

Anderson, R. M. "Mammals of the Province of Quebec." Ottawa: Society for the Preservation of Canadian Natural History, 1938: 50–131.

Anonymous. [Accounts of Lions]. *Gentlemen's Magazine,* 1749: 89.

Anonymous. [Accounts of Lions]. *Gentlemen's Magazine,* 1750: 8.

Anonymous. [Accounts of Lions]. *Gentlemen's Magazine,* 1772: 169.

Anonymous. "Adirondack Panthers." *Forest & Stream* 10, 1878: 138.

Anonymous. "Adventures with Cougars." *American Field* 21, 1884: 541.

Anonymous. "After a Panther—Banks of the Red River." *American Field* 28, 1887: 390.

Anonymous. "The American Lion." *American Field* 17, 1882: 411.

Anonymous. "The American Panther." *American Nature* 4(11), 1871:692.

Anonymous. "The American Panther." *Penny Magazine* 5, October 22, 1836: 413–414.

Anonymous. "Big Game Near Memphis, Tennessee." *Chicago Field* 13(1), 1880: 11.

Anonymous. "A Camp-Fire Symposium on Cats." *American Field* 21, 1884: 86.

Anonymous. "A Combat with a Puma." *American Field* 28, 1887: 607.

Anonymous. "The Cougar." *Cabinet of Natural History* 1, 1830: 243–245.

Anonymous. "Does the Panther Scream?" *Forest & Stream* 15, 1880: 307.

Anonymous. [Editorial]. *Frontier Palladium.* Malone, N.Y.: August 1, 1850.

Anonymous. "Encounter with a Panther." *Cabinet of Natural History* 1, 1830: 137–140.

Anonymous. "An Encounter with Mountain Lions." *American Field* 24(21), November 21, 1885: 486.

Anonymous. "Fierceness of the Mountain Lion." *Forest & Stream* 77(27), December 30, 1911: 941.

Anonymous. *Forest & Stream* 30, 1888: 493.

Anonymous. "Habits of the Panther." *American Naturalist* 18, 1884: 1160–1164.

Anonymous. "Habits of the Panther." *Forest & Stream* 20, 1883: 344.

Anonymous. "Indian Fur Value Shown in Invoice Left by (Francis) Vigo of Vincennes Three Lifetimes Ago." *Outdoor Indiana* 10(10), November 15, 1943: 3.

Anonymous. "The Killing of a Panther [Franklin, Franklin County, N.Y.]." *Malone Palladium,* January 2, 1868.

Anonymous. "Kills a Big Cougar." *Forest & Stream* 83(20), November 14, 1914: 629.

Anonymous. "Mountain Lion Killed in St. Clair County: Huge 109-Pounder Slain by A. D. Hare in His Pasture Near Springville." *Alabama Conservation* 19, 1948.

Anonymous. "Mysterious Monster *(Felis concolor)*." *Field & Stream* 20, 1883: 48.

Anonymous. "On the Hunting of the Puma." *Longman's Magazine,* September 1886.

Anonymous. "A Panther Hunt." *Forest & Stream* 12, 1879: 157 [originally from *Knickerbocker's Magazine,* 1855].

Anonymous. "The Panther in Canada." *Biological Review of Ontario* 1(3), July 1894: 49–50.

Anonymous. "Panthers in Alabama." *Alabama Conservation* 27(5), 1956: 26.

Anonymous. "A Texas Panther Hunt." *Forest & Stream* 4(2), February 18, 1875: 19.

Anonymous. "These Were Former Pennsylvanians." [Pennsylvania] *Game News* 15(9), December 1944: 21.

Anonymous. "White Mountain Lions." *American Field* 22, 1883: 201.

B., P. "Mountain Lions and Deer." *Forest & Stream* 30, 1888: 243.

Bach, Ernest. "Destruction of Game by Predatory Animals." *Outdoor Life* 43(3), March 1919: 166.

Backus, William. "Persistent Reports Bring Us the Mountain Lion." *New Jersey Outdoors* 6(7), January 1956: 12–13.

Bailey, Vernon. "Cave Life of Kentucky." *American Midland Naturalist* 14(5), 1933: 47.

Barnhurst, D., and F. G. Lindzey. "Detecting Female Mountain Lions with Kittens." *Northwest Science* 63, 1989: 35–37.

Batty, J. H. "The *Felis concolor* or Panther." *American Sportsman* 4(4), New Series No. 30, Saturday, April 25, 1874: 51.

Batz, Bob Jr. "Do Panthers Really Roam the Big East? This Week's Eastern Cougar Conference Continues the Exploration of Whether They Do, Could and Should." *Pittsburgh Post-Gazette,* April 25, 2004: G-1, 10–11.

Batz, Bob Jr. "What's New, Pussycat? A Mountain Lion Sanctuary." *Pittsburgh Post-Gazette,* April 25, 2004: G11.

Beier, Paul. "Cougar Attacks on Humans in the United States and Canada." *Wildlife Society Bulletin* 19, 1991: 403–412.

Beier, Paul. "Determining Minimum Habitat Areas and Habitat Corridors for Cougars." *Conservation Biology* 7(1), March 1993: 94–108.

Beier, Paul. "Dispersal of Juvenile Cougars in Fragmented Habitat." *Journal of Wildlife Management* 59(2), 1995.

Beier, Paul, with Dave Choate and Reginald Barrett. "Movement Patterns of Mountain Lions During Different Behaviors." *Journal of Mammalogy* 76(4), 1995.

Belden, R. C., and Bruce W. Hagedorn. "Feasibility of Translocating Panthers into Northern Florida." *Journal of Wildlife Management* 57, 1993: 388–397.

Berg, R. L., L. L. McDonald, and M. D. Strickland. "Distribution of Mountain Lions in Wyoming as Determined by Mail Questionnaire." *Wildlife Society Bulletin* 11, 1983: 265–268.

Bigony, Mary-Love. "Cat of Controversy." *Texas Parks & Wildlife,* April 1993: 4–11.

Boardman, G. A. "St. Croix Mammals." *Calais Times,* Calais, Maine, November 22, 1899.

Bodo, Pete. "Ghost of Supposedly Extinct Cat Leaves a Real Devil of a Void." *New York Times,* September 12, 1993: VIII 13.

Brazier, F. "A Mountain Lion Near Regina." *Blue Jay* 18, 1960: 182.

Brocke, Rainer H., and Fred G. Van Dyke. "Eastern Cougars: The Verifiability of the Presence of Isolated Individuals Versus Populations (Comment on Downing, *Cryptozoology,* 3:31–49, 1984)." *Cryptozoology* 4, 1985:102–105.

Brodie, William. "The Panther in Ontario." *Biological Review of Ontario* 1(2), 1894: 27–28.

Bruce, E. C. "A Dish of Capon." *Harper's New Monthly Magazine,* April 1861.

Bue, G. T., and M. H. Stenlund. "Recent Records of the Mountain Lion, *Felis concolor,* in Minnesota." *Journal of Mammalogy* 34, 1953: 390–391.

Bull, Charles Livingston. "The Puma." *The Century Magazine,* November 1913.

Cahalane, Victor H. "Cougars *(Felis concolor)* in the U.S. Are Barely Holding Their Own." *Audubon,* May 67(2), 1965: 108–109.

Calcutt, John. "The American Panther." *Biological Review,* Toronto 1(2), April 1894: 23–26.

Cardoza, James E., and Susan A. Langlois. "The Eastern Cougar: A Management Failure?" *Wildlife Society Bulletin* 30(1), 2002: 265–273.

Carroll, Christine. "Cat Fight." *Texas Monthly,* June 1993:50–61.

Carter, B. C., and T. G. Dilworth. "A Simple Technique for Revealing the Surface Pattern of Hair." *American Midland Naturalist* 85(1), 1971: 260–262.

"Causes of Discontent in Virginia, 1676." *Virginia Magazine of History and Biography,* 1894–95: 289.

Cawthon, Jack. "The Day the Panther Prowled." *Virginia Conservation* 21, November 1957: 12–13.

Chapman, Frank M. "Who Treads Our Trails." *National Geographic,* September 1927.

Chichester, Bertram. "Cougar Trails." *Rod and Gun in Canada* (Montreal) 45(3), August 1943: 12–13.

Cist, Charles. *Cincinnati Miscellany or Antiquities of the West, and Pioneer History and General and Local Statistics.* Cincinnati: Caleb Clark, Printer, 1845: Vol. 1, 79–80 and 219–220.

Clark, David W., Steffany C. White, Annalea K. Bowers, Leah D. Lucio, and Gary A. Heidt. "A Survey of Recent Accounts of the Mountain Lion *(Puma concolor)* in Arkansas." *Southeastern Naturalist* 1(3), 2002: 269–278.

Clarke, C. H. D. "Cougar in Saskatchewan." *Canadian Field-Naturalist* 56(3), March 1942: 45.

Clarke, C. H. D. "The Puma in Ontario." *Ontario Fish and Wildlife Review* 8(4), Winter 1969: 7–12.

Clayton, Chris. "Iowa Officials Seek Legislation Protecting Stray Mountain Lions; A State Wildlife Chief Is Asking the Public Not to Harm Cougars Unless They Present a Threat." *Omaha World-Herald,* September 30, 2001: Sunrise 3B.

Clayton, John. "Account of Virginia." *Philosophical Transactions of the Royal Society,* No. 210, May 1694.

Clayton, John. "Virginia Field and Game Sports: Description of Them by the Botanist Clayton in 1739." *Virginia Magazine of History and Biography* 7, 1899–1900: 172–174.

Coleman, L. E. "Melanistic Phases of Felidae in Captivity: Preliminary Survey Results." *Carnivore Genetics News* 2, 1974: 209–211.

Conger, W. B. "The Real Cougar." *Nature* 31(8), October 1938: 491–492.

Coper, Edward D. "On the Extinct Cats of America." *American Naturalist* 14(12), December 1880: 834–858.

"The Cougar. *Felis concolor.*" *Cabinet of Natural History and American Rural Sports,* 1832.

"Cougar Kills a Boy." *Okanogan Independent,* Okanogan, Wash.: December 20, 1924.

"Cougar photograph." *Detroit Free Press,* September 13, 1997.

Cram, G. W. "Notes on Some New England Carnivores." *Journal of Mammalogy* 6, 1925:199.

Cram, Gardner. "Panthers in Maine." *Forest & Stream* 56(6), February 16, 1901: 123.

Crane, Jocelyn. "Mammals of Hampshire County, Massachusetts." *Journal of Mammalogy* 12(3), August 1931: 267–273.

Culver, Melanie, W. E. Johnson, J. Pecon-Slattery, and S. J. O'Brien. "Genomic Ancestry of the American Puma *(Puma concolor)." Journal of Heredity* 91, 2000: 186–197.

Cumberland, Roderick E., and Jeffrey A. Dempsey. "Recent Confirmation of a Cougar, *Felis concolor,* in New Brunswick." *Canadian Field-Naturalist* 108(2), 1994: 224–226.

Cunningham, E. B. "A Cougar Kills an Elk." *Canadian Field-Naturalist* 85, 1971: 353–354.

D., E. T., and H. R. R. "Habits of the Mountain Lion." *Forest & Stream* 30, 1888: 289.

Dagg, A. I. "The Walk of Large Quadrupedal Mammals." *Canadian Journal of Zoology* 57, 1979: 1157–1163.

Dahne, Bob. "The Truth About Black Panthers." *Florida Wildlife* 12(6), November 1958: 26–27, 48–49.

Davis, William B., and J. L. Robertson Jr. "The Mammals of Culbertson County, Texas." *Journal of Mammalogy* 25(3), August 1944: 254–273.

Dawson, Jim. "Big Black Cats." *The Outsider* 14, 1980: 6–7.

Dear, L. S. "Cougar or Mountain Lion Reported in North-Western Ontario." *Canadian Field-Naturalist* 69(1), 1955.

Dearborn, Ned. "An Old Record of a Mountain Lion in New Hampshire." *Journal of Mammalogy* 8, November 1927: 311–312.

Decker, D. J., and J. W. Enck. "Human Dimensions of Wildlife: Knowledge for Agency Survival in the 21st Century." *Human Dimensions of Wildlife* 1(2), 1996: 60–71.

Decker, D. J., C. C. Krueger, R. A. Baer Jr., B. A. Knuth, and M. E. Richmond. "From Clients to Stakeholders: A Philosophical Shift for Wildlife Management." *Human Dimensions of Wildlife* 1(1), 1996: 70–82.

Dobie, Frank J. "Tales of the Panther." *Saturday Evening Post* 216(24), December 11, 1943: 23, 27, 60–61.

Doel, Rev. John. "The Panther in Canada." *Biological Review of Ontario* 1(2), 1894: 18–23.

Douglass, E. M. "Oxalate Nephrosis in Captive Pumas." *Modern Veterinary Practice* 61, 1980: 758.

Doutt, J. Kenneth. "Mountain Lions in Pennsylvania?" *American Midland Naturalist* 82, July 1969: 281–285.

Doutt, J. Kenneth. "Mountain Lions in Pennsylvania?" *American Society of Mammalogists,* June 18, 1968.

Doutt, J. Kenneth. "Observations on Mammals Along the East Coast of Hudson Bay and the Interior of Ungava." Pittsburgh: Annals of the Carnegie Museum 33, 1954: 243.

Downing, Robert L. "The Search for Cougars in the Eastern United States." *Cryptozoology,* 1984: 31–49.

Duggan, Joe. "Examinations Reveals [sic] Shot Cat Was Healthy." *Lincoln Journal Star* [Neb.], November 2, 2000: 1.

Dutcher, Jim. "The Secret Life of America's Ghost Cat." *National Geographic* 182(1), July 1982.

East, B. "Cougar Comeback in the East." *American Forests* 85(11), 1979: 54–59.

"The Eastern Puma: Evidence Continues to Build." International Society of Crytozoology Newsletter 8(3), Autumn 1989: 1–8.

Eaton, R. L. "The Status, Management and Conservation of the Cougar in the United States." *World's Cats* 1, 1973: 68–89.

Eaton, R. L. "Why Some Felids Copulate So Much." *World's Cats* 3, 1976: 73–94.

Eaton, R. L., and K. A. Velander. "Reproduction in the Puma: Biology, Behavior and Ontogeny." *World's Cats* 3, 1977: 45–70.

"Eminence Men Forfeit $2,000 Each in 1994 Cougar Killing Case." *Missouri Wildlife* 57(6), December 1996/January 1997.

Ernest, H. B., W. M. Boyce, V. C. Bleich, B. May, S. J. Stiver, and S. G. Torres. "Genetic Structure of Mountain Lion *(Puma concolor)* in California." *Conservation Genetics* 4, 2003: 353–366.

Ernest, Holly. "DNA Analysis for Mountain Lion Conservation." *Outdoor California,* May/June 2000.

Ernest, Holly. "DNA Sampling and Research Techniques." *Outdoor California,* May/June 2000.

Evans, W. F. "The Super-Strength of the Mountain Lion." *Outdoor Life* 49, 1922: 244–345.

Fair, Jeff. "The Wolf Test." *Appalachia,* December 15, 1992: 9–23.

Finley, W. L. "Cougar Kills a Boy." *Journal of Mammalogy* 6(3), August 1925: 197–199.

Fitzhugh, William. "Letters of William Fitzhugh." *Virginia Magazine of History & Biography* 2, 1894: 269.

Foran, D. R., K. R. Crooks, and S. C. Minta. "DNA-Based Analysis of Hair to Identify Species and Individuals for Population Research and Monitoring." *Wildlife Society Bulletin* 25, 1997: 840–847.

Foran, D. R., K. R. Crooks, and S. C. Minta. "Species Identification from Scat: An Unambiguous Genetic Method." *Wildlife Society Bulletin* 25, 1997: 835–839.

Ford, Ray. "The Cougar Leaves a Calling Card." *The Globe and Mail,* Toronto, June 19, 1999: D5.

Frome, Michael. "Panthers Wanted—Alive, Back East, Where They Belong." *Smithsonian* 10(3), June 1979: 82–87.

Garrison, Bill. "Cougar: Dead or Alive?" *Country,* December 1980: 24–36.

G., E. "Capt. Bell's Panther Story." *Forest & Stream* 15, 1880: 110.

G., S. W. "Panthers in Vermont." *Forest & Stream* 5, 1875: 300.

Gelder, Austin. "Hunter's Remote Camera Captures Picture of Mountain Lion." *Arkansas Democrat-Gazette,* August 23, 2003.

Gerson, Helen B. "Cougar, *Felis concolor,* Sightings in Ontario." *Canadian Field-Naturalist* 102(3), 1988: 419–424.

Goertz, John W., and Roland Abegg. "Pumas in Louisiana." *Journal of Mammalogy* 47(4), November 1966: 727.

Goodwin, George Gilbert. "Big Game Animals of the Northeastern United States." *Journal of Mammalogy* 17(1), 1936: 48–50.

Goodwin, George Gilbert. "New Records and Some Observations of Connecticut Mammals." *Journal of Mammalogy* 13(1), 1932: 36–40.

Graham, S. R. "Lion of the Rockies." *Outdoor Life* 41, 1918: 91–94 and 171–174.

Gregory, Tappan. "Lion in the Carmens." *The Chicago Naturalist.* Chicago Academy of Science 1(3), 1938: 70–81 and 110–120.

Guynn, David C., Robert L. Downing, and George R. Askew. "Estimating the Probability of Non-Detection of Low Density Populations." *Cryptozoology* 4, 1985: 55–60.

Hamburg, O. D. S. "Hand to Hand with a Panther." *Forest & Stream* 3, 1874: 67.

Hancock, L. "Is the Controversial Cougar Worth Saving?" *Canadian Geographer* 96, 1978: 46–53.

Handley, C. O. Jr. "The Subspecies of *Felis concolor* Linnaeus." *Eastern Cougar Newsletter* 4, 1981: 2–3.

Handley, C. O. Jr., R. Stafford, and E. H. Geil. "A West Virginia Puma." *Journal of Mammalogy* 42(2), 1961: 277–278.

Harden, Blaine. "Deer Draw Cougars Ever Eastward." *New York Times,* November 12, 2002.

Hardison, Stewart. "Carolina Cougar: An Update." *Wildlife in North Carolina* 40, January 1976: 14–17.

Harlin, J. E. "A Cougar Trailing Incident." *Outdoor Life* 43(6), June 1919: 356–357.

Harper, Francis. "Okefenokee Swamp as a Reservation." *Natural History* 20, January/February 1920: 29–40.

Harper, Francis. "Tales of the Okefenokee." *American Speech* 1, May 1926: 408–420.

Hentcy, Kathleen. "Do Cougars Feel at Home in Vermont?" *Sunday Rutland Herald,* September 18, 1994.

Hibben, Frank C. "The Mountain Lion and Ecology." *Ecology* 20, 1939: 584–586.

Hitchcock, Harold B. "Panthers in Vermont?" *Vermont Natural History.* Montpelier: Vermont Institute of Natural Science, 1986: 9–11.

Hitchcock, Harold B. "A Vermont Road Kill Report: And Other Selected Evidence." *Panther Prints,* Newsletter of the Friends of the Eastern Panther, 1993.

Hobbs, Robert M. "What! Our King of Beasts Is a Coward?" *Northwest Sportsman* 4, 1967: 13–17.

Holt, David. "The Great Cat Scat Mystery." *Eastern Woods & Waters* 9, 1993.

Holt, Ernest G. "Swimming Cats." *Journal of Mammalogy* 13(1), February 1932: 72–73.

Hornocker, Maurice G. "The American Lion." *Natural History* 79(9), 1970: 40–49, 68–71.

Hornocker, Maurice G. "Learning to Live with Mountain Lions." *National Geographic* 182(1), July 1992.

Hornocker, Maurice G. "Winter Territoriality in Mountain Lions." *Journal of Wildlife Management* 33, 1969: 457–464.

Horsford, B. "The Panther's Leap." *Forest & Stream* 20, 1883: 305.

Hughes, J. C. "The American Panther, *Felis concolor.*" *Forest & Stream* 21(6), September 1883: 103.

Hugo, Nancy. "A Catamount Tale." *Virginia Wildlife,* February 1987: 9–13.

Huyghe, Patrick. "Maine Event." *Audubon,* May–June 1994:18, 20.

Jackson, C. F. "Notes on New Hampshire Animals." *Journal of Mammalogy* 3(1), 1922: 13–15.

Jaimet, Kate. "Cougar Believed Extinct May Be Roaming Quebec." *National Post,* Don Mills, Ontario, October 15, 2002.

Jefferson, Thomas. "A Memoir on the Discovery of Certain Bones of a Quadruped of the Clawed Kind Discovered in the Western Parts of Virginia." *Transactions of the American Philosophical Society* 4, 30, 1797.

Johnson, Kirk. "The Mountain Lions of Michigan." *Endangered Species Update* 19(2): 27–31, 2002.

Johnson, Kirk. "The Return of the Great Plains Puma." *Endangered Species Update* 17, 2000: 108–114.

Johnson, M. L., and L. H. Couch. "Determination of the Abundance of Cougar." *Journal of Mammalogy* 35, 1954: 255–256.

Johnson, W. E., Melanie Culver, J. A. Iriate, E. Eizirik, K. L. Seymour, and S. J. O'Brien. "Tracking the Evolution of the Elusive Andean Mountain Cat *(Oreailurus jacobtta)* from Mitochondrial DNA." *Journal of Heredity* 89, 1998: 227–232.

Jones, G. W. "Virginia Was Once England's Wild West." *Nature* 38(6), 1945: 317–320.

K., H. J. "A Chase in Missouri." *Forest & Stream* 30, 1888: 493–494.

Kahn, Jason. "Cougar Kitten Shot Near Adirondack Park." *Northern Forest Forum* 2, 1994.

Keaton, J. B. "Bolivar My Cougar Chum." *Outdoor Life,* December 1940.

Kelly, J. Michael. "Cougars Gone But Not Forgotten." *ESF Quarterly,* Winter 1993.

Kenney, Edward L. "Cougar Buffs Say Delaware Could Be Big Cat Capital." *News-Journal,* Wilmington, Del., June 5, 2003.

Kirk, Jay. "Aslan Resurrected: Searching for Wild Panthers in a Domesticated World." *Harper's Magazine,* April 2004: 49–64.

Knox, Margaret L. "Mountain Lions Meeting Humans Too Often." *Philadelphia Inquirer,* December 30, 1990.

Kurten, B. "Fossil Puma (Mammalia: Felidae) in North America." *Netherlands Journal of Zoology* 26, 1976: 502–534.

Lambert, H. "There Ain't No 'Painters' in West Virginia." *West Virginia Conservation* 19(1), March 1955: 10–12.

Lancia, R. A., C. E. Braun, M. W. Collopy, R. D. Dueser, J. G. Kie, C. J. Martinka, J. D. Nichols, T. D. Nudds, W. R. Porath, and N. G. Tilghman. "ARM! for the Future: Adaptive Resource Management in the Wildlife Profession." *Wildlife Society Bulletin* 24, 1996: 436–442.

LaPointe, D. "The Cat That Isn't." *Michigan Natural Resources Magazine* 47, 1978: 28–30.

Larson, J. S. "Panthers in Maryland?" *The Maryland Conservationist* 43(4), 1963.

Laycock, George. "Cougars in Conflict." *Audubon,* March 1988: 88–95.

Lazenby, John. "The Cat Is Back." *Vermont Life,* Winter 1994.

Leach, J. P. "The Felidae." *American Field* 17, 1882: 432.

Leach, N. P. "Panthers in New England." *Forest & Stream* 73, 1909: 412.

Lee, David S. "Unscrambling Rumors: The Status of the Panther in North Carolina." *Wildlife in North Carolina,* July 1977: 6–9.

Lee, David S., and Ben A. Saunders. "The Status of the Panther *Felis concolor* in North Carolina." Association of Southeastern Biologists Bulletin 25(2), April 1978: 73.

Leopold, Aldo, Lyle K. Sowls, and D. L. Spencer. "A Survey of Overpopulated Deer Ranges in the United States." *Journal of Wildlife Management* 11, 1947: 162–177.

Lesowski, J. "Two Observations of Cougar Cannibalism." *Journal of Mammalogy* 44, 1963: 586.

Lester, Todd, Chris Bolgiano, Jaquetta Lester, Traci Hickson, et al. Eastern Cougar Foundation Newsletter. North Spring, W.V.: 1994–present.

Letourneau, Gene. "Man Claims Photo Proves Maine Has Mountain Lions." *Maine Sunday Telegram,* February 6, 1994.

Lett, William Pittman. "The Cougar or Panther." *Ottawa Naturalist* 1(9), December 1887: 127–132.

Lewis, J. C. "Evidence of Mountain Lions in the Ozarks and Adjacent Areas, 1948–68." *Journal of Mammalogy* 50, 1969: 371–372.

Lindzey, F. G., W. D. Van Sickle, B. B. Ackerman, D. Barnhurst, T. P. Hemker, and S. P. Lang. "Cougar Population Dynamics in Southern Utah." *Journal of Wildlife Management* 58, 1994: 619–624.

Linsley, Rev. James H. "Catalogue of the Mammals of Connecticut." *American Journal of Science & Arts* 83, 1824: 348.

Logan, K. A., L. L. Irwin, and R. Skinner. "Characteristics of a Hunted Mountain Lion Population in Wyoming." *Journal of Wildlife Management* 50, 1986: 648–654.

Lohr, C., W. B. Ballard, and A. Bath. "Attitudes Toward Gray Wolf Reintroductions in New Brunswick." *Wildlife Society Bulletin* 24, 1996: 414–420.

Low, Jim. "Kansas City Cougar Probably Was Wild, from the West; Body Condition and Stomach Contents Point to a Free-Ranging Life." *Missouri Outdoors,* March 28, 2003.

Lucas, J. "The Mountain Lion." *Sports Afield,* December 1948.

Lutz, John, and Linda Lutz. Eastern Puma Network News. Baltimore: July 1989–1994.

Lyon, Marcus Ward Jr. "Mammals of Indiana." *American Midland Naturalist* 17, 1936.

Maehr, David S., E. D. Land, D. B. Shindle, O. L. Bass, and T. S. Hoctor. "Florida Panther Dispersal and Conservation." *Biological Conservation* 106, 2002: 187–197.

Maehr, David S., M. J. Kelly, Chris Bolgiano, Todd Lester, and Helen McGinnis. "Eastern Cougar Recovery Is Linked to the Florida Panther: Cardoza and Langlois Revisited." *Wildlife Society Bulletin* 31, 2003: 849–853.

Mann, T. "The Phantom of Elk Mountain." *South Dakota Conservation Digest* 26(1), 1959: 2–5.

Manville, R. H. "Reports of Cougar in New York." *Journal of Mammalogy* 32, 1951: 227.

Manville, R. H. "The Vertebrate Fauna of the Huron Mountains, Michigan." *American Midland Naturalist* 39(3), 1948: 615–640.

Marge, W. B. "Some Extinct Wild Animals of Tidewater." *Maryland Tidewater News,* Solomons, Md., 2(1), June 1945: 1 and 3.

McCabe, R. A. "The Scream of the Mountain Lion." *Journal of Mammalogy* 30, 1949: 305–306.

McGinnis, Helen. "On the Trail of a Pennsylvania Cougar." *Pennsylvania Game News,* February 1982: 2–8.

McGinnis, Helen J. "A Puma Puzzle." *Mississippi Outdoors,* July/August 1990.

McGuire, J. A. "The Cougar." *Outdoor Life* 37, 1916: 536–544.

McKay, Alex. "The Panther—Still Roaming?" *Adirondack Life* 5, 1974.

McNamee, Thomas. "Chasing a Ghost." *Audubon,* March 1981: 31–35.

Merriam, Clinton Hart. "Remarks on the Fauna of the Great Smokey Mountains." *American Journal of Science,* Series 3, 36(216), 1888:458–460.

Mills, Enos A. "The Mountain Lion." *Saturday Evening Post* 190(38), 1918: 125–126.

Milne, J. W. "The Panther in Canada." *Biological Review of Ontario* 1(4), 1894: 81–83.

"Minutes of the Council and General Court 1622–1629." *Virginia Magazine of History and Biography* (21), 1913: 45–47.

Mooney, Tom. "Vermonters Say Panthers Are Back." *Providence Journal-Bulletin,* April 19, 1995.

Morley, Jack. "A Sea-Going Couger." *Outdoorsman* 86(6), Whole No. 511, November/December 1944: 25–26.

Morris, R. F. "The Land Mammals of New Brunswick." *Journal of Mammalogy* 29(2), 1948: 165–176.

Mosby, J. "Save Arkansas Cougars—Where?" *Arkansas Gazette,* December 31, 1988: 8D.

"Mountain Lion History a Mystery: Do You Know Where This Cat Came From?" *Missouri Conservationist,* September 30, 1999.

Murie, Olaus J. "The Cougar at Bay." *Outing Magazine* 60(5), August 1917: 605–609.

Murphy, D. D., and B. D. Noon. "Coping with Uncertainty in Wildlife Biology." *Journal of Wildlife Management* 55, 1991: 773–782.

Murrill, William A. "American Wild Cats." *Forest & Stream* 97, 1927: 476–478 and 504.

Musgrave, Mark E. "The Mountain Lion Is Just a 'Fraidy Cat.'" *Farm and Fireside* 51(6), 1927: 8–9 and 61.

Nelson, E. W. "The Larger North American Mammals." National Geographic Society. Washington, D.C.: November 1916: 385–472.

Nelson, E. W. "List of the Pumas, with Three Described as New." *Journal of Mammalogy* 10(4), 1929: 345–350.

Nero, R. W., and R. E. Wrigley. "Status and Habits of the Cougar in Manitoba." *Canadian Field-Naturalist* 91, 1977: 28–40.

Noble, R. E. "A Recent Record of the Puma *(Felis concolor)* in Arkansas." *Southwestern Naturalist* 16, 1971: 209.

Orr, James E. "The Last Panther." *Rod & Gun and Motor Sports in Canada* 10(3), August 1908: 266.

Orr, James E. "Old Time Stories of Old Ontario." *Rod & Gun and Motor Sports in Canada* 12(11), April 1911: 1439–1446.

Orr, James E. "Old Time Stories of Ontario." *Rod & Gun and Motor Sports in Canada* 10(3), August 1909: 259–261.

Orr, James E. "Some Old Time Reminiscences of Old Ontario." *Rod & Gun and Motor Sports in Canada* 10(9), August 1909: 840–842.

Osgood, Frederick L. "The Mammals of Vermont." *Journal of Mammalogy* 19(4), November 1938: 435–441.

"Panther Killed." *The Pocahontas Times,* Marlinton, W.Va., Vol. 94, October 1976.

Peach, Arthur W. "The Vermont Panther." *Vermont Life,* Autumn 1955.

Peregrinus. "A Panther Hunt in Pennsylvania." [Dennie's] *Port Folio,* Philadelphia, 31(266), June 1824: 494–499.

Phleps, C. L. "The Panther." *Forest & Stream* 23, 1884: 264.

Pierce, James. "A Memoir on the Catskill Mountains." *American Journal of Science & Art* 6, 1823: 93.

Pike, Jason R., J. H. Shaw, D. M. Leslie, and M. G. Shaw. "A Geographic Analysis of the Status of Mountain Lions in Oklahoma." *Wildlife Society Bulletin* 27(1), 1999: 4–10.

Pocock, R. I. "The Classification of Existing Felidae." *American Magazine of Natural History* Series 8, 20, November 1917: 329–350.

Powell, Addison M. "The American Panther, or Puma." *Outdoor Life* 42(4), October 1918: 243–245.

Powell, Rev. S. A. "Vermont Deer and Panther." *Forest & Stream* 25, 1885: 306.

Preble, Edward A. "The American Cougar." *Nature* 38(3), March 1945: 137.

Preble, Edward A. "A Biological Investigation of the Athabasca-MacKenzie Region." *North American Fauna* 27, Washington, D.C.: Bureau of Biological Survey, U.S. Department of Agriculture, 1908.

Presnall, C. "Applied Ecology of Predation on Livestock." *Journal of Mammalogy* 29, 1948: 155–161.

Quinn, T. "Using Public Sighting Information to Investigate Coyote Use of Urban Habitat." *Journal of Wildlife Management* 59, 1995: 238–245.

R. "Panthers and Deer." *Forest & Stream* 25, 1885: 286.

Radetsky, Peter. "Cat Fight." *Discover,* July 1992.

Rafinesque, Constantine S. "Extracts from the Journal of Mr. Charles Le Raye, Relating to Some New Quadrupeds of the Missouri Region." *American Monthly* 1(6), October 1817: 435–437.

Rafinesque, Constantine S. "On North American Cougars." *Atlantic Journal and Friend of Knowledge,* 1832–33: 51–56.

Reed, Ted, editor. *Panther Prints,* the Official Newsletter of the Friends of the Eastern Panther. Exeter, N.H.: 1990–94.

Regan, Timothy W., and David S. Maehr. "Melanistic Bobcats in Florida." *Florida Field Naturalist* 18(4), 1990: 84–87.

Reilly, E. M. Jr. "New York's Big Spooky Cats." *The Conservationist* 18(4), 1964: 2–4.

Rich, J. G. "The Panther's Scream." *Forest & Stream* 31, 1888: 25.

Ringbolt, Ralph. "A Panther's Serenade." *Forest & Stream* 4(12), April 29, 1875: 181.

Riome, S. D. "Evidence of Cougars Near Nipawin, Saskatchewan." *Blue Jay* 31, 1973: 100–102.

Rioux, Dwayne. "Cougar Sighting? Possible Mountain Lion Prints Studied by State Game Officials." Central Maine Newspapers (*Morning Sentinel* and *Kennebec Journal*), Augusta, Maine, November 19, 2000.

Robinette, W. L., J. S. Gashwiler, and O. W. Morris. "Food Habits of the Cougar in Utah and Nevada." *Journal of Wildlife Management* 23, 1959: 261–273.

Robinette, W. L., J. S. Gashwiler, and O. W. Morris. "Notes on Cougar Productivity and Life History." *Journal of Mammalogy* 42, 1961: 204– 217.

Roof, Jayde C., and David S. Maehr. "Sign Surveys for Florida Panthers on Peripheral Areas of Their Known Range." *Florida Field Naturalist* 16(4), 1988: 81–104.

S., O. D. "Hand to Hand with a Panther." *Forest & Stream* 3(5), September 10, 1874: 67.

Sanja, Mike. "Storyteller." *Pennsylvania Game News* 64, March 1993: 14–18.

SAS Institute, Inc. *SAS Stet Users Guide 6,* 4th Edition. Cary, N.C.: SAS Institute, 1990.

Sass, Herbert Ravenel. "The Panther Prowls the East Again!" *Saturday Evening Post,* March 13, 1954: 133–136.

Sasse, D. B. "Status of Pet Mountain Lions *(Puma concolor)* in Arkansas." *Journal of the Arkansas Academy of Science* 55, 2001:188.

Schorger, A. W. "A Wisconsin Specimen of Cougar." *Journal of Mammalogy* 19(2), May 1938: 252.

Schultz, J. W., and W. J. MacHaffie. "Panthers Climb Trees." *Forest & Stream* 30, 1888: 350 and 411.

Sealander, J. A. "Mountain Lion in Arkansas." *Journal of Mammalogy* 32, 1951: 364.

Sealander, J. A. "A Provisional Checklist and Key to the Mammals of Arkansas (with Annotations)." *American Midland Naturalist* 56,1956: 257–296.

Seddon, P. J., and P. S. Soorae. "Guidelines for Subspecific Substitutions in Wildlife Restoration Projects." *Conservation Biology* 13, 1999: 177–194.

Seidenstecker, J. C. IV, Maurice G. Hornocker, W. V. Wiles, and J. P. Messick. "Mountain Lion Social Organization in the Idaho Primitive Area." *Wildlife Monographs* 35, 1973.

Seidensticker, John, and Susan Lumpkin. "Mountain Lions Don't Stalk People. True or False?" *Smithsonian,* February 1992: 113–122.

Sekeres, Matthew. "Cougar Attacked Me: Cornwall-Area Man." *The Ottawa Citizen,* August 15, 2001.

Shelton, Tom. "Lion." *Wildlife in North Carolina,* September 1973.

Shoemaker, Henry W. "The Panther in Pennsylvania." *Pennsylvania Game News* 13(11), February 1943.

Shoemaker, Henry W. "Those Pennsylvania Panthers." *Frontiers* (Academy of Natural Sciences of Philadelphia), 19, 1954.

Simmons, Morgan. "Evidence Mounting That Elusive Cougars Are Back in Smokies Park." *Knoxville News-Sentinel,* September 22, 2002.

Simms, William Gilmore. "The Cub of the Panther, a Mountain Legend." *The Old Guard,* 12 installments, 1869.

Sinclair, A. R. E. "Science and the Practice of Wildlife Management." *Journal of Wildlife Management* 55, 1991: 767–773.

Sinclair, E. A., E. L. Swenson, M. L. Wolfe, D. C. Choate, B. Gates, and K. A. Crandall. "Gene Flow Estimates in Utah's Cougars Imply Management Beyond Utah." *Animal Conservation* 4, 2001: 257–264.

Smith, R. W. "The Land Mammals of Nova Scotia." *Middle American Naturalist* 24(1), 1940: 213–241.

Smith, Sam J. "Do Mountain Lions Scream?" *Outdoor Life* 42(5), November 1918: 325–326.

Snow, Dave. "A Report of a Cougar Near Port Rexton, Newfoundland." *Osprey* 25, 1994.

Spalding, D. J., and J. Lesowski. "Winter Food of the Cougar in South-Central British Columbia." *Journal of Wildlife Management* 35(2), 1971: 378–381.

Squires, W. A. "Changes in Mammal Populations in New Brunswick." *Acadian Naturalist* 2, 1946: 26–44.

Squires, W. A. "The Eastern Panther Is Not Extinct." *Canadian Geographical Journal* XLI (4), October 1950.

Stearns, Don. "Susquehanna County's Last Mountain Lion." *Montrose Independent,* February 24, 1966.

Stocek, Rudolph F. "The Cougar, *Felis concolor,* in the Maritime Provinces." *Canadian Field-Naturalist* 109, 1995.

Sweanor, L. L., K. A. Logan, and Maurice G. Hornocker. "Cougar Dispersal Patterns, Metapopulation Dynamics, and Conservation." *Conservation Biology* 14, 2000: 798–808.

T., W. "The American Jaguar and Panther (Cougar)." *American Field* 22, 1884: 7.

Tench, C. V. "Cougar Adventures." *Rod & Gun in Canada,* February 1933: 15–17 and 28.

Thomson, Sheila C. "Sight Record of a Cougar in Northern Ontario." *Canadian Field-Naturalist* 88, 1974.

Thoreau, Henry David. "Chesuncook." *Atlantic Monthly,* Boston, June/July/August, 1858.

Thornton, J. F. "Mountain Lion Comeback in Alabama." *Alabama Conservation,* March/April 1956.

Tischendorf, Jay. "The Eastern Panther on Film? Results of an Investigation." *Cryptozoology* 9, 1990: 74–78.

Tischendorf, Jay, editor. *Eastern Panther Update.* Fort Collins, Colo.: 1992–1994.

Tischendorf, Jay, and Donald F. McAlpine. "Melanism in Bobcats: An Addendum." *Florida Field Naturalist* submission, 1994.

Torres, S. G., T. M. Mansfield, J. E. Foley, T. Lupo, and A. Brinkhaus. "Mountain Lion and Human Activity in California: Testing Speculations." *Wildlife Society Bulletin* 24, 1996: 451–460.

Tougias, Robert. "The Eastern Cougar: Legend or Survivor." *Fur-Fish-Game,* December 1993.

Toweill, D. E. "Food Habits of Cougars in Oregon." *Journal of Wildlife Management* 41(3), 1974: 576–578.

Trautman, M. B. "The Numerical Status of Some Mammals Throughout Historic Time in the Vicinity of Buckeye Lake, Ohio." *Ohio Journal of Science* 39(3), May 1939: 136.

Turner, John W., Michael L. Wolfe, and Jay F. Kirkpatrick. "Seasonal Mountain Lion Predation on a Feral Horse Population." *Canadian Journal of Zoology* 70, 1992: 929–934.

Ulmer, Fred A. Jr. "Melanism in the Felidae, with Special Reference to the Genus Lynx." *Journal of Mammalogy* 22, 1941: 285–288.

Van Dyke, Fred G., and Rainer H. Brocke. "Searching Technique for Mountain Lion Sign at Specific Locations." *Wildlife Society Bulletin* 15(2), 1987: 256–259.

Van Dyke, Fred G., and Rainer H. Brocke. "Sightings and Track Reports as Indices of Mountain Lion Presence." *Wildlife Society Bulletin* 15(2), 1987: 251–256.

Van Dyke, Fred G., Rainer H. Brocke, and Harley G. Shaw. "Use of Road Track Counts as Indices of Mountain Lion Presence." *Journal of Wildlife Management* 50, 1986: 102–109.

Van Dyke, Fred G., Ranier H. Brocke, H. G. Shaw, B. B. Ackerman, T. P. Hemker, and F. G. Lindzey. "Reactions of Mountain Lions to Logging and Human Activity." *Journal of Wildlife Management* 50(1), 1986: 102–109.

Virginia Gazette, March 4, 1773: 3.

Vose, C. L. "Cougar on the Bridge." *Forest & Outdoors* 5(5), May 1939: 140.

W., G. S. "Panthers in Vermont." *Forest & Stream* 5, 1875: 300.

Waddell, J. M. "A Panther Hunt in the Canebrake." *Forest & Stream* 28(15), May 5, 1887: 323.

Walker, C. W., L. A. Harveson, M. T. Pittman, M. E. Tewes, and R. L. Honeycutt. "Microsatellite Variations in Two Populations of Mountain Lions *(Puma concolor)* in Texas." *Southwestern Naturalist* 45, 2000: 196–203.

Walker, J. H. "Pioneers and Panthers." *Pennsylvania Game News* 40, February 1960.

Wallace, Joseph. "Has the Big Cat Come Back?" *Sierra,* May–June 1986: 20–21.

Walsh, W. "Panthers Are Popular." *Pennsylvania Game News* 27(1), January 1956: 4–10.

Warren, R. J. "The Challenge of Deer Overabundance in the 21st Century." *Wildlife Society Bulletin* 25, 1997: 213–214.

Weddle, F. "The Ghost Cats of the Yukon." *Defenders of Wildlife News* 40(5), 1965: 53.

White, T. "Cougar Shot at Cutknife, Saskatchewan." *Blue Jay* 34, 1976: 181.

White, T. "Cougars in Saskatchewan." *Blue Jay* 21, 1963: 32–33.

White, T. "History of the Cougar in Saskatchewan." *Blue Jay* 25, 1967: 84–89.

Wobeser, G. "Forensic (Medico-Legal) Necropsy of Wildlife." *Journal of Wildlife Diseases* 32, 1996: 240–249.

Wright, Bruce S. "The Cougar in Eastern Canada." *Canadian Audubon* 27, 1965: 144–148.

Wright, Bruce S. "The Cougar Is Alive and Well in Massachusetts." *Massachusetts Wildlife* 24, 1973: 2–8, 19.

Wright, Bruce S. "Don't Shoot to Prove There Is One." *Hunting and Fishing in Canada,* November 1954.

Wright, Bruce S. "The Fundy Lions." *Field & Stream* 54, September 1948: 118–119.

Wright, Bruce S. "Further Notes on the Panther in the Northeast." *Canadian Field-Naturalist* 67, 1953.

Wright, Bruce S. "The Latest Specimen of Eastern Panther." *Journal of Mammalogy* 42, 1961.

Wright, Bruce S. "Rediscovering the Eastern Panther." *Animals* 6(4), March 1965: 85.

Wright, Bruce S. "Return of the Cougar." *Audubon,* November/December 1960: 262–265 and 292–296.

Wright, Bruce S. "Survival of the Northeastern Panther *(Felis concolor)* in New Brunswick." *Journal of Mammalogy* 29, 1948.

Wright, Bruce S. "The Wild Cats of North America." *Animals,* March 3, 1964: 357–363.

Wright, George M. "Cougar Surprised at Well-Stocked Larder." *Journal of Mammalogy* 15, 1934: 321.

Wright, W. N. "Lynx and Lion." *American Magazine* 62(5), September 1906: 523–529.

Young, Stanley P. "Early Wildlife Americana." *American Forests* 49(8), 1943: 387–389 and 414.

Young, Stanley P. "Mountain Lion Eats Its Kittens." *Journal of Mammalogy* 8(2), May 1927: 158–160.

Young, Stanley P. "The Return of the 'Indian Devil.'" *Pennsylvania Game News* 25(12), December 1954: 8–14.

Young, W. D. "Does the Cougar Scream?" *Outing Magazine* 70(4), July 1917: 480–482.

Z [Letter Writer]. "Mr. Urban." *Gentlemen's Magazine* (42), 1772: 169.

Zuidema, M. "Are There Mountain Lions in Michigan?" *Fur-Fish-Game,* March 2002.

SOCIETY, GOVERNMENT, AND ACADEMIC REPORTS

Adorjian, A. S., and G. B. Kolenosky. "A Manual for the Identification of Hairs of Selected Ontario Mammals." Toronto: *Ontario Department of Lands and Forests Research Report* (Wildlife) 90.

Allen, Glover M. "Extinct and Vanishing Mammals of the Western Hemisphere." Special Publications of the American Committee for International Wildlife Protection 11, December 11, 1942: 233–252.

Allen, Glover M. "Fauna of New England." Boston: *Proceedings of the Boston Society of Natural History* 7, 1904: 21.

Allen, J. A. "Catalogue of the Mammals of Massachusetts: With a Critical Revision of the Species." Cambridge, Mass.: Museum of Comparable Zoology 8, 1869: 153.

Allen, J. A. "Geographic Variation Among North American Mammals, Especially in Respect to Size." Washington, D.C.: Department of the Interior, U.S. Geological and Geographic Survey, Territory 2(4), 1876: 321–322.

Allen, J. A. "Remarks on the Second Collection of Mammals from New Brunswick." Washington, D.C.: *Bulletin of the American Museum of Natural History* 6, 1894: 359–364.

Altherr, Thomas L. "The Catamount in Vermont Folklore and Culture, 1760–1900." In *Proceedings of the Eastern Cougar Conference,* by J. W. Tischendorf and Steven J. Ropski. Erie, Pa.: June 3–5, 1994. Fort Collins, Colo.: American Ecological Research Institute, 1996.

Ames, A. E. "Mammalia of Minnesota." Washington, D.C.: *Bulletin of the Minnesota Academy of Natural Science,* 1874: 68–71.

Bangs, Outram. "The Land Mammals of the Peninsula of Florida and the Coast Region of Georgia." Boston: *Proceedings of the Boston Society of Natural History* 28, 1898.

Beier, Paul, J. E. Borreco, and R. E. Marsh, editors. "Cougar Attacks on Humans: An Update and Some Further Reflections." *Proceedings in the 15th Vertebrate Pest Conference.* Davis, Calif.: University of California at Davis, 1992: 365–367.

Belden, R. C. "How to Recognize Panther Tracks." *Proceedings of the Annual Conference of the Southeastern Fish and Wildlife Agencies* 32, 1978:112–115.

Bischof, R., and B. Morrison. "Status Report on Mountain Lions in Nebraska." In *Proceedings of the Sixth Mountain Lion Workshop,* edited by L. A. Harveson, P. M. Harveson, and R. W. Adams. San Antonio, Tex.: 2000.

Boddicker, M. L. "Mountain Lion: Prevention and Control of Wildlife Damage." Manhattan, Kans.: Great Plains Agricultural Council Cooperative Extension Service, Kansas State University.

Bogue, G., and M. Ferrari. "The Predatory 'Training' of Captive Reared Puma." *World's Cats* 3, Contributions to Status, Management and Conservation. Seattle: *Proceedings of the Third International Symposium on the World's Cats,* University of Washington, April 26–28, 1974, 1976: 36–45.

Bole, B. Patterson Jr., and Philip N. Moulthrop. "The Ohio Recent Mammal Collection in the Cleveland Museum of Natural History." Cleveland: Cleveland Museum of Natural History Science Publication 5(6), September 1942: 83–182.

Bolgiano, Chris, Todd Lester, Donald W. Linzey, and David S. Maehr. "Field Evidence of Cougars in Eastern North America." In *Proceedings in the Sixth Mountain Lion Workshop,* edited by L. A. Harveson, P. M. Harveson, and R. W. Adams. Austin: 2000.

Braun, Clait E., editor. "Mountain Lion–Human Interaction: Symposium and Workshop." Denver: Colorado Division of Wildlife, April 22–26, 1991.

Brayton, A. W. "Report on the Mammalia of Ohio." Columbus: *Geological Survey of Ohio* 4, 1882: 1–185.

Brocke, Ranier H. "Reintroduction of the Cougar *Felis concolor* in Adirondack Park: A Problem Analysis and Recommendations." Albany: Final Report to the New York State Department of Environmental Conservation, 1981.

Brocke, R. H., K. A. Gustafson, and A. R. Major. "Restoration of Lynx in New York: Biopolitical Lessons." *Transactions of the North American Wildlife and Natural Resources Conference* 55, 1990: 590–598.

Brooks, Fred E. "Mammals of West Virginia." Charleston: West Virginia State Board of Agriculture, Report 20, December 20, 1910: 9–30.

Butler, Amos W. "A Century of Changes in the Aspects of Nature." Indianapolis: *Proceedings in the Indiana Academy of Science,* 1895: 31–40.

Cahalane, Victor H. "A Preliminary Study of Distribution and Numbers of Cougar, Grizzly and Wolf in North America." New York: New York Zoological Society, 1964.

Cameron, A. W. "Mammals in the Islands of the Gulf of St. Lawrence." Ottawa: *Natural Museum of Canada Bulletin* 154, Biology Series 53, 1958.

Cartwright, M. E. "Strategic Deer Management Plan." Little Rock: Arkansas Game and Fish Commission, 1999.

Chamberlain, M. "Mammals of New Brunswick." Fredericton, New Brunswick: *Bulletin of the Natural History Society of New Brunswick* 3(4), 1884: 37–40.

Chamberlain, M. "Mammals of New Brunswick." Fredericton, New Brunswick: *Bulletin of the Natural History Society of New Brunswick* 10(2), 1892: 30–33

Colvin, Verplank. "Seventh Annual Report on the Progress of the Topographical Survey of the Adirondack Region of New York to the Year 1879." Albany: Assembly Document 87, March 7, 1879: 159–160.

Committee on Rare and Endangered Wildlife Species. "Rare and Endangered Fish and Wildlife of the United States," Revised Edition. Washington, D.C.: United States Bureau of Sport Fisheries and Wildlife, Resource Publication 34, 1968.

"Conservation Review Update." Newsletter of the Michigan Chapter of the Wildlife Society, Fall 2003.

Cragin, Francis W. "Notes on Some Mammals of Kansas . . ." Topeka: *Bulletin of Washburn College* 1(2), January 1885: 42–47.

Cronan, John M., and Albert Brooks. "The Mammals of Rhode Island." Providence: Rhode Island Department of Natural Resources, Wildlife Pamphlet 6, 1968.

Culbertson, Nicole. "Status and History of the Mountain Lion in the Great Smokey Mountains National Park." Gatlinburg, Tenn.: Management Report 16, National Park Service, 1976.

Culver, Melanie, W. E. Johnson, J. Pecon-Slattery, and S. J. O'Brien. "Genomic Ancestry of American Puma *(Puma concolor).*" Genetic Diversity and Evolution Symposium. University Park, Pa.: Pennsylvania State University, June 1999.

Davis, George W., and Leonard E. Foote. "A History of Wild Game in Vermont." Vermont Fish and Game Service, State Bulletin 11, 1944.

Davis, R. "Giving the Eastern Cougar a Second Chance: A Feasibility Study of Reintroducing the Cougar *(Puma concolor)* into Allegheny National Forest." In *Proceedings of the Eastern Cougar Conference,* edited by J. W. Tischendorf and Steven J. Ropski. Erie, Pa.: June 3–5, 1994. Fort Collins, Colo.: American Ecological Research Institute, 1996: 243–245.

Davis, W. B. "The Mammals of Texas." Austin: *Texas Game and Fish Commission Bulletin* 41,1966.

Dearborn, Ned. "Food of Some Predatory Animals in Michigan." Ann Arbor: School of Forestry and Conservation, University of Michigan, Bulletin 1, 1932: 50.

Deems, E. F. Jr., and D. Pursley, editors. "North American Furbearers: Their Management, Research and Harvest Status in 1976." Washington, D.C.: International Association of Fish & Wildlife Agencies, 1976.

Downing, Robert L. "The Cougar in the East." In *Proceedings of the Eastern Cougar Conference,* edited by J. W. Tischendorf and Steven J. Ropski. Erie, Pa.: June 3–5, 1994. Fort Collins, Colo.: American Ecological Research Institute, 1996: 163–166.

Downing, Robert L. "The Current Status of the Cougar in the Southern Appalachian [sic]." In *Proceedings of Nongame and Endangered Wildlife Symposium.* Athens, Ga.: August 13–14, 1981.

Downing, Robert L. "Eastern Cougar Recovery Plan." Atlanta: U.S. Fish and Wildlife Service, 1982.

Downing, Robert L. "Investigation to Determine the Status of the Cougar in the Southern Appalachians." In *Proceedings of the Eastern Cougar Conference,* edited by J. W. Tischendorf and Steven J. Ropski. Erie, Pa.: June 3–5, 1994. Fort Collins, Colo.: American Ecological Research Institute, 1996: 46–49.

Dusi, J. L. "Mammals: Endangered Species." Tuscaloosa: *Bulletin of the Alabama Museum of Natural History* 2, 1976: 90.

"Eagle, Peregrine, Red-Cockade, and Cougar Among Protected Species in Virginia." *Endangered Species Technical Bulletin* 4(2), February 1979: 3, 6.

Eaton, R. L., and J. R. van Oosten. "The Status and Conservation of North America's Cats." Washington, D.C.: Wild Canid Survival and Research Center, Symposium on Endangered and Threatened Species of North America, 1974.

Evermann, B. W., and Amos W. Butler. "Preliminary List of Indiana Mammals." Indianapolis: *Proceedings of the Indiana Academy of Science,* 1893: 120–139.

Faulkner, C. E. "The Legal Status of Wild Cats in the United States." Portland, Ore.: Transcript of the North American Wildlife and Natural Resource Conference, 1971.

Faull, J. H. "The Natural History of the Toronto Region, Ontario, Canada." Toronto: Canadian Institute, 1913: 14.

Foote, Leonard E. "A History of Wild Game in Vermont." Montpelier: Vermont Fish and Game Service, State Bulletin, Pittman-Robertson Series 11, 1944: 46.

Fuller, D. "Report on the Period of Gestation of the Puma, *Felis concolor.*" London: *Proceedings of the Committee of Science & Correspondence,* Zoological Society 2, 1832: 62.

Ganong, W. F. "On Reported Occurrences of the Panther *(Felis concolor)* in New Brunswick." Fredericton, New Brunswick: *Bulletin of the Natural History Society of New Brunswick* 21, 1903: 82–86.

Garman, H. "A Preliminary List of the Vertebrate Animals of Kentucky." Salem, Mass.: *Bulletin of the Essex Institute* 26 (1,2,3), January, February, March, 1894.

Gilpin, J. B. "On the Mammalia of Nova Scotia." Halifax: *Transactions of the Nova Scotia Institute of Science* 1(3), 1864: 8–15.

Gilpin, J. B. "On the Mammalia of Nova Scotia." Halifax: *Transactions of the Nova Scotia Institute of Science* 2(2), 1868: 58–69.

Goldman, Edward A. "A New Puma from Texas." Washington, D.C.: *Proceedings of the Biological Society* 49, August 22, 1936: 137–138.

Goldman, Edward A. "A Substitute Name for *Felis concolor youngi.*" Washington, D.C.: *Proceedings of the Biological Society of Washington* 51, March 18, 1938: 63.

Golley, F. B. "South Carolina Mammals." Charleston: Charleston Museum, Contribution XV, 1966.

Greenwell, J. R. "The Place of the Eastern Puma in the Natural History of the Larger Felids." In *Proceedings of the Eastern Cougar Conference,* edited by J. W. Tischendorf and Steven J. Ropski. Erie, Pa.: June 3–5, 1994. Fort Collins, Colo.: American Ecological Research Institute, 1996: 9–29.

Gregory, Tappan. "Mammals of the Chicago Region." Chicago: Chicago Academy of Science 7 (2 and 3), July 1936: 21.

Hahn, Walter Lewis. "The Mammals of Indiana." Indianapolis: 33rd Annual Report, Indiana Department of Geology and Natural Resources, 1909: 540–542.

Hall, Archibald. "On the Mammals and Birds of the District of Montreal." Montreal: *Canadian Natural and Geological and Proceedings in Natural History Society of Montreal* 6, 1861: 284–309 and 298–299.

Harper, Francis. "The Mammals of the Okeefenokee Swamp Region of Georgia." Boston: *Proceedings of the Boston Society of Natural History* 37, 1927: 317–320.

Harveson, L. A., P. M. Harveson, and R. W. Adams, editors. Austin: *Proceedings in the Sixth Mountain Lion Workshop,* 2000.

Harvey, M. J., and S. W. Barkley. "Distribution and Status of Endangered Mammals in Arkansas." Little Rock: Arkansas Game and Fish Commission, 1979: 10.

Hebert, D., and L. Lay, editors. "Cougar-Human Interactions in British Columbia." In Southern California Chapter of The Wildlife Society. *Proceedings of the Fifth Mountain Lion Workshop,* February 27–March 1, 1996, 1997: 44–45.

Heist, Edward J., Jennifer Bowles, and Alan Woolf. "Record of a North American Cougar *(Puma concolor)* from Southern Illinois." *Transactions of the Illinois State Academy of Science* 94(4), 2001: 227–229.

Henderson, F. Robert. "Update: Puma in Kansas?" Manhattan: Kansas State University Cooperative Extension Service, 1992.

Herrick, C. L. "Mammals of Minnesota." Minneapolis: *Bulletin of the Geological and Natural History Survey* 7, 1892: 68–70.

Herrman, Augustin. "Map of Virginia & Maryland." 1673.

Hibbard, Claude W. "A Checklist of Kansas Mammals." Lawrence: *Transactions of the Kansas Academy of Sciences* 47, 1943: 61–88.

Hitchcock, Charles H. "Catalogue of the Mammals of Maine." Portland: *Proceedings in the Portland Society of Natural History* 1, 1862: 65.

Hollister, Ned. "The Louisiana Puma." Washington, D.C.: *Proceedings of the Biological Society of Washington* 24, June 16, 1911: 141.

Hollister, Ned. "Notes on Wisconsin Mammals." *Bulletin of the Natural History Society of Wisconsin* 4(3–4), 1908: 141.

Howell, Arthur H. "A Biological Survey of Alabama." *North American Fauna* 45. Washington, D.C.: Bureau of Biological Survey, U.S. Department of Agriculture, 1921: 1–88 and 41–42.

Iriarte, J. Augustin, William L. Franklin, Warren E. Johnson, and Kent H. Redford. "Biogeographic Variation of Food Habits and Body Size of the American Puma." *Oecologia* 85(2), 1990: 185–190.

Jackson, Hartley H. T. "Conserving Endangered Wildlife Species." *Transactions of the Wisconsin Academy of Science Arts and Letters* 35, 1943: 61–90.

Jackson, Hartley H. T. "A Preliminary List of Wisconsin Mammals." *Bulletin of the Wisconsin Natural History Society* 6(1–2), 1908: 14.

Jackson, Hartley H. T. "The Wisconsin Puma." *Proceedings in the Biological Society of Washington* 68, 1955: 149–150.

Jenkins, J. H. "The Status and Management of the Bobcat and Cougar in the Southeastern United States." In *Proceedings of the Symposium on the Native Cats of North America; Their Status and Management,* edited by S. E. Jorgensen and L. D. Mech. Minneapolis and St. Paul: U.S. Fish & Wildlife Service Bureau of Sport Fisheries and Wildlife, 1971.

Jewell, P. A. "The Concept of Home Range in Mammals." London: Symposium of the Zoological Society of London 18, 1966: 85–109.

Johnson, Maynard S. "Common Injurious Mammals of Minnesota." St. Paul.

Jones, J. K. Jr. "Distribution and Taxonomy of Mammals of Nebraska." Lawrence: University of Kansas Publications, Museum of Natural History 16, 1964.

Jordan, D. B. "Identification and Evaluation of Candidate Florida Panther Population Reestablishment Sites." In *Proceedings of Florida Panther Conference,* edited by D. B. Jordan. U.S. Fish and Wildlife Service, 1994: 106–120.

Jordan, D. B. "Preliminary Analysis of Potential Florida Panther Reintroduction Sites." United States Fish and Wildlife Service, 1993.

Jorgensen, S. E., and L. D. Mech, editors. *Proceedings of the Symposium on the Native Cats of North America; Their Status and Management.* Minneapolis and St. Paul: U.S. Fish and Wildlife Service Bureau of Sport Fisheries and Wildlife, 1971.

Kellogg, Remington. "Annotated List of Tennessee's Mammals." *Proceedings in the U.S. Natural History Museum, Smithsonian Institute* 84(3022), 1939: 245–303.

Kellogg, Remington. "Annotated List of West Virginia's Mammals." *Proceedings in the U.S. Natural History Museum, Smithsonian Institute* 86(3051), 1937: 443–479.

Kennicott, Robert. "Catalogue of Animals Observed in Cook County, Illinois." Springfield, Ill.: *Transactions of the Illinois Agricultural Society* 1, 1855: 578–595.

Kirtland, Jared P. "A Catalogue of the Mammalia, Birds, Reptiles, Fishes, Testacea and Crustacea in Ohio." *2nd Annual Report of the Geological Survey of Ohio,* 1838: 160–200.

Knox, M. V. B. "Kansas Mammalia." *Transactions of the Kansas Academy of Science* 4, 1875: 18.

Kopman, H. H. "Wildlife Resources of Louisiana." New Orleans: *State Department of Conservation Bulletin* 10, 1921: 29.

Lancia, R. A., T. D. Nudds, and M. L. Morrison. "Opening Comments: Slaying Slippery Shibboleths." *Transactions of the North American Wildlife and Natural Resources Conference* 58, 1993: 505–508.

Lapham, I. A. "Systematic Catalogue of the Mammals of Wisconsin." *Transactions of the Wisconsin Agricultural Society* 2, 1853: 337–340.

Lewis, J. C. "Evidence of Mountain Lions in the Ozark, Boston, and Ouachita Mountains." *Proceedings of the Oklahoma Academy of Science for 1968,* 1970: 182–184.

Lindzey, F. G. "Mountain Lion." In *Wild Furbearer Management and Conservation in North America,* edited by M. Novak, J. A. Baker, M. E. Obbard, and B. Malloch. Toronto: Ontario Ministry of Natural Resources, 1987: 657–658.

Linzey, Donald W. "Cougars in the Southern Appalachians." In *Proceedings of the New River Symposium,* Boone, N.C., April 15–16, 1999:10–15.

"Lion-Human Interactions Reported on or Near Department Managed Lands." Sacramento: California Department of Fish and Game, 1998.

Lowery, George H. Jr. "A Checklist of the Mammals of Louisiana and Adjacent Waters." Baton Rouge: Occasional Papers, Museum of Zoology, Louisiana State University 13, November 22, 1943: 234–235.

Lowery, George H. Jr. "Distribution of Mammals of Louisiana with Respect to the Physiography of the State." *Proceedings in the Louisiana Academy of Science* 8, 1944: 63.

Lowery, George H. Jr. "A Preliminary Report on the Distribution of Mammals of Louisiana." Baton Rouge: Department of Zoology, Louisiana State University, *Proceedings in the Louisiana Academy of Science* 3 (1), March 1936: 11–39.

Lutz, J., and L. Lutz. "The Eastern Puma." In *Proceedings of the Eastern Cougar Conference,* edited by J. W. Tischendorf and Steven J. Ropski. Erie, Pa.: June 3–5, 1994. Fort Collins, Colo.: American Ecological Research Institute, 1996: 127–138.

Maehr, David S. "Florida Panther Movements, Social Organization, and Habitat Utilization." Tallahassee: Florida Game and Fresh Water Fish Commission Study No. 7502 [Federal No. E-1-11-2],1989, 1990.

Majors, T. J., D. C. Brock, and G. A. Heidt. "A Mail Survey to Determine the Status of the Black-tailed Jackrabbit, Ringtail Cat, Long-tailed Weasel, Badger, and Eastern Spotted Skunk in Arkansas." *Proceedings of the Arkansas Academy of Science* 50, 1996: 127–130.

Maliepaard, H. S. "A Report of Wildcats in Saskatchewan." In *Proceedings of the Symposium on the Native Cats of North America; Their Status and Management,* edited by S. E. Jorgensen and L. D. Mech. Minneapolis and St. Paul: U.S. Fish and Wildlife Service Bureau of Sport Fisheries and Wildlife, 1971.

McBride, Roy T., R. M. McBride, J. L. Cashman, and David S. Maehr. "Do Mountain Lions Exist in Arkansas?" *Proceedings of the Annual Conference of the Southeastern Fish and Wildlife Agencies* 47, 1993: 394–402.

McGinnis, Helen S. "Reports of Pumas in Pennsylvania, 1890–1981." In *Proceedings of the Eastern Cougar Conference,* edited by J. W. Tischendorf and Steven J. Ropski. Erie, Pa.: June 3–5, 1994. Fort Collins, Colo.: American Ecological Research Institute, 1996: 92–125.

McWilliams, W. H., G. C. Reese, R. C. Connor, V. A. Rudis, and T. L. Schmidt. "Today's Eastern Forests: What Have 350 Years of European Settlement Wrought?" *Transactions of the North American Wildlife and Natural Resources Conference* 62, 1997: 220–235.

Mead, J. R. *"Felis concolor."* Topeka: *Transactions of the 30th and 31st Annual Meetings, Kansas Academy of Science, 1897–1898,* edited by Librarian 18, 1899: 278–279.

Mearns, E. A. "The Native Mammals of Rhode Island." Circular of the Newport Natural History Society 1, July 1900: 1–4.

Mearns, E. A. "Notes on the Mammals of the Catskill Mountains, New York, with Genereal Remarks on the Fauna and Flora of the Region." Washington, D.C.: *Smithsonian Institute, Natural Museum Proceedings* 21(1147), 1898: 341–360.

Merriam, Clinton Hart. "The Mammals of the Adirondack Region." Foster, N.Y., 1884: 29–39.

Merriam, Clinton Hart. "Preliminary Revision of the Pumas (*Felis concolor* group)." *Proceedings of the Washington Academy of Science,* December 11, 1901: 577–600.

Merriam, Clinton Hart. "The Vertebrates of the Adirondack Region, Northeastern New York." *Transactions of the Linnaean Society of New York* 1, 1882.

Michigan Wildlife Habitat Foundation. "Cougar Caught on Video." *The Wildlife Volunteer,* September/October 2001: 3.

Miller, G. S. Jr. "Preliminary List of New York Mammals." *Bulletin of the New York State Museum* 6(29), 1899: 270–390.

Miller, G. S. Jr., and R. Kellogg. "List of North American Recent Mammals." Washington, D.C.: Smithsonian Institution, *United States Natural Museum Bulletin* 205, 1955.

Mills, William C. "Explorations of the Baum Prehistoric Village Sites." *Ohio Archaeological and Historical Quarterly* 15(1), 1906: 28 and 65.

"Minutes of the Council and General Court, 1623" [1622–1629]. *Virginia Magazine of History & Biography* 21, 1913: 45–47.

"Mountain Lions in Texas: Staff Briefing Report." Texas Parks and Wildlife Department, January 16, 1992.

Mumford, Russell E. "Distribution of Mammals in Indiana." Indiana Academy of Science, Monograph No. 1, 1969.

Nash, C. W. "Manual of the Vertebrates of Ontario." Toronto: Department of Education, Section 4, 1908: 96.

Nelson, William. Letter to St. George Tucker, August 19, 1810, Rare Books and Manuscripts Department. Williamsburg: College of William and Mary, 1918.

"North Florida Panther Reintroduction Study: Progress Report." Florida Game and Fresh Water Fish Commission, February 1993.

Norton, Arthur H. "Mammals of Portland, Maine, and Vicinity." *Proceedings in the Portland Society of Natural History* 4, 1930: 49–51.

Nowak, Ronald M. "The Cougar in the United States and Canada." New York: Report to the New York Zoological Society; Washington, D.C.: U.S. Fish and Wildlife Service, 1976.

Nowak, Ronald M. "Some Thoughts on Panther Study: A Personal View." *Endangered Species Technical Bulletin* 18, 1993.

Oberholser, Harry Church. "Notes on the Mammals and Summer Birds of Western North Carolina." Biltmore, N.C.: Biltmore Forestry School, September 30, 1905.

Padley, W. Douglas, editor. *Proceedings in the Fifth Mountain Lion Workshop.* Fort Collins, Colo.: Southern California Chapter of the Wildlife Society, 1996.

Paradiso, J. L. "Status Report on Cats of the World." Washington, D.C.: United States Department of the Interior, Bureau of Sport Fisheries and Wildlife, Special Science Report—Wildlife 157, 1972.

Penn, William. "Letter to the Committee." London: 1683.

"Perfect Description of Virginia" [1694]. *Virginia Historical Register,* 1849: 76.

Peterson, S. "Puma Attacks Child and Man." *Idaho Wildlife Review* 4(3), 1952: 15.

Phillips, M. K., and D. W. Smith. "Gray Wolves and Private Landowners in the Greater Yellowstone Area." *Transactions of the North American Wildlife and Natural Resources Conference* 63, 1998: 443–450.

Pritchard, P. E. H., editor. *Proceedings of the Florida Panther Conference.* Gainesville: Florida Audubon Society, 1976.

Puckette, W. L. "An Occurrence of the Puma *Felis concolor* from Svendsen Cave, Marion County, Arkansas." *Proceedings of the Arkansas Academy of Science* 29, 1975: 52–53.

Report of the State Conservation Commission. New Orleans: State of Louisiana, April 1, 1914, to April 1, 1916: 42.

Rhoads, S. N. "Contributions to the Zoology of Tennessee." Philadelphia: *Proceedings of the Academy of Natural Science* 48, 1896: 175–205.

Robertson, P., and C. D. Altman Jr. "Texas Mountain Lion Status Report." In *Proceedings of the Sixth Mountain Lion Workshop,* edited by L. A. Harveson, P. M. Harveson, and R. W. Adams. San Antonio: 2000.

Ropski, Steven J., and Jay Tischendorf, editors. *Proceedings of the 1994 Eastern Cougar Conference.* Erie, Pa.: June 3–5, 1994. Fort Collins, Colo.: American Ecological Research Institute, 1996.

Ruff, F. J. "The White-Tailed Deer of the Pisgah National Game Preserve." U.S. Department of Agriculture, Forest Service Mimeo Report.

Russ, William. "Mountain Lion Status Survey." Austin: Texas Parks and Wildlife Department, Job No. 69, Federal Aid Project No. W-103-19, Nongame Wildlife Investigations, 1989.

Russ, William. "Mountain Lion Status Survey." Austin: Texas Parks and Wildlife Department, Job No. 69, Federal Aid Project No. W-125-4, Wildlife Research and Surveys, 1993.

Rusz, P. "The Cougar in Michigan: Sightings and Related Information." Bath, Mich.: Bengal Wildlife Center Technical Publication, Michigan Wildlife Habitat Foundation, February 2001.

Ruth, Toni K., et al. "Evaluating Mountain Lion Translocation, Final Report." U.S. Fish and Wildlife Service and Hornocker Wildlife Research Institute, 1993.

Samuels, E. A. "Mammalogy and Ornithology in New England." Washington, D.C.: Report, Commission on Agriculture, Government Printing Office, 1863.

Schoerger, A. W. "Extinct and Endangered Mammals and Birds of the Upper Great Lakes Region." *Transactions of the Wisconsin Academy of Science, Arts and Letters* 34, 1942: 23–44.

Schortemeyer, J. L., David S. Maehr, J. W. McCowen, E. D. Land, and P. D. Manor. "Prey Management for the Florida Panther: A Unique Role for Wildlife Managers." *Transactions of the North American Wildlife and Natural Resources Conference* 56, 1991: 512–526.

Scott, F. W. "Update COSEWIC Status Report on Cougar *(Felis concolor couguar),* Eastern Population." Ottawa: Committee on the Status of Endangered Wildlife in Canada, Environment Canada, 1998.

Scott, W. E. "Rare and Extinct Mammals of Wisconsin." *Wisconsin Conservation Bulletin* 4(10), October 1939: 21–28.

Seagears, C. "Feline Flying Saucer." *New York State Conservation* 10(3), 1956: 48–49.

Seal, U. S. "A Plan for Genetic Restoration and Management of the Florida Panther *(Felis concolor coryi)*." Apple Valley, Minn.: Report to the U.S. Fish and Wildlife Service, Conservation Breeding Specialist Group, SSC/IUCN, 1994.

Sealander, J. A., and P. S. Gipson. "Status of the Mountain Lion in Arkansas." *Proceedings of the Arkansas Academy of Science* 27, 1973: 38–41.

Shaw, H. G. "A Mountain Lion Field Guide." Phoenix: Arizona Game and Fish Department, Special Report 9, 1979.

Sitton, L. W. "Mountain Lion Predation on Livestock in California." Lake Tahoe, Calif.: Annual Fish and Wildlife Society Conference, 1978.

Smith, E. R., J. B. Funderburg, and T. L. Quay. "A Checklist of North Carolina Mammals." North Carolina Wildlife Reserve Commission, 1960.

Smith, H. L., and P. L. Verkruysse. "The White-tailed Deer in Ontario: Its Ecology and Management." Ontario Ministry of Natural Resources, 1983.

Smith, K. G., J. D. Clark, and P. S. Gipson. "History of Black Bears in Arkansas: Over-Exploitation, Near Elimination, and Successful Reintroduction." *Proceedings of the Tenth Eastern Workshop on Black Bear Restoration and Management* 10, 1990: 5–14.

"Statutes at Large." Continuation of "Hening's Statutes," Laws of Virginia.

Stone, Livingston. "Incidents in Shasta City, California, Vol. 5." *Proceedings of the United States National Museum,* 1882: 520.

Stone, Witmer. "The Mammals of New Jersey." Trenton: *Annual Report of the New Jersey State Museum,* 1907: 33–110.

Stoner, Dayton. "Extant New York State Specimens of the Adirondack Cougar." Albany: New York State Museum Circular 25, 1950.

Surber, Thaddeus. "The Mammals of Minnesota." St. Paul: Minnesota Department of Conservation, Division of Fish and Game, 1932: 12.

Swanson, G., Thaddeus Surber, and T. S. Roberts. "The Mammals of Minnesota." *Minnesota Department of Conservation Technical Bulletin* 2, 194.

Swem, Earl. "Contributions to the Bibliography of Agriculture in Virginia." *Virginia State Library Bulletin* 11(1–2), 1918.

Swem, Earl Gregg. "Virginia Historical Index."

Taverna, Kristin, et al. "Eastern Cougar *(Puma concolor couguar):* Habitat Suitability Analysis for the Central Appalachians." Charlottesville: Appalachian Restoration Campaign, 1999.

Tischendorf, Jay W. "Bruce S. Wright, the Ghost Cat and Other Players." In *Proceedings of the Eastern Cougar Conference,* edited by Jay W. Tischendorf and Steven J. Ropski. Erie, Pa.: June 3–5, 1994. Fort Collins, Colo.: American Ecological Research Institute, 1996: 39–45.

Tischendorf, Jay W., and Steven J. Ropski, editors. *Proceedings of the Eastern Cougar Conference,* Gannon University, Erie, Pa., June 3–5, 1994. Fort Collins, Colo.: American Ecological Research Institute, 1996.

Trautman, Milton B. "The Ohio Country from 1750 to 1977—A Naturalist's View." Columbus: Ohio State University, *Ohio Biological Survey, Biological Notes* 10, 1977.

Trethewey, D. E. "The Cougar in New Brunswick." Fish & Wildlife Newsletter, Fredericton, New Brunswick: Department of Natural Resources, July 1970.

True, Frederick W. Annual Report for the Board of Regents of the Smithsonian Institution for the Year Ending June 30, 1899. Washington, D.C.: United States National Museum, 1891: 591–608.

True, Frederick W. "The Puma or American Lion: *Felis concolor* of Linnaeus." Report for the U.S. Natural Museum, 1889: 591–608.

United States Fish and Wildlife Service. "Eastern Cougar Recovery Plan." Atlanta: U.S. Fish and Wildlife Service, 1982.

Van Hyning, T., and Frank C. Pellett. "Mammals of Iowa." *Extract of the Proceedings of the Iowa Academy of Science,* 1910: 218.

Van Zyll de Jong, C. G., and E. van Ingen. "Status of the Eastern Cougar *(Felis concolor couguar)* in Canada." Committee on the Status of Endangered Wildlife in Canada (Ottawa), 1978.

Virginia Writers' Project. "Folklore Collection by Workers of the Writers' Program of the Public Works Administration." Charlottesville: University of Virginia Library, Manuscript Collection 1547, 1936–43.

Wailes, Benjamin Leonard Covington. "Report on the Agriculture and Geology of Mississippi." East Barksdale State Printer, 1854: 315.

Watkins, John. "Notices of the Northerly Parts of Louisiana in a Letter to Dr. Barton." *Transactions of the American Philosophical Society* 6 (Part 1), 1804: 69–72.

Werdlin, L. "The Radiation of Felids in South America: When and Where Did It Occur?" Rome: Fifth International Theriological Congress, Abstract of Papers and Posters, 1989, 290–291.

Williams, Stephen L., Suzanne B. Mclaren, and Marion A. Burgwin. "Paleo-Archeological and Historical Records of Selected Pennsylvania Mammals." Pittsburgh: Annals of Carnegie Museum 54, 1985.

Witsell, T., G. A. Heidt, P. L. Dozhier, T. Frothingham, and M. Lynn. "Recent Documentations of Mountain Lion *(Puma concolor)* in Arkansas." *Proceedings of the Arkansas Academy of Science* 53, 1999: 157–158.

Wood, Norman A. "An Annotated Checklist of Michigan Mammals." Ann Arbor: Occasional Papers, Museum of Zoology, University of Michigan, 1914.

Wood, Norman A. "The Mammals of Washtenaw County, Michigan." Ann Arbor: Occasional Papers, Museum of Zoology, University of Michigan 123, 1922: 1–23.

Wright, Bruce S. "The Cougar in New Brunswick." Symposium on the Native Cats of North America, 1971.

Wright, George M., Joseph S. Dixon, and Ben H. Thompson. "Fauna of the National Parks of the United States. A Preliminary Survey of Faunal Relations in National Parks." Washington, D.C.: U.S. Department of the Interior, Contribution of Wildlife Survey, Fauna Series 1, 1933: 35–139.

Wydevan, A. P., and J. E. Ashbrenner. "History and Status of Cougars in Wisconsin." In *Proceedings of the Eastern Cougar Conference,* edited by J. W. Tischendorf and Steven J. Ropski. Erie, Pa.: June 3–5, 1994. Fort Collins, Colo.: American Ecological Research Institute, 1996: 39–45.

Young, Stanley. "Hints on Mountain Lion Trapping." United States Department of Agriculture Leaflet 94, April 1933.

Youngman, P. M. "Mammals of the Yukon Territory." Ottawa: National Museum of Canada, Natural Science, Publications in Zoology 10, 1975.

THESES, DISSERTATIONS, AND UNPUBLISHED MANUSCRIPTS

Anderson, C. R. "Cougar Ecology, Management, and Population Genetics in Wyoming." Ph.D. dissertation. Laramie: University of Wyoming, 2003.

Carter, Cathy, and Richard Rummel. "Status of the Florida Panther in Mississippi." Unpublished report to the Mississippi Museum of Natural Science, 1980.

Culver, Melanie. "Molecular Genetic Variation, Population Structure, and Natural History of Free-Ranging Pumas *(Puma concolor)*." Ph.D. dissertation. College Park, Md.: University of Maryland, 1999.

Hancock. Lynn. "A History of Changing Attitudes to *Felis concolor*." Burnaby, British Columbia: Simon Fraser University, 1980.

Hardin, S. E. "The Status of the Puma *(Puma concolor)* in Missouri, Based on Sightings." Unpublished M.S. thesis. Springfield, Mo.: Southwest Missouri State University, 1996.

Hauck, K. "Prey and Habitat Availability to Support a Cougar *(Puma concolor)* Population in the Whiskey Jack Forest (Kenora Management Unit)." M.S.F. thesis. Thunder Bay, Ontario: Lakehead University, Faculty of Forestry, 2000.

Houser, Rhonda S. "The Use of Geographic Information Systems to Model Habitat for *Puma concolor cougar* [sic] in the Northern Blue Ridge of Virginia." M.S. thesis. Richmond: Virginia Commonwealth University, 2002.

Loxterman, J. L. "The Impact of Habitat Fragmentation on the Population Genetic Structure of Pumas *(Puma concolor)* in Idaho." Ph.D. dissertation. Pocatello: Idaho State University, 2001.

McBride, Roy T. "The Status and Ecology of Mountain Lion *(Felis concolor Stanleyana)* of the Texas-Mexico Border." Alpine, Tex.: Sul Ross University, 1976.

McRae, B. "Effects of Habitat Discontinuities on Genetic Structure Among Puma Populations in the Southwestern U.S.A." Ph.D. dissertation. Flagstaff: Northern Arizona University, 2004.

Miller, Janet. 1998. "Evidence for an Eastern Cougar Reassessment." M.S. thesis. Oxford, Ohio: Miami of Ohio University, 1998.

Palmer, R. S. "Mammals of Maine." Honor's thesis. Orono, Maine: University of Maine, 1937.

Russ, W. P. "The Rare and Endangered Terrestrial Vertebrates of Virginia." Blacksburg, Va.: Virginia Polytechnical Institute, 1973.

Tischendorf, Jay. "The Puma in the Central Mountains and Plains." 1993.

Van Dyke, Fred Gerald. "A Western Study of Cougar Track Surveys and Environmental Disturbances Affecting Cougars Related to the Status of the Eastern Cougar." Ph.D. dissertation, Syracuse: State University of New York, Syracuse, 1983.

LETTERS, MEMORANDA, PRESS RELEASES, TELEPHONE CONVERSATIONS, AND EMAILS

Bowman, G. Personal communication with Kirk Johnson, Gulliver, Mich., 2000.

Cantner, Dan E. Official letter from Division of Wildlife Resources, State of West Virginia, to Howard N. Larson, Regional Director, U.S. Fish and Wildlife Services, Boston, May 7, 1976.

Clark, Jamie R., Director, U.S. Fish and Wildlife Service, letter to Todd Lester, Washington, D.C., June 21, 2000.

"Cougar Questions." Massachusetts Department of Fisheries, Wildlife and Environmental Law Enforcement press release. Boston, November 16, 2000.

Deputy Regional Director, U.S. Fish and Wildlife Service. "Eastern Cougar (?)." Official communication to "The File," April 14, 1976.

Deputy Regional Director, U.S. Fish & Wildlife Service, "Eastern Cougar (?)." Official communication to Regional Director, Boston, April 15, 1976.

Edde, J. Personal communication with Kirk Johnson, Bessemer, Mich., 2000.

Endangered Species Program Specialist. "West Virginia's Cougar." Memorandum to "The File," April 20, 1976.

Ernest, Holly. Letter on DNA analysis to Cedric Alexander, Davis, California, January 19, 2004.

Fitzhugh, E. Lee. Email message to Todd Lester, Davis, California, September 1, 1998.

Hughes, B. Personal communication with Kirk Johnson, Gulliver, Mich., 2000.

Ledbetter, Nancy S. "Arkansas Game and Fish Commission Mountain Lion Position Statement." Little Rock, July 18, 2003.

Lester, Todd. Letter to Bruce Babbitt, Secretary, U.S. Department of the Interior, North Spring, W.V., March 20, 2000.

Loftus, E. F. Eyewitness testimony, Harvard University, Cambridge, Mass., 1979.

Maehr, David S. Personal communication with Chris Bolgiano, 2000.

McCarthy, J. Personal communication with Kirk Johnson, Ann Arbor, Mich., 2001.

Minzey, T. Personal communication with Kirk Johnson, Cadillac, Mich., 2000.

Nelson, William. Letter to St. George Tucker, August 19, 1810.

Perez, R. Personal communication with Kirk Johnson, Saginaw Bay, Mich., 2000.

Regional Director, U.S. Fish and Wildlife Service. "File Copy" of memorandum to Dan Cantner, Wildlife Resources Division, Department of Natural Resources, State of West Virginia, April 22, 1976.

Robinson, L. Personal communication with Kirk Johnson, Mio, Mich., 2000.

Rusz, P. Personal communication with Kirk Johnson, Bath, Mich., 2001.

Sprague, B. Personal communication with Kirk Johnson, White Pine, Mich., 2001.

Thomas, Steve. Official letter from Kentucky Department of Fish and Wildlife Resources to Chris Bolgiano, Frankfort, Kentucky, April 20, 2001.

Tyrrell, J. B. "The Mammalia of Canada." Toronto: Read Before the Canadian Institute, April 7, 1888.

Van Zyll de Jong, C. (Stan) G. Personal communication with Rod Cumberland, Ottawa, Ontario, February 16, 1993.

Yates, Bonnie C. Official U.S. Fish and Wildlife letter to Cedric Alexander, Ashland, Oregon, September 12, 1994.

Yates, Bonnie C. Personal communication with Chris Bolgiano, Davis, California, 2004.

Zuidema, M. Personal communication with Kirk Johnson, Escanaba, Mich., 2000.

WEBSITES

http://www.easterncougar.org
http://www.easterncougarnet.org

Index